Oracle Enterprise Manager Grid Control
Advanced OEM Techniques for the Real World

Oracle In-Focus Series

Porus Homi Havewala

Oracle Enterprise Manager Grid Control
Advanced OEM Techniques for the Real World

By Porus Homi Havewala

Copyright © 2010 by Rampant TechPress. All rights reserved.
Printed in the United States of America.
Published in Kittrell, North Carolina, USA.
Oracle In-focus Series: Book 39
Series Editor: Donald K. Burleson
Production Manager: Robin Rademacher and Jennifer Stanley
Production Editor: Valerre Aquitaine
Cover Design: Janet Burleson
Printing History: January 2011 for First Edition

ISBN 10: 0-9844282-0-8
ISBN 13: 978-0-9844282-0-5
Library of Congress Control Number: 2010941002

Table of Contents

Using the Online Code Depot

Purchase of this book provides complete access to the online code depot that contains sample code scripts. Any code depot scripts in this book are located at the following URL in zip format and ready to load and use:

rampant.cc/emg.htm

If technical assistance is needed with downloading or accessing the scripts, please contact Rampant TechPress at rtp@rampant.cc.

Conventions Used in this Book

It is critical for any technical publication to follow rigorous standards and employ consistent punctuation conventions to make the text easy to read. However, this is not an easy task. Within database terminology, there are many types of notation that can confuse a reader. For example, some Oracle utilities such as STATSPACK and TKPROF are always spelled in CAPITAL letters, while Oracle parameters and procedures have varying naming conventions in the database documentation. It is also important to remember that many database commands are case sensitive, are always left in their original executable form and never altered with italics or capitalization. Hence, all Rampant TechPress books follow these conventions:

- Parameters: All database parameters will be lowercase italics. Exceptions to this rule are parameter arguments that are commonly capitalized (KEEP pool, TKPROF); these will be left in ALL CAPS.

- Variables: All procedural language (e.g. PL/SQL) program variables and arguments will also remain in lowercase italics (dbms_job, dbms_utility).

- Tables & dictionary objects: All data dictionary objects are referenced in lowercase italics (dba_indexes, v$sql). This includes all v$ and x$ views (x$kcbcbh, v$parameter) and dictionary views (dba_tables, user_indexes).

- SQL: All SQL is formatted for easy use in the code depot, and all SQL is displayed in lowercase. The main SQL terms (select, from, where, group by, order by, having) will always appear on a separate line.

- Programs & Products: All products and programs that are known to the author are capitalized according to the vendor specifications (CentOS, VMware, Oracle, etc.). All names known by Rampant TechPress to be trademark names appear in this text as initial caps. References to UNIX are always made in uppercase.

Acknowledgements

This type of highly technical reference book requires the dedicated efforts of many people. Even though we are the authors, our work ends when we deliver the content. After each chapter is delivered, several Oracle DBAs carefully review and correct the technical content. After the technical review, experienced copy editors polish the grammar and syntax.

The finished work is then reviewed as page proofs and turned over to the production manager, who arranges the creation of the online code depot and manages the cover art, printing distribution, and warehousing.

In short, the authors play a small role in the development of this book, and we need to thank and acknowledge everyone who helped bring this book to fruition:

- **Paulo Ferreira Portugal** for technical expertise and review.

- **Robin Rademacher and Jennifer Stanley** for the production management including the coordination of the cover art, page proofing, printing, and distribution.

- **Valerre Q Aquitaine** for help in the production of the page proofs.

- **Janet Burleson** for exceptional cover design and graphics.

- **John Lavender** for assistance with the web site, and for creating the code depot and the online shopping cart for this book.

- **Don Burleson** for providing me with the opportunity to write this book.

With my sincerest thanks,

Porus Homi Havewala

System Requirements and Installation

Introduction

I would like to extend a warm welcome to all my readers. I have been working with Oracle Enterprise Manager Grid Control since Version 1 in 2004 and its predecessors such as Server Manager since 1996, and I have been steadily impressed by the rapid increase in capabilities of the toolset along with all its management packs, connectors and plug-ins.

I am a big fan of the increasing scope of Oracle Enterprise Manager – I call it fantabulous on my Enterprise Manager blog (more on that later), so I thought of writing a book to introduce more DBAs and managers to the capabilities of this product.

There are other Grid Control books on the market. They tell you about the basics of installation, configuration and so on. However, I believe this book is unique since it is based on my experience as an Oracle and Enterprise Manager DBA and shows you practical examples of how DBAs use Grid Control to achieve various database management tasks and make their lives easier in the bargain.

It is easy to get lost in the advanced topics of Enterprise Manager and not realize how it can help you with your major day-to-day DBA activities. This is why the book is called *Advanced Practical Techniques* because these are the practical things that help a DBA in their daily activities.

This book explains the various power possibilities and advanced techniques of using Oracle Enterprise Manager (OEM) Grid Control in a large corporate environment, such as setting up and scheduling RMAN backups of databases, creating Data Guard standbys, cloning databases and Oracle Homes and patching databases, which are all normal but tedious tasks for a DBA that can be automated and enhanced using Grid Control.

I have observed that there are a number of large corporate sites looking into the possibilities of OEM Grid Control. There are also a number of corporate sites where the DBA/Management staff has no idea of Grid Control. This book will serve as a solid introduction to the many possibilities of this enterprise management software from Oracle. This book also takes a look at the new Oracle Enterprise Manager 11g Grid Control, released in April 2010, and is perhaps the first book in the market to do so.

About OEM

OEM Grid Control is Oracle's flagship enterprise-class management and monitoring toolset for corporate-wide Oracle databases and other third-party databases, application servers, and application software such as Oracle E-Business, Peoplesoft, and Siebel. It also works with the host servers themselves, disparate storage systems such as SAN or NAS filers, and also load balancers with an ever-expanding list of plug-ins by Oracle or by third-party vendors.

The list just keeps growing. Grid Control 10g Release 5 has support for over 40 non-Oracle technologies including storage and network devices. And today, more than 22,000 customers use Enterprise Manager globally.

With the introduction of Grid Control 11g Release 1 (covered in the last chapter in this book), the world of Enterprise Manager now encompasses the Sun Ops Center and has reached new heights of integrated application-to-disk management, including advanced techniques of transaction management. Now take a look back in time.

DBAs have been using the SQL*Plus command line to administer the database since the days of the earliest versions of the Oracle database. The command line was fine when databases were less complex and had fewer features. However, as time moved on and databases became more complex, the need for a GUI-based tool was apparent, especially when Windows point-and-click applications were gaining popularity in the early-to-mid 90s.

Around 1996, Oracle made a first attempt at releasing a GUI tool to manage its databases. This was Oracle Server Manager, which featured a command line as well as a GUI interface. Some DBAs attempted to use the GUI interface even then and I was one of them, but most eventually used only the command line interface of Server Manager, called Server Manager/Line Mode or SVRMGRL. This was because at that time it was easier and quicker to get things done at the command line, and the other factor was that the first few releases of the GUI interface had limited administrative capabilities.

Oracle then released a new version, OEM or Oracle Enterprise Manager. This progressed to OEM 2.2 in the days of Oracle 8i at the start of the millennium. About two years later in 2002, OEM 9.2 was released, which was when larger numbers of DBAs first started using Enterprise Manager seriously. However, the console product was Java-based and had to be installed as a separate product on every workstation that accessed the central repository of OEM.

This OEM 9.2 console was very memory-intensive with crashes on the Windows platform dogging many DBAs. There was a standalone console mode without a repository and a mode that connected to a central repository. Many DBAs used the standalone mode without the repository; as a result, there was no central repository of database information in many sites even though OEM 9.2 was being used.

In 2004, Oracle rewrote the entire product with a new architecture based on its application server technology. Significantly, the console was now browser-based and could be accessed from any workstation on the corporate network without the need to install software on any workstation or any other installation other than the repository and server agents. The standalone mode was no longer possible, thus forcing the use of a centralized repository. This was when Enterprise Manager really took off, and the rest, as they say, is history.
The OEM product that allowed management of multiple databases and servers was named Grid Control, after Oracle's use of the "g" letter in their 10g database, and the heavy emphasis it laid on the Grid as the future of computing.

There are various power possibilities with OEM Grid Control, and this book attempts to explain the most common. DBAs can understand how Grid Control can assist in the daily database administration activities that were described earlier – all the normal but tedious tasks for a DBA. They would like the automation of jobs without scripts, removing much of the dependence on UNIX shell scripts and cron jobs.

Grid Control can also be used by System Administrators for most of them would appreciate its host performance monitoring capabilities, performance history of host CPU and memory utilization being stored in the repository, and the host configuration comparison capabilities for troubleshooting.

IT managers would be interested in how Grid Control can help them achieve an overall and holistic view of the corporate infrastructure system and provide reports and information on security compliance, application level performance dashboards, SLAs, database versions in use, licensing usage, conformation to standards, unnecessary storage allocation, and unused databases, particularly for development and testing. They would certainly be interested in how OEM Grid Control can create databases in a matter of minutes rather than hours or days.

A Word About Licensing

Throughout this book, I make mention of Oracle licensing and, in particular, how it relates to certain OEM features, add-ons and packs.

While the licensing information I provide is, to the best of my knowledge, correct at the time of writing this book, software licensing is subject to change. Your company may also have enterprise agreements that encompass the licensing of some of the Oracle software products I identify in this book as requiring additional licensing costs.

In any event, it is your responsibility to ensure that you and your company are licensed to use the Oracle software (or any software) that you install.

What You Need to Download

OEM Grid Control is available as a separate download from the Oracle Technology Network (OTN). On the Internet, go to http://technet.oracle.com and then select Downloads...Enterprise Manager. If you are not already a member, you may have to create your account details.

Note that it is a free site. The direct Enterprise Manager Downloads page is: http://www.oracle.com/technology/ software/products/oem/index.html.

You must first download and install the Full (Base) Installer (Agent, Repository, OMS, and Management Packs) for your platform. In this case, this is Release 2 (10.2.0.2.1) for Microsoft Windows (32-bit). For the new OEM 11g Release 1 version, please refer to the last chapter of this book for the installation techniques as well as the new features. OMS stands for the Oracle Management Service, which is the guts of the Enterprise Manager system.

After the Full (Base) Release 2 is installed, you can upgrade using the Patch Installer (Agent, OMS, and Management Packs) for Release 5 (10.2.0.5). This Release 5 patch can also be downloaded from the same page.

Enterprise Manager can be installed on a number of certified platforms such as Linux, Solaris, Windows, HP-UX and AIX. It is not necessary to use the same platform as your target databases. For example, your company may have the majority of the production databases on Solaris, but you can easily use a Linux or Windows platform on which to install the Enterprise Manager Repository and Management Service.

You can refer to the *OEM Grid Control Installation and Basic Configuration 10g Release 2 (10.2) Guide*, downloadable from the documentation section of OTN (select Documentation...Enterprise Manager). This guide will tell you the exact versions of the operating systems you can use for the Grid Control install and also what types of targets are supported; for example, single-instance databases from Release 8.1.7.4 onwards are supported, and in the case of clustered RAC databases, only releases from 9.2.0.6 onwards are supported.

You should be aware that although OEM supports older versions of its databases, not every OEM feature may be available for that database version. This depends on the version of the OEM repository compared to the Oracle database version you are monitoring using the OEM product. This is one of many reasons you should maintain your Oracle databases on the most recent release and version.

Oracle has recently provided recut base installers on OTN for 10.2.0.1.1 (Linux x86 and Solaris SPARC64) and 10.2.0.2.1 (Windows 32bit) Grid Control. These installers now allow you to use Oracle 11g databases as the repository database with the Grid Control with existing database and additional management service installation options. These options will be seen shortly during the install.

Previously, to use an 11g database as the repository, you had to go through a series of detailed steps using the "install software only" techniques that were described in My Oracle Support (Note 763351.1 contains links to published procedures). So, to avoid such unnecessary steps, please make sure you use the recut versions of the base installer.

Using 11g as the Repository Database

You have an option: either use the Grid Control installation option with a new database for the repository, or install Grid Control using an existing database for the repository.

If you select a new database, it is the cleanest and fastest install since Grid Control installs the database software, creates a new database for the repository, and then installs the Management Service and the Agent. So in all, three homes will be created on the host on which you have installed Grid Control.
The drawback of this method is that you are limited to the release of the database that is provided by the installation, known as the seed or embedded database. In the case of Grid Control Release 2 (10.2.0.2) for Microsoft Windows, the embedded database is a 10g Release 1 database (10.1.0.4).

It is far better to install the EM repository on the 11g database release rather than the 10.1 Release, the main reason being that if your repository is on 11g, it will be supported longer by Oracle and you can defer longer the upgrade of your EM repository. So it is recommended to create an 11g database initially, and then use this database as an existing database when running the Grid Control installation option using an existing database for the repository. Since you have the recut version of the base Grid Control install, an 11g database can be used.

Database Creation and Configuration

For successful Management Repository creation, the 11g database software you installed must be the Oracle Enterprise Edition version of the software and not the Standard Edition or any other edition. This is because various sophisticated database options are used by the repository, such as partitioning which is used for automatic rollup of metric data and truncation of older metric data partitions. Database options such as partitioning require the Enterprise Edition version of the software.

Using the Database Configuration Assistant (DBCA), you can create an 11.1 general purpose or transaction-processing database. Name the database as EMREP, which stands for Enterprise Manager Repository, or some other meaningful name. In the course of moving through the DBCA screens, make sure you untick Configure Enterprise Manager so it is not configured for Database Control or for Grid Control.

This new database will be the repository database for Grid Control and the actual repository will be created later by the OMS install, so you do not want any Database Control repository to be created by the DBCA installer.
For small (100 monitored targets), medium (1000 targets) and large (more than 10000 targets) sites, use an *sga_target* of 0.5 GB, 1.5 GB and 2.5 GB, respectively, for the new database as per Oracle recommendations. Other recommended values for memory settings can be seen in the *Grid Control Installation and Configuration Guide 10g Release 5* (10.2.0.5.0).

During the database creation, you can keep the enhanced 11g default security settings, which include the enabling of auditing and a new default password profile, and also select Enable Automatic Maintenance Tasks when the screen prompts you. The latter is for the automatic collection of optimizer statistics and proactive advisor reports that run in a predefined maintenance window. These and a number of other benefits are the reasons why the 11g release for the repository is being used.

After the database is created, unlock the SYSMAN account since this will be used for the repository creation. You can also unlock the DBSNMP account that is used for monitoring of the repository database by Grid Control. You can do this at the end of the DBCA database creation in the password management screen.

It is required that the fine-grained access control option in the database must be set to *true*. You can select from *v$options* for making sure this setting is correct:

```
SQL>
select
 parameter, value
from
 v$option
where
 parameter like '%grain%access%'
/
```

```
PARAMETER                        VALUE
-----------------------------    ---------------
Fine-grained access control      TRUE
```

There are also certain initialization parameters that must be set for a successful management repository database creation. These are listed in the "Software Requirements...Oracle Management Repository Software Requirements...Check Database Initialization Parameters" section of the *Grid Control Installation and Configuration Guide 10g Release 5 (10.2.0.5.0)*, and are as follows:

```
Parameter                    Recommended Value

job_queue_processes          10
db_block_size                8192
timed_statistics             TRUE
open_cursors                 300
session_cached_cursors       200
aq_tm_processes              1
compatible                   <currently installed Oracle Database
                             release> (default)
undo_management              AUTO
undo_retention               10800
undo_tablespace              <any acceptable name>
processes                    150
log_buffer                   1048576
statistics_level             TYPICAL
_b_tree_bitmap_plans         false (hidden parameter)
```

If necessary, change the parameters in the *spfile* using the SQL command *alter system set .. scope = spfile* and bounce the database for them to take effect. You can also change these parameters as necessary during the execution of DBCA itself before the database is created except for the hidden parameter in the above list.

To see the default value of the hidden parameter *_b_tree_bitmap_plans*, you can use the SQL statement as follows:

```
column name format A30
column value format A10
select
```

```
      a.ksppinm name, b.ksppstvl value
  from
      sys.x$ksppi a, sys.x$ksppcv b
  where
      a.indx = b.indx
  and
      a.ksppinm like '\_%bitmap%plan%' escape '\'
/
```

```
NAME                                VALUE
---------------------------------   ----------
_b_tree_bitmap_plans                FALSE
```

Another way to find the values of hidden parameters in an 11g database is to issue the command in SQL*Plus:

```
SQL>
create
 pfile from memory;

File created.
```

This creates a parameter file *INITemrep.ORA* in the *$ORACLE_HOME/database* directory in Windows that contains all the hidden parameter settings. Now, to change the hidden parameter as recommended for the repository database, issue this SQL command:

```
SQL>
alter
 system set "_b_tree_bitmap_plans" = false;

System altered.
```

Execute the *dbmspool* package as follows on the database. This is also a requirement:

```
SQL>
@?/rdbms/admin/dbmspool.sql

Package created.
Grant succeeded.
View created.
Package body created.
```

At this stage, you should be ready to install Grid Control.

First, check the environment variables in your session to verify that there are no references to existing Oracle homes or any Java locations in the operating system. Remove all such references for the installing session.

Ensure that the *PATH* value has no entries that might interfere with Oracle software installation. Oracle Installer provides its own Java and Perl utilities, so make sure no existing references will interfere. This may involve changing environment variables like *classpath, path, perl5lib,* and so on if they are set and contain references to other Oracle homes or JDK installations. Do this by using the *set* command in the Windows command prompt.

```
set oracle_home=
set classpath=
set perl5lb=
etc.
```

Now you can start the Oracle Installation by calling *setup* from that same command prompt after changing the environment:

```
C:\>cd c:\Gc_102021_win\Disk1

C:\Gc_102021_win\Disk1>dir
 Volume in drive C is ACER
 Volume Serial Number is E034-D176

 Directory of C:\Gc_102021_win\Disk1

11/01/2009  10:21 AM    <DIR>          .
11/01/2009  10:21 AM    <DIR>          ..
11/01/2009  10:16 AM    <DIR>          install
11/01/2009  10:19 AM    <DIR>          oms
11/01/2009  10:21 AM    <DIR>          rdbms
11/01/2009  10:21 AM    <DIR>          response
01/03/2006  11:13 PM            65,536 setup.exe
11/01/2009  10:21 AM    <DIR>          stage
               1 File(s)         65,536 bytes
               7 Dir(s)  32,204,349,440 bytes free

C:\Gc_102021_win\Disk1>setup
```

The Installation Type screen appears (Figure 1.1).

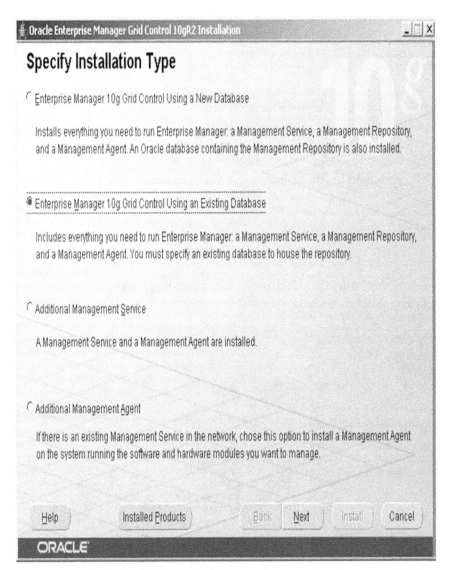

Figure 1.1: *Installation Type – Using an Existing Database*

Select the Installation type as Enterprise Manager 10g Grid Control Using an Existing Database. Move to the next screen.

On the next screen (Figure 1.2), specify the installation location as *C:\OracleHomes*. This will be the master directory into which the Management Server and Agent Homes will be saved.

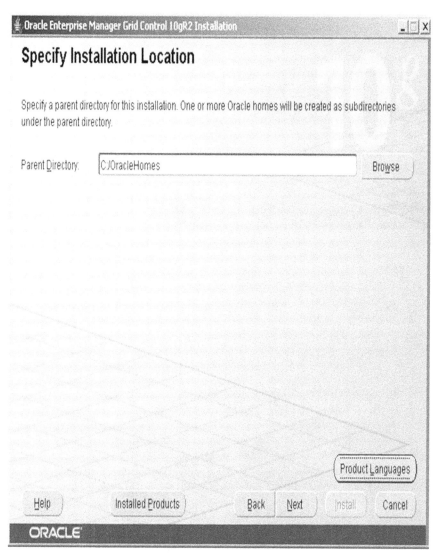

Figure 1.2: *Installation Location*

You can also change the environment variables at this point by clicking on the Installed Products button, and then moving to the Environment tab (Figure 1.3) where you can deselect the Oracle Homes you do not want in the path.

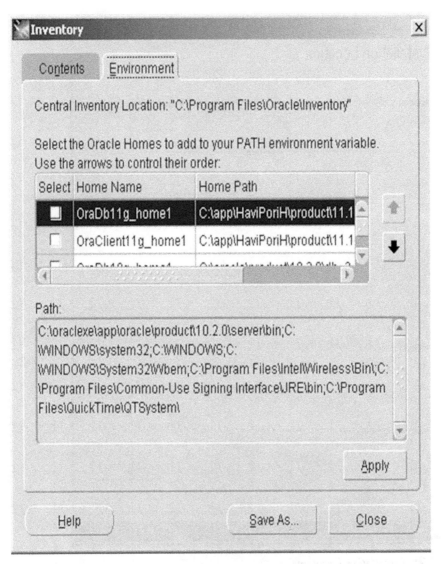

Figure 1.3: *Changing the Environment*

Next, the Installer performs certain prerequisite checks as per the product being installed (Figure 1.4) and informs you if there are any outstanding issues.

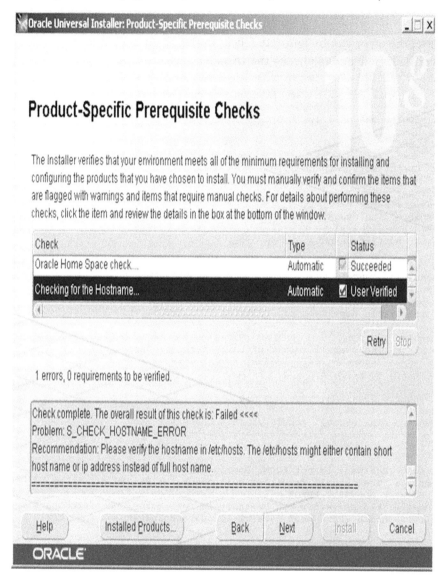

Figure 1.4: *Prerequisite Checks*

Since the hostname of the server being used is not a fully qualified name, i.e. the domain is not being used, a recommendation to verify the hostname has appeared in Figure 1.4.

In this case, the error can be ignored. Click on the Error checkbox to change it to user-verified. The actual checks the Installer performs can be seen below:

```
Checking if Oracle software certified on the current O/S...

Expected result: One of 4.0,4.1,5.0,5.1,5.2,6.0
Actual Result: 5.1
Check complete. The overall result of this check is: Passed
================================================================
Checking for the service pack...

Expected result: 1
Actual Result: 2
Check complete. The overall result of this check is: Passed
================================================================
Checking for sufficient physical memory...

Expected result: 512MB
Actual Result: 2038MB
Check complete. The overall result of this check is: Passed
================================================================
Checking for Oracle Home incompatibilities ....

Actual Result: NEW_HOME
Check complete. The overall result of this check is: Passed
================================================================
Oracle Home Space check....

Expected result: 2764.8GB in volume C:\
Actual Result: 30481GB
Check complete. The overall result of this check is: Passed
================================================================
Checking for the Hostname...

Actual Result: Hostname is not FQDN, Domain name is null.
Check complete. The overall result of this check is: Failed <<<<
Problem: S_CHECK_HOSTNAME_ERROR
Recommendation: Please verify the hostname in /etc/hosts. The /etc/hosts
might either contain short host name or ip address instead of full host
name.
================================================================
```

On the next screen (Figure 1.5), enter the details of the 11g database that you want to use for the repository. This can be on the same machine or a different machine, which is important for scaling out, as will be seen in the next chapter.

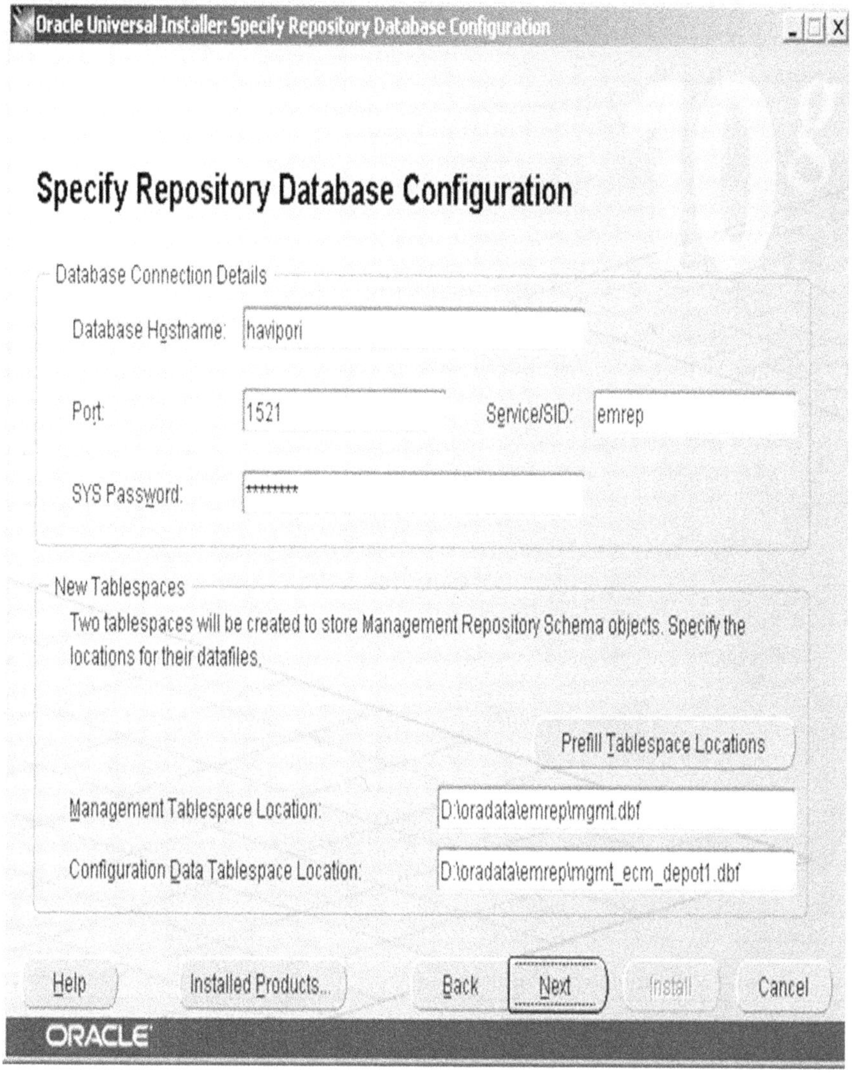

Figure 1.5: *Repository Database Configuration*

On this screen, you are asked to specify the locations of two tablespaces where management repository schema objects will be stored. Change the default locations of the two tablespaces to the following:

```
D:\oradata\emrep\mgmt.dbf
D:\oradata\emrep\mgmt_ecm_depot1.dbf
```

Next, the following warning screen (Figure 1.6) appears. This may happen if by chance you had configured your database for Enterprise Manager Database Control when creating it.

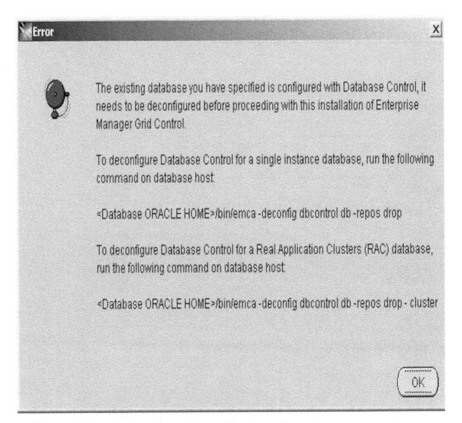

Figure 1.6: *Request to Deconfigure Database Control*

To resolve this issue, start a new command window and run the following commands:

```
cd C:\app\HaviPoriH\product\11.1.0\db_1\bin

set ORACLE_HOME=C:\app\HaviPoriH\product\11.1.0\db_1

set ORACLE_SID=emrep

emca -deconfig dbcontrol db -repos drop

STARTED EMCA at Nov 1, 2009 12:39:48 PM
```

```
EM Configuration Assistant, Version 11.1.0.5.0 Production
Copyright (c) 2003, 2005, Oracle.  All rights reserved.

Enter the following information:
Database SID: emrep
Listener port number: 1521
Password for SYS user:
Password for SYSMAN user:
Do you wish to continue? [yes(Y)/no(N)]: y

Nov 1, 2009 12:40:11 PM oracle.sysman.emcp.EMConfig perform
INFO: This operation is being logged at
C:\app\HaviPoriH\cfgtoollogs\emca\emrep\
emca_2009_11_01_12_39_47.log.

Nov 1, 2009 12:40:33 PM oracle.sysman.emcp.EMDBPreConfig
performDeconfiguration
WARNING: EM is not configured for this database. No EM-specific actions can
be performed.
Nov 1, 2009 12:40:33 PM oracle.sysman.emcp.ParamsManager
checkListenerStatusForDBControl
Nov 1, 2009 12:40:33 PM oracle.sysman.emcp.EMReposConfig invoke
INFO: Dropping the EM repository (this may take a while) ...
Nov 1, 2009 12:44:49 PM oracle.sysman.emcp.EMReposConfig invoke
INFO: Repository successfully dropped
Enterprise Manager configuration completed successfully
FINISHED EMCA at Nov 1, 2009 12:44:49 PM
```

Once you have pressed the OK button, the following warning may appear about the use of dispatchers (Figure 1.7).

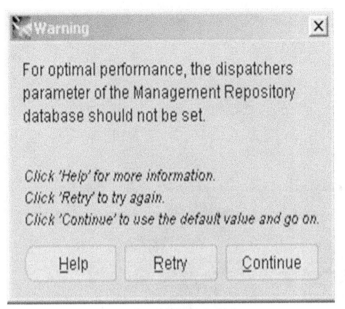

Figure 1.7: *Warning About Dispatchers*

If your database is using dedicated connections, you can ignore this warning and continue.

On the next screen (Figure 1.8), you are asked to enter additional configuration information, such as the SMTP server in your corporation if you want to receive email notifications from Enterprise Manager, the Oracle Support login, and the proxy details for connecting through a firewall. You can provide these details now or you can always set them later in Grid Control.

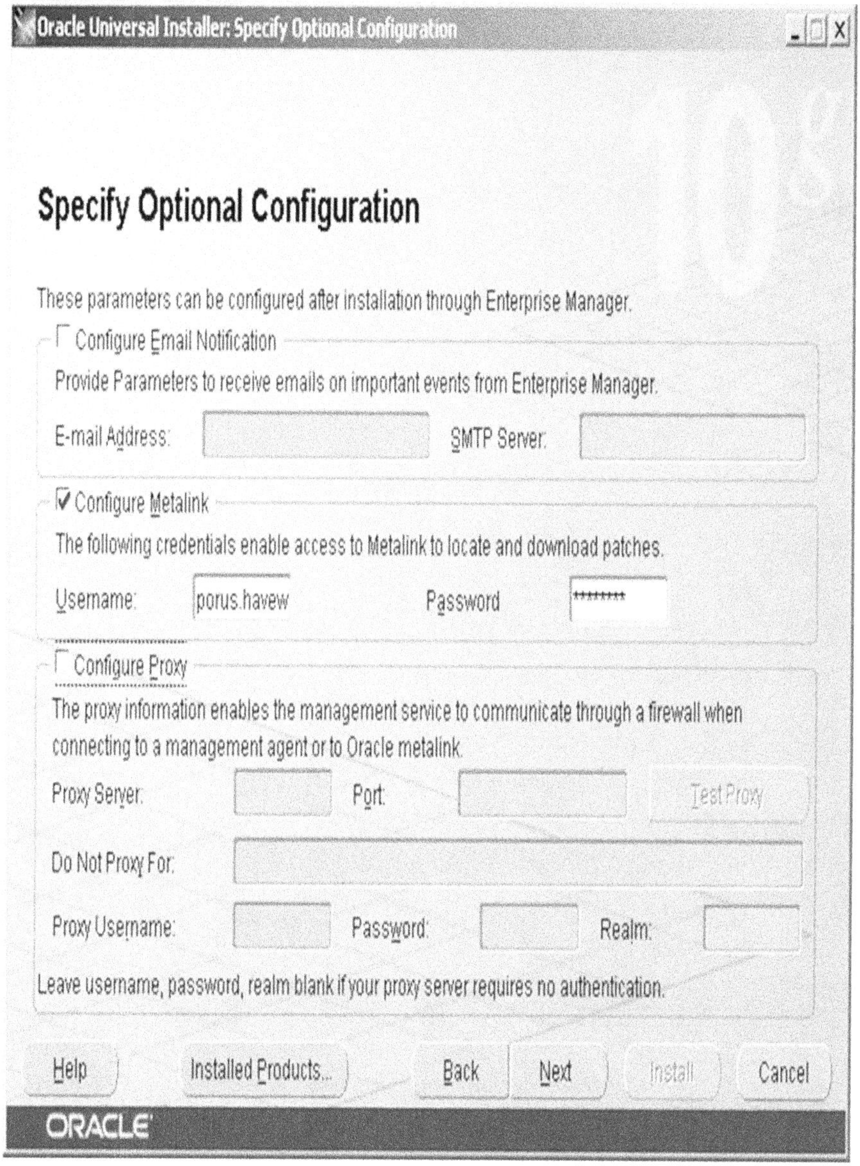

Figure 1.8: *Optional Configuration*

The next screen (Figure 1.9) prompts you to enter the password for the management service for secure communications and the all-important SYSMAN password. SYSMAN is the owner of the OEM Grid Control repository.

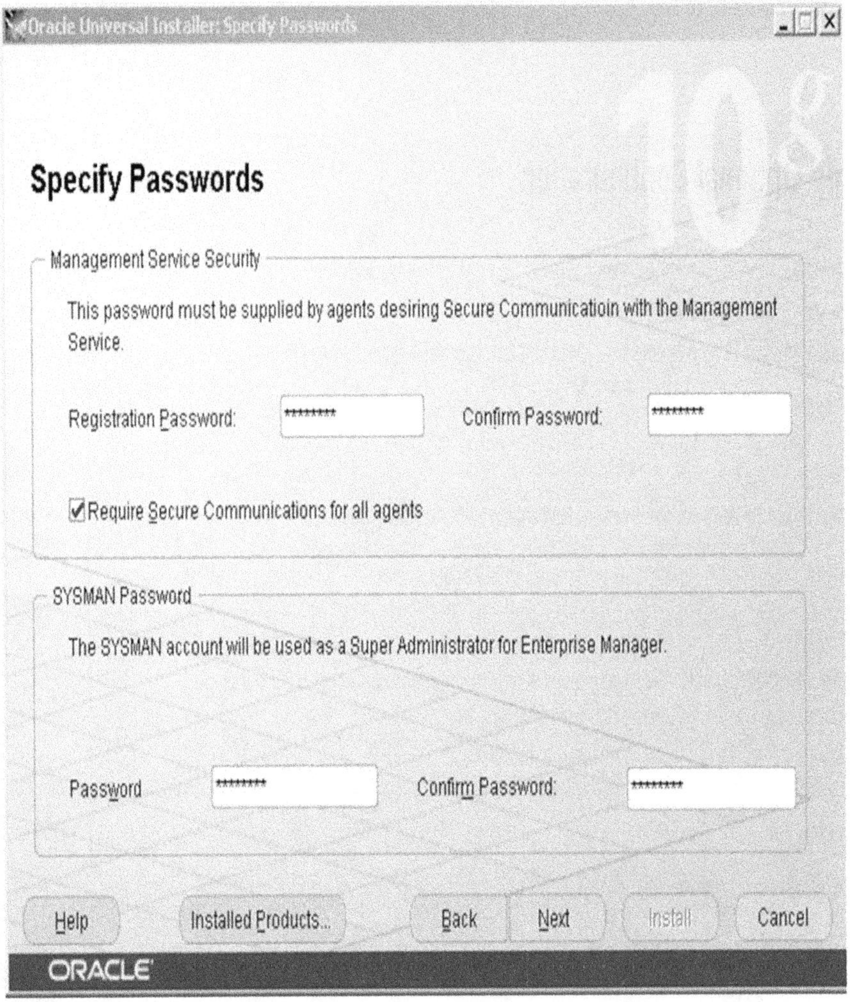

Figure 1.9: *Passwords*

Finally, the installation summary screen appears (Figure 1.10) where you can verify the space requirements. In this case, two homes will be created: the OMS Home and the Agent Home.

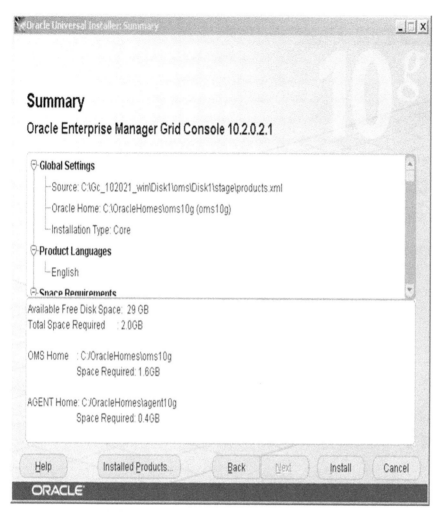

Figure 1.10: *Installation Summary*

The installation now proceeds (Figure 1.11) with the first stage of installing the Grid Control console and the Management Service.

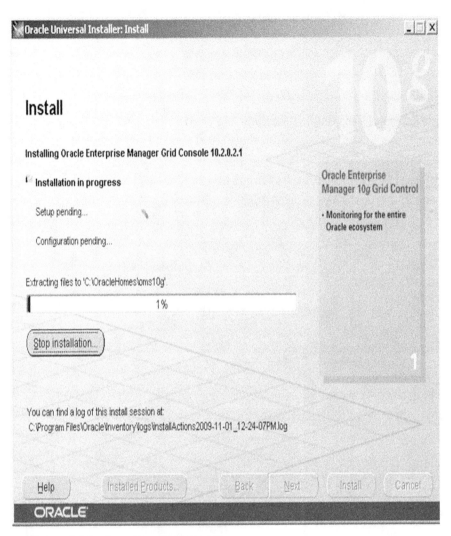

Figure 1.11: *Installing Grid Console*

This is followed with the installation of the Management Agent (Figure 1.12) as follows:

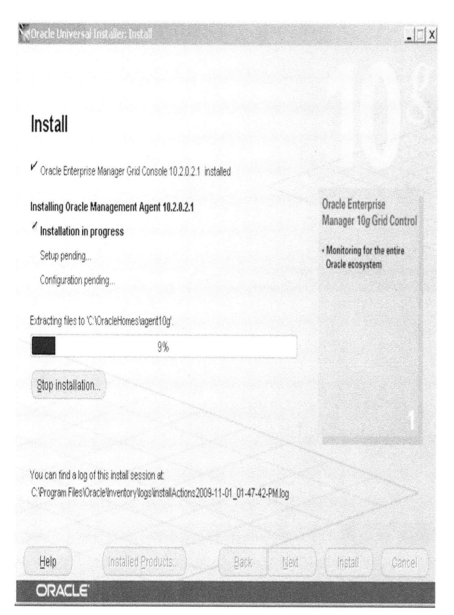

Figure 1.12: *Installing Management Agent*

After the installations are completed, the Configuration Assistants start running (Figure 1.13) and this is the step which will require the most time to complete.

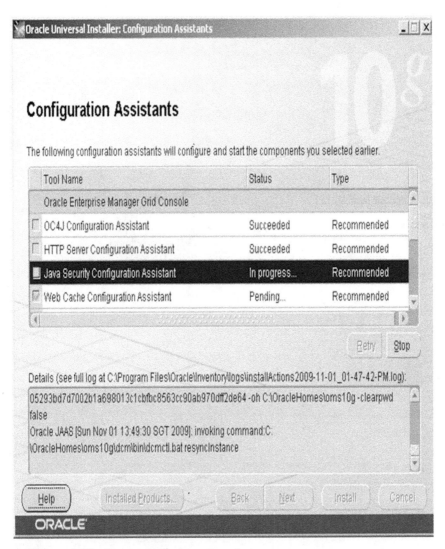

Figure 1.13: *Running Configuration Assistants*

The installation finishes once the Configuration Assistants have completed successfully. You can verify the installation by logging into the Grid Control console, i.e. the URL is provided at the end of the installation. Log on as SYSMAN, the repository owner. A typical Grid Control console appears as in Figure 1.14.

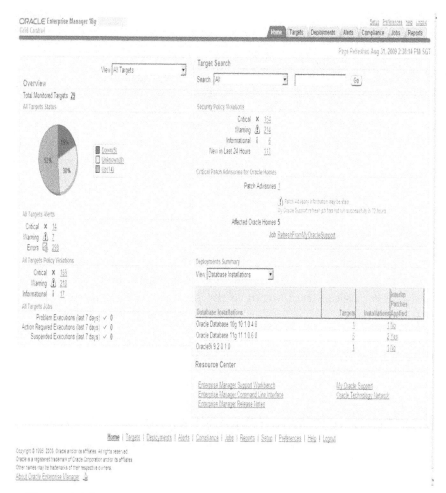

Figure 1.14: *Console Home Page*

Installing the 10.2.0.5 Patch

After the Full (Base) Release 2 is installed, you can upgrade using the Patch Installer (Agent, OMS, and Management Packs) for Release 5 (10.2.0.5). This Release 5 patch can also be downloaded from the same direct Enterprise Manager Downloads page on OTN as follows: http://www.oracle.com/technology/software/products/oem/index.html.

Stop the OMS and Agent as follows:

```
cd c:\OracleHomes\agent10g\bin
emctl stop agent

cd c:\OracleHomes\oms10g\opmn\bin
opmnctl stopall
```

You can now apply the 10.2.0.5.0 patchset to the OMS and then the agent as per the README instructions in the patch. Next, restart the OMS and the Agent.

```
cd c:\OracleHomes\agent10g\bin
emctl start agent

cd c:\OracleHomes\oms10g\opmn\bin
opmnctl startall
```

Finally, you can log in to the Grid Control console again and use the About Enterprise Manager link at the bottom of the page to verify that the upgraded version is 10.2.0.5.0.

You can also use *opatch lsinventory* at the command prompt. This will display the recut base product installer version in addition to the patchset version. You can test this in both the OMS and Agent Home inventories.

Using a New Database for the Repository

If you had decided to use the seed database for the repository by selecting the installation type as Enterprise Manager 10g Grid Control Using a New Database (Figure 1.15), you would proceed like this:

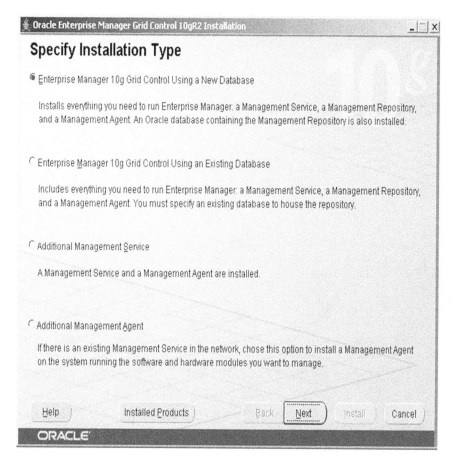

Figure 1.15: *Installation Type Using a New Database*

This would then bring up the screen to specify the configuration details for the database that you are creating (Figure 1.16). You name the database and specify the location for the database files.

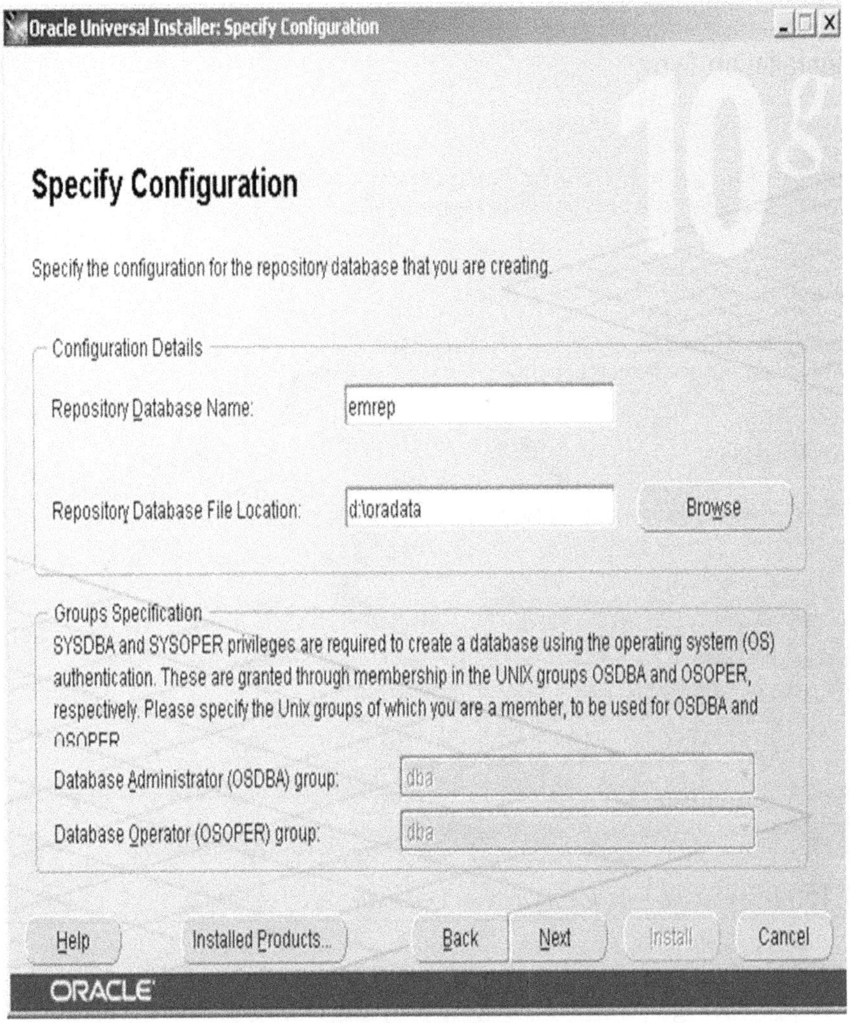

Figure 1.16: *Specify Configuration for New Database*

In Figure 1.17, you are asked to specify the management service security password and also the database passwords for SYS, SYSTEM and SYSMAN.

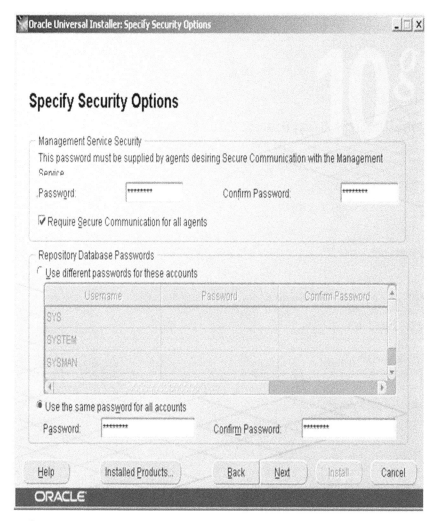

Figure 1.17: *Specify Security Options for New Database*

The installation summary for the new repository database installation option is seen in Figure 1.18. As expected, a third home will be created for the database under *C:\OracleHomes*. This directory will now have three homes in all: the Repository Database Home, the OMS, and the Agent.

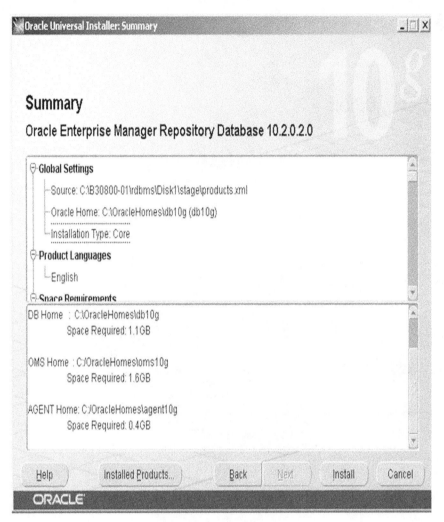

Figure 1.18: *Installation Summary for New Database*

The installation now proceeds with the first step of installing the Repository database (Figure 1.19). The rest of the steps are the same as in the installation option of using an existing database and will not be repeated here.

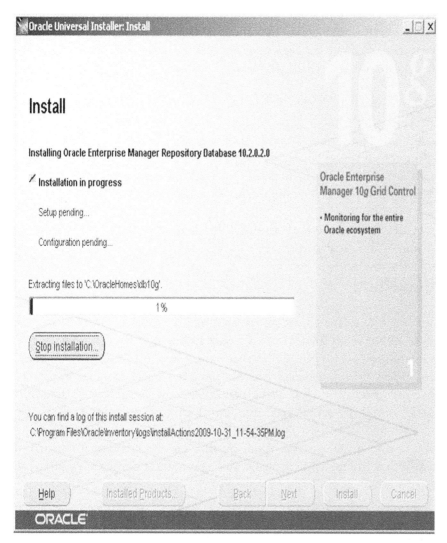

Figure 1.19: *Installing Repository Database*

Installing the Agent on Your Target Servers

You now have a functioning Grid Control installation that includes an OMS Home and an Agent Home, and you are using an 11g database in another database home as the repository database.

The Agent that is installed on the Grid Control server collects information about the health and performance of the targets on the server and sends that information to the Oracle Management Service (OMS), which then stores that information in the Grid Control repository.

What about your other production target servers? They also need to communicate to the Oracle Management Service. So the next phase of the installation is to install the Enterprise Manager Agent on every development, test and production server on your enterprise and in that order, if possible, for testing purposes. You must make sure that the O/S version on each server is patched to a level supported by the OEM Agent before installing the Agent.

Oracle provides various methods to install the Agent on the target servers and here are some of the most common.

The GUI Method

The traditional way to install the agent is to use the Oracle Installer on every target server, either from the CD or from the installation files you have copied across. This is the GUI method. If there are a small number of servers on which the agent is to be installed, you can use the Oracle Installer in this way and choose the installation type Additional Management Agent (the last option on the Installation Type screen seen in Figure 1.15).

This allows you to install just the agent on the server and point it back to the OMS host. When the install completes, the agent starts communicating to the OMS.

The drawback of this method is that it is time-consuming, meaning you have to sit through and interact with all the GUI screens, and not automated. However, it is the most straightforward method and easily understandable by the most novice of DBAs.

You can achieve some level of automation by using a response file and the silent method of installation, which answers the interactive questions for you. Actually, the silent installer mode is used effectively in the second method of agent install, which is described in the next section. This method effectively automates even the transfer of the installer files to the target server and is the logical next step evolution of agent installs.

The Agent Pull Method

The next method, which has been the most common in the past few years, is the Agent Pull method. This installation type makes use of the *agentDownload.<platform>* script, which is provided in your Grid Control installation under the directory *<OMS Home>\sysman\agent_download\10.2.02.0\<platform>*. This file is *agentDownload.vbs* on the Windows platform, which is a Visual Basic script that executes in Windows. You can execute this on your target servers that are using the Windows platform.

But what about your other target platforms, such as the various flavors of UNIX, e.g. Solaris, HP-UX, or AIX and Linux, e.g. Oracle Enterprise Linux, Red Hat Linux, SUSE Linux and such? The agent installation files for these multiple other platforms are not provided in this directory, but only the files for the platform on which you have installed the OMS – for example, Windows.

This means if you wish to install agents on UNIX or Linux platform servers, you have to download the agent software for those platforms and place these files on your central OMS server under the *<OMS Home>\sysman\agent_download* directory. Full instructions for this are provided in the section "Downloading Management Agent Software for Different Platforms" in the *Grid Control Installation and Configuration Guide 10g Release 5 (10.2.0.5.0)*.

Once you do this, you can use this method to install the agent on the different platforms you have downloaded. If Oracle were to provide the files for the agent installation on all UNIX-Linux-Windows platforms in every base installation set of files, the file size would be immense; hence, this pragmatic approach of downloading is needed.

There is another requirement. The *agentdownload.<platform>* script requires the pre-installation of GNU Wget, which is a free software package used for retrieving files using the Internet HTTP, HTTPS and FTP protocols. The Wget software is written in portable C, so you can easily install it on any UNIX-like operating system or even Windows. Download it from the Internet.

When executed, the *agentdownload.<platform>* script uses the *wget* utility to access the Oracle Universal Installer and the installation response file, and downloads or pull them from the OMS host to the Agent Install Host. Then the installer is executed in silent (non-interactive) mode using the values specified in the response file.

To access the actual install binaries which remain located on the OMS host, the Agent Install Host specifies their location via HTTP or HTTPs in the script itself. Note that the *wget* utility is a mandatory requirement for this method, so for environments lacking the utility and not allowing extra software utilities to be downloaded and installed on production servers due to hardening exercises, this deployment method may not be suitable.

This Agent Pull method is certainly faster, but requires *wget* to be installed on the target server, so there is some manual effort. This method of installing the agent has been used in large corporations with thousands of servers and is definitely a reliable method.

Agent Push or Agent Deploy Method

Agent Push, or Agent Deploy as it is now called, is a J2EE application within the Grid Control console. This application can be used easily for mass deployment of the OEM Agent since it allows you to specify multiple hosts.
The application uses the SSH protocol to transfer files and execute remote commands on your target server, and concurrently, SSH equivalence is required; you must run a script to set up this equivalence between the Oracle Management Service (OMS) server and the target servers.

This script is *sshUserSetup.sh* (renamed to *sshUserSetupNT.sh* in Windows) and you can find it in the following directory on your OMS server installation: *<OMS HOME>/sysman/prov/resources/scripts*. The SSH equivalence is needed so that password authentication will not be required during the execution of the Agent Deploy process. Note that this equivalence must be set only between the target hosts and the OMS and not among the target hosts themselves since that would be a security breach.

The Agent Deploy method is much faster than other methods, but requires SSH equivalence that could be a security issue in large corporations, especially financial institutions. So the method may not be entirely suitable for corporations that do not allow SSH equivalence due to strict security controls.

NFS Agent Installation

From Grid Control 10g Release 2 onwards, it has been possible to install a single agent on a shared NFS filesystem whereby you can have multiple servers share that same Agent Home's binaries to run the agent on each of those servers.

The shared agent in this scenario is called the Master agent. The *nfsagentinstall* script is used to install the other agents, which are called the NFS agents on the target servers. Each target server stores configuration files specific to itself in a *state* directory, the location of which can be selected during the *nfsagentinstall* script install.

The main drawback is that this method of agent install is not supported on clustered targets. Another limitation is that there can only be one NFS agent installation per server. Any installation of multiple agents on the same server will result in an error. The NFS Agent method is fast for installs, but may be slow when the agent runs since the Master agent is shared across all NFS agents, especially if using older NFS technology. The NFS technology in Netapps Filers may be more appropriate.

The method requires a shared NFS filesystem across all servers. This may not be a possibility in many corporations.

Agent Cloning

The Agent Cloning method is the latest method and could be the preferred option. This method is described in the "Management Agent Cloning" section of the *Grid Control Installation and Basic Configuration 10g Release 2 (10.2) Guide*. The method is simply to clone an existing agent install. The benefit is that you know the agent you want to clone works properly, and it can also be pre-patched to the appropriate level required. For example, you can have a 10.2.0.5 agent patched and ready for cloning.

However, note that even this agent cloning method is not supported for deploying agents onto clustered servers. You must use one of the other agent deployment methods that is supported for clusters. You can only use this method from the command line and not from the Grid Control console. The steps are simple. First you zip or tar the Agent Home directory, transfer this archive to the destination location, and expand it there. Next, you simply run the following commands inside the new home directory:

```
<Agent Home>/oui/bin/runInstaller -clone -forceClone ORACLE_HOME=<full path
of new Agent Home> ORACLE_HOME_NAME=<Name of the new Agent Home> -noconfig -
silent
```

The next step is to execute the Agent Configuration Assistant. This step configures the agent. The targets on the server are also discovered by the agent during this step. This is done by the following command:

```
<Agent Home>/bin/agentca -f
```

Then execute the *root.sh* script in the new Agent Home to set up the operating system level file and directory permissions as required:

```
<Agent Home>/root.sh
```

By default, the newly cloned agent is not in the secure mode. If the OMS requires secure communications, you must manually secure the agent as follows:

```
<Agent Home>/bin/emctl secure agent
```

This could be the preferred method for stand-alone servers (not clustered), but requires manual effort.

Another point to note is that if there are firewalls between the target servers and the central management services, then the firewall ports need to be opened by the networking department, and this would take more time.

Agents in Gold Copies

Of course, in a large corporation where there are many servers, the very best way to install OEM Grid Control Agents on every server is simply to change the corporate policy so that the agent is pre-provisioned on every new server created for deployment in new or existing projects.

This is the concept of the Gold Copy – a master server installation of the operating system and all the software required, such as the OEM Agent. This master server is then placed in a software library in OEM Grid Control and can be cloned out to new servers including the operating system, the Agent Home, the Oracle Home and even the Oracle Database. OEM Grid Control would be of great use in this scenario by virtue of the Provisioning and Patch Automation Management Pack. More on that later in the book.

Agent Deployment Best Practices

The following document from OTN explains the best practices for agent deployment and is also worth reading:

- 10g R2 Management Agent Deployment Best Practices: An Oracle White Paper, http://www.oracle.com/technology/products/oem/pdf/10gr2_agent_deploy_bp.pdf.

Conclusion

In this first chapter, the basic steps of the installation of the Oracle Enterprise Manager Grid Control system have been examined. Different methods were explored, such as installing with an existing database or installing with a new database.

The former is useful when it is required to use a newer release of the database for the repository instead of the seed 10.1 database that is supplied with the base install of OEM Grid Control. The new release 11g has a number of performance and storage enhancements and will be supported much longer than the earlier release of 10g. It was also noted how agents could be installed on the target servers using the various methods of Agent Push, Pull, Cloning, and so on. The new Oracle Enterprise Manager 11g Grid Control, released in April 2010, has considerably different installation requirements that will be introduced in the last chapter in this book.

This book has purposely not delved any deeper into installation and configuration topics; indeed, others have written tomes on the subject and Oracle documentation on installation is also impressive and all-encompassing. Instead, the preference is to deal with practical issues in this book, which will be delved into straight away.

The next chapter will look at the first practical topic taken from real life examples: scalable architecture for large sites. It will show how to set up a Grid Control site that can monitor and manage thousands of servers including the set up of the Big IP Load Balancers that can be used for this purpose. Welcome to the real world!

Scalable Architecture for Large Sites

In the world of Oracle Enterprise Manager Grid Control when large sites are mentioned, this means an enormous collection of targets which are being monitored and managed. This chapter will now show how to architect such sites so that OEM can perform its management and monitoring tasks with the maximum efficiency and scalability.

First Production Grid Control Site in the World

As a real-life example, study the first OEM Grid Control production site in the world, which was a large telecommunications company in Australia. Our corporate database team was involved in this major project in close association with Oracle Corporation Support consultants in Sydney and Melbourne who guided us in on-site Beta testing as well as the first production implementation of Grid Control Release 1, and later the upgrade to Release 2.

The objective of the project was to set up a centralized OEM Grid Control site at the company headquarters in Melbourne. The central site would be responsible for managing the many thousands of servers and databases in the entire company. Database teams responsible for these servers and databases were located all over Australia, and these teams were to use the central Grid Control console for their day-to-day database administration work.

Obviously, the central site needed to be horizontally scalable to handle new servers and databases as necessary when they were brought into the management framework of these teams.

Benefits to Management

As a whole, the centralized Grid Control project appealed to the management due to certain basic requirements:

1. Oracle licenses were increasing in use in different departments and teams, and this was becoming more and more difficult to keep track of. More and more projects were implementing Oracle in production.

   A corporate-wide view of all Oracle versions and licenses was required to assist with enterprise-level license agreements with Oracle and the central Grid Control console would offer such a view.

2. Many projects requested for excessive SAN storage space at the start of their implementations. As and when they moved into production, it was found that the space was either not allocated at the UNIX level, or it was over-allocated at the database level, meaning tablespaces had been created with a lot of free unused space.

   All this space was virtually wasted, and it was charged for at a high annual cost by the storage vendor. Management wanted to reduce this unnecessary expenditure. On request from management, the Oracle support consultants developed customized Grid Control storage usage reports to assist with this requirement.

   The reports they developed were ultimately included by Oracle Corporation in Release 2 of Grid Control since they were very informative to the corporate management and helped to reduce storage expenditure by millions of dollars.

3. The stated goal of the corporate database architect was to have one single database management tool in the entire company rather than disparate tools from different vendors.

   This was in the interest of company-wide standardization. Oracle Enterprise Manager Grid Control would be the single corporate tool towards this end.

4. The other factor driving the centralized Grid Control site was seen to be the fact that database managers in the organization were impressed with many of the features in Grid Control.

   These features included the powerful diagnostic and tuning capabilities to improve performance in the database, the easy setup and scheduling of RMAN backups without using UNIX scripts or the crontab, and the easy cloning of entire Oracle Homes and Oracle databases to new project servers or development/test servers from the centralized Gold copy of the Oracle Home or Oracle database. All these incredible possibilities of Grid

Control would ultimately decrease many hours of database consulting time used for internal projects.

Before the Grid Control project came into existence, the database teams had performed all these tasks manually, taking a lot of time. The manual steps were also subject to human errors which caused further project delays.

So due to the factors listed above, the centralized Grid Control site was seen as a necessity for the future of the corporate databases. The goal was to perform myriads of database management activities for thousands of database servers and to monitor them continuously.

Several database teams would use the centralized site for this purpose. This signified that the central site would have to be well architectured so it could scale in consecutive stages as future targets from different departments that would be added to the central system.

Architectural Design: The Incorrect Approach

The architectural design that was used to attain this type of horizontal scalability in Grid Control is the current subject and the reason why Grid Control is considered to be exceptionally different from older versions in terms of design and scalability. This recommended architectural design would be useful to sites that are considering the use of Grid Control, but are not correctly architectured. The design would serve as a real life handbook for these sites, and possibly a lifesaver.

Normally, when a DBA team or their management decides to implement Grid Control, they would use a test or development server to install the product on UNIX, or Linux, or Windows. In this scenario, all Grid Control components would be installed on a single server.

Next, the database team would install the OEM Agents using the push or pull method on development and test database servers. They would initially test the functionality of Grid Control, and then decide to install an agent on a production server for the first time. Some more Grid Control usage tests would then be run on production databases. The DBAs would be more and more pleased when they realize what Grid Control can do.

After some discussions and decision meetings, management ultimately decides to move Grid Control to production. However, at this time, a fundamental mistake is made. It is wrongly assumed that what works for a few development servers would also work with hundreds of production servers. So the database team is asked to install Grid Control on a single production server. All components are installed on this server; in some cases, the Grid Control install is even shared with a production or test database on the same box.

OEM Agents are next installed on the production and test database servers pointing back to the production Grid Control installation. For an initial short cooling-off period, things are fine and Grid Control works. Then the workload is slowly increased by the DBAs; a greater number of databases start to be managed by Grid Control. More and more monitoring is performed. The DBAs use it for setting up and scheduling RMAN backups, Dataguard standbys, and for cloning of databases and homes.

Ultimately, the entire Grid Control system slows down with all these activities and finally comes to a full stop.

Reasons for Project Failure

To identify the reason for this occurrence and the failure of the initial project, you need to understand the Grid Control internal architecture. The main working component engine of Grid Control is the Oracle Management Service (OMS). This is a J2EE application deployed on Oracle Application Server 10g.

Member components are the Oracle HTTP Server, the Oracle Application Server Containers for J2EE (OC4J), and the OracleAS Web Cache. From this, it is understood that Grid Control is a reduced version of Application Server. At the operating system level, a UNIX process can be found which is the actual OC4J_EM process. This is also seen when the *opmnctl* command is executed:

```
./opmnctl status
Processes in Instance: EnterpriseManager0.EMMgt001.in.ourcorporate.com
--------------------+--------------------+-------+---------
ias-component       | process-type       |   pid | status
--------------------+--------------------+-------+---------
WebCache            | WebCacheAdmin      |  2071 | Alive
WebCache            | WebCache           |  2099 | Alive
```

```
OC4J             | OC4J_EM      | 27705 | Alive
OC4J             | home         |   N/A | Down
dcm-daemon       | dcm-daemon   |   N/A | Down
LogLoader        | logloaderd   |   N/A | Down
HTTP_Server      | HTTP_Server  |  2072 | Alive
```

As an aside, the OMS runs on the Application Server, so it can be controlled very much like the Application Server.

You can use the OEM Application Server control or at the command line, use *opmnctl* (Oracle Process Management Notification Control) or *dcmctl* (Distributed Configuration Management Control). Besides this, you can use the OEM Control (*emctl*) utility.

It is obvious that OC4J_EM is a single UNIX process with its own PID. The process uses limited memory, and this is set by the file *$ORACLE_HOME/opmn/conf/opmn.xml*.

It is possible to increase the memory used by the process, but it will always remain a single process. This one process is then used to perform multiple Grid Control tasks such as managing databases and servers, Dataguard setups, cloning and so on.

Recommendations for Production

From this, you can begin to understand why such a setup using a single process will not scale. Suppose there was a world in which the database itself ran on a single process: the db writer, the log writer, the archiver, and other functions were all being executed by a single process. Then in that world, the database would certainly not be as efficient and scalable as it is in your world.

This brings you to one conclusion: only limited scalability will be achieved if all Grid Control components are placed on a single server. Doing this limits you to one OC4J_EM process with its inherent limits of memory and processor speed. If this process was under heavy load, it would reach its limits quickly and the process would slow down, not respond, or even reboot.

Database team members would not be able to log in to the Grid Control console for their own DBA activities. Therefore, implementing a single

OC4J_EM process means there is no redundancy and this would not be appropriate for a production Grid Control installation.

In production scenarios, it is generally not recommended to place all the Grid Control components on a single server, and these components should also not be shared with a production or test database on the same server. Grid Control should preferably be allocated its own server or its own set of servers via a well-architected and documented solution.

It is advisable to spend quality time to plan any Grid Control installation that is meant for production since it is a management solution for the enterprise and should be treated as a professional project and not as a minor database tool to be implemented on a single workstation. The initial planning study should be fully endorsed and supported by senior management, and they should unconditionally approve the budget for the architectured solution.

There is a major difference between Grid Control and past incarnations of OEM. Previously, Enterprise Manager was not N-tiered, and so it was not as scalable as it is today. The oldest version was Server Manager, which was a PC executable. Just prior to Grid Control was OEM 9i. This was a Java program that hogged the PC's memory and caused numerous crashes and restarts as a result.

The New Architecture of Grid Control

With the release of Grid Control, Oracle altered the internal architecture and changed it to the N-tier model. Grid Control was then divided into three components: the repository database, the Management Service (OMS), and the OEM Agent. The OMS, which was the main engine, now ran on the application server as an OC4J component, and therefore, became inherently scalable.

The reason that makes this possible is that Grid Control is not tied to one single PC or one single server. It runs as an OC4J application on the application server tier. Multiple OC4J_EM applications can be placed on the application server on numerous servers, and these can all be directed to the same OEM repository. This is the secret of the vast scalability of Grid Control.

Horizontal scaling was opened for the first time to the OEM world. Larger numbers of targets could be managed by adding more OMS servers to the OEM site. This can be illustrated more clearly by looking at an example of a real life implementation at a large site.

In this implementation, industry standard and open architecture were utilized. Linux servers with the following configuration were used (Table 2.1).

Specification Type	Specification Details
Hardware	Any hardware vendor
OS	Linux (version should be certified for Grid Control)
CPU	4 (2.2 GHZ or above)
Memory Requirement	8GB
Disk Space	10GB Free Space

Table 2.1: *Hardware and Software Configuration*

There was no need to deploy high-end expensive servers, typically with 24 CPUs or above, and 32 GB or more memory. More economical 4-CPU machines with eight GB memory were used so as to enable the system to scale horizontally and not vertically.

In Table 2.1, a free space requirement of 10 GB is outlined. This is for the Oracle software installation including the Oracle Database Home, the Oracle Management Service Home, and the Agent Home. This space does not include the repository database that is to be placed on a SAN or a NAS (Netapps filer).

The OEM repository database would require approximately 60 to 70 GB of disk space. There should be an equal amount of space reserved for the flash recovery area since this is where all archive logs and RMAN backups will be stored. Oracle strongly recommends database backups to disk, which is the concept of the flash recovery area. This enables fast disk-based recovery.

The idea is to trade expensive downtime for inexpensive disks because the flash recovery area can be configured on less expensive storage. In reality, although a large number of targets may be monitored and managed, you find that the repository database size rarely goes above 60 to 70 GB if out-of-the-box Grid Control functionality is being used.

A new feature in Grid Control ensures that the OEM repository database (10g) manages itself so far as space is concerned. It performs rollups of metric data at pre-determined intervals. The result is that the metric data that is being collected continuously from the targets will not dramatically increase the database size. However, since it is possible for the DBA to create extra metrics for monitoring each target, it is possible that this may lead to an increase in the repository database size which could be greater than this figure.

The Installation Technique

In the installation phase on a large site as the very first step, the Grid Control software is installed on one of the servers using the Grid Control Installation CDs. Select the OEM 10g Grid Control using a new database installation type to do this.

The repository database is created on this first server which becomes the repository server. In the Full install, the OMS and the OEM Agent are also installed on the same repository server. Three Homes are created on this server during the install for the three components. The OMS that has been installed on this server can be ignored at this stage.

As was described in the previous chapter, it is possible to use an existing preinstalled 11g database as the repository by selecting the installation type *OEM 10g Grid Control*. The next step is to install additional management services on the other servers by using the same Grid Control Installation CDs.

Select the *Additional Management Service* installation type. When the additional service is being installed, it is possible to point at an existing repository. Point to the repository database on the first server.

It is assumed that the repository database is already operational at this stage and the repository has been successfully installed in the *sysman* schema. In this type of install, only the OMS and the OEM Agent Homes are created on the server. Repeat this process on three or more additional servers. The servers now form the management service pool.

The architecture can be augmented further with a standby database server running Oracle Dataguard, or possibly an Oracle RAC cluster on multiple nodes. The latter will help in a horizontal scale-out of the repository database performance.

Scale-Out and Load Balancing

However, it is to be noted that in Grid Control, performance scale-out is more of a necessity on the management service level rather than the database level. The OC4J_EM is where the bulk of the Grid Control work is performed; therefore, scalability is more desired on the management services.

In the case of a large Grid Control setup, the architecture should include three or more load balanced management servers. Load balancing is a very important requirement of this architecture. You could use, for this purpose, a hardware load balancer like a BIG-IP Application Switch Load Balancer from F5 Networks. At the time of this writing, BIG-IP's flagship product is the BIG-IP network appliance. Initially a network load balancer, this product has now been enhanced with more functionality such as access control and application security.

Set up the load balancer with its own IP address and domain name, such as gridcontrolcentral.in.ourcorporate.com. This, in turn, points to the IP addresses of the three management services. At the point when a service request is received at the IP address or domain name of the load balancer - this can be at a certain port set up at the balancer level - the balancer distributes the incoming service request to any of the three active management servers in its pool and at the particular port specified.

Ports are used by Grid Control for different purposes. A certain port is utilized by the console logons. Another port is used for the Agent uploads of target metric data. The actual port numbers can be seen in the *portlists.ini* file that is created during the Grid Control install in the OMS or Agent Home /*install* subdirectory.

Set up the load balancer for all these ports; as a result, load balancing will occur for Grid Control console logons as well as for Agent uploads of target metric data. This would also give a level of redundancy to the Grid Control implementation.

Suppose as a result of heavy load, a management service was to stop functioning, thereby necessitating a manual restart of the OC4J_EM process using *opmnctl*. At this point, the other active management services will continue to service requests distributed by the load balancer.

The pool members are monitored by the load balancer at predetermined intervals on an ongoing basis. The non-reachable IP would be discovered in this manner, and will then be ignored by the load balancer until it becomes reachable again. Therefore, failure of any of the existing management server instances is tolerated by the Grid Control system due to the load balancer directing all subsequent service requests to the active surviving instances.

Subsequently, when the monitor detects that the node is online again, it automatically adds the node or service back into the pool. It is possible to use software load balancing instead of hardware load balancing. This type of balancing uses software configuration, i.e. network domain names, to route requests to the three management services. However, it is recommended to use hardware load balancing since this is a more robust solution, even though it is more expensive.

The total architecture solution should include a hardware load balancer for the purpose of load balancing as well as automatic failover capabilities, as described above. As an added precaution, a standby load balancer can also be deployed to ensure further redundancy at the Big IP load balancer level. This standby load balancer is set up to mirror any configuration change in the production load balancer, enabling it to take over seamlessly on the event of any failure in the production machine.

Such high availability architecture, where even the load balancer is deployed redundantly, is important when there are a number of production database teams using the centralized Grid Control to manage and monitor production systems.

The Grid Control scalable architecture that has been explained so far can be illustrated in Figure 2.1:

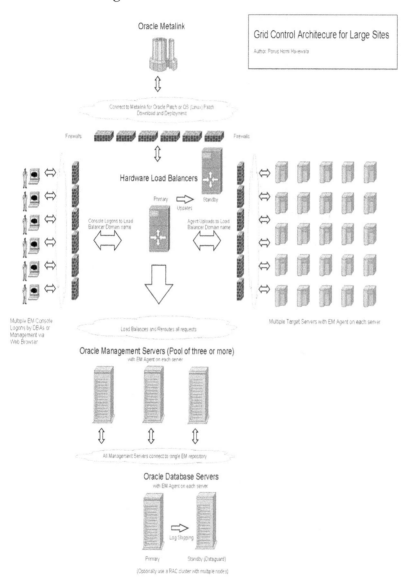

Figure 2.1: *Grid Control Architecture for Large Sites*

IP Assignments to Load Balancers

Assign internal IPs to both the primary and standby load balancers to manage them, and also assign a floating IP address pointing to either the primary or standby load balancer depending on which balancer is active. It is then possible to manage the load balancer through the floating IP using the URL address as listed in Table 2.2.

This management utility is the Big-IP web console. Log in to this console using the admin password or the support password. You can create new users in the Big-IP web console with read-only rights if necessary.

Use the Big-IP root password to log in at the Linux level using SSH. The load balancer runs Linux in a reduced command set shell known as the command line interface (CLI) of Big-IP. This uses commands that are nominally different from normal Linux. As an example, the command *bigtop* is used to monitor the load balancer in the CLI.

Table 2.2 shows the use of the internal IPs and floating IP. Although each IP address is unique, it is shown as nnn.nnn.nnn.nn for the purpose of illustration:

Hostname	IP Address	Description	Management URL (Big IP Web Console)
EMBal001	nnn.nnn.nnn.nn	IP Address Unit 1	https://<IP Address Unit 1>/bigipgui/bigconf.cgi
EMBal002	nnn.nnn.nnn.nn	IP Address Unit 2	https://<IP Address Unit 2>/bigipgui/bigconf.cgi
EMBal003	nnn.nnn.nnn.nn	IP Address Floating	https://<IP Address Floating>/bigipgui/bigconf.cgi

Table 2.2: *IP Address Table for Load Balancers*

Any one of the two load balancer units, EMBal002 and EMBal002, could be active and performing the load balancing.

There are three addresses that are associated with the two units: Unit 1 IP, Unit 2 IP, floating IP. The floating IP, being a shared IP address, exists on the unit that is active at the time. Therefore, in order to manage the active device, connect to https://FloatingIP. If the intention is to manage the units directly, it is possible to do this by accessing them via https://Unit1IP or https://Unit2IP.

The other servers in the Grid Control configuration are illustrated by the following table (Table 2.3):

Hostname	Ip Address	Description
EMMgt001	nnn.nnn.nnn.nn	EM Management Server (OMS 1)
EMMgt002	nnn.nnn.nnn.nn	EM Management Server (OMS 2)
EMMgt003	nnn.nnn.nnn.nn	EM Management Server (OMS 3)
EMMgt100	nnn.nnn.nnn.nn	EM Virtual Management Server (Virtual OMS)
EMDB001	nnn.nnn.nnn.nn	EM Database Server (DBS 1) Primary (Dataguard) or RAC
EMDB002	nnn.nnn.nnn.nn	EM Database Server (DBS 2) Standby (Dataguard) or RAC

Table 2.3: *IP Address Table for OMS and DB Servers*

Virtual Servers and Pools

Big-IP utilizes virtual servers, pools, associated nodes (members) and guiding rules to achieve the load balancing. Set up a virtual OMS server at the Big-IP level with its own IP address, which points to a pool of Oracle management servers with their IP addresses. The world outside points to the virtual OMS server's IP address or domain name for the purpose of Grid console logons as well as the Agent uploads from multiple targets.

Use the IP address:port combination to set up the pool of Oracle Management Servers so one pool can be set up for Grid console logons and a second pool for Agent uploads to the OMS. The recommendations on load balancing in the OEM Advanced Configuration Guide can be studied. With these in mind, and with due consideration of the points above, the Big-IP management console was used to perform the setup as described below.

EMAgentUploads and *EMConsoles* were created as two new pools. The three OMS nodes were added to both pools. It is also possible to add a node which is in the process of being setup by marking it as forced down in Big-IP so no monitoring takes place. The two new pools differ at the port level. Pool *EMAgentUploads* uses port 4889 for Agent uploads, whereas pool *EMConsoles* uses port 7777 for console access with 7777 being the default port for Oracle Web Cache. It is also possible to define the persistence (stickiness) at the pool level. This controls whether subsequent service requests are routed to the same pool member or a different one.

It was decided that Grid console logons as such will not require stickiness, since it is immaterial as to which OMS is used by the console upon connection by the DBA. However, on the other hand, Agent uploads could benefit from this stickiness. Therefore, the pools were modified accordingly; the Agent uploads pool was set up with simple persistence, and no persistence was configured for the console logons pool.

Two new Virtual OMS servers were created: one using port 4889 for Agent uploads using the *EMAgentUploads* pool, and the other using port 7777 for the web cache EM console using the *EMConsoles* pool. Both virtual servers used the same reserved IP address; however, the ports were different.

It is also possible to set up Big-IP monitors that continuously inspect the status of pool members. One such monitor, EMMon, was set up using the send string of *GET /em/upload* and the receive rule of Http XML File receiver as per instructions in the OEM Advanced Configuration Guide.

It was found, however, that this monitor did not work for the 7777 ports. The monitor only worked for the 4889 ports. So a new monitor, EMConsoleMonitor, needed to be created, based on http, with the send string of *GET /*. This successfully started to monitor the 7777 ports.

We now found that the URL http://EMMgt100:7777/em was working successfully and load balanced Grid console logons to the three management servers in the pool. URL http://EMMgt100:4889/em was tested and also successfully load balanced to the three servers. This, however, was to be used for Agent uploads only. Consequently, when corporate network alias gridcontrolcentral.in.ourcorporate.com was pointed to the virtual OMS server EMMgt100, the Big-IP load balancer was now active in production.

Issues Faced in Production

It was observed that the initial changes that were successful at the Big-IP management console did not work at the URL level – the URLs did not work. This was fixed only when the Big-IP was failed over to its standby and back again. The reason for this was that the configuration changes had not been propagated to the standby load balancer.

If you perform any configuration changes on the active load balancer, these changes should be propagated to the standby load balancer. This is done via the Big-IP configuration utility. Select Redundant Properties and click on Synchronize Configuration. The standby balancer configuration is immediately forced to be the same as the active including all pools, virtual servers, and rules. The standby will, therefore, be ready to take over the load balancing in the event of a failover.

Also note that when the admin password is changed, you must change the password on the peer controller to match in order for configsync to work. This is because the admin user is configured as the configsync user.

A manual failover can also be performed. It is recommended to mirror all connections before any failover to the standby Big IP; but, of course, this has a CPU performance hit. Select this option under the properties of Virtual server..Mirror connections.

We recall that a management service was installed on the Grid Control repository server during the initial install. The management service function has been disassociated from the repository function in this architecture, so it is not recommended to use the extra management service installed on the repository server. The server is dedicated only for the repository. This is reflected in the load balancer setup: only the three standalone management servers were configured in the Big-IP load balancer pools.

Since the surplus management service is a Java process that runs on the repository server, it consumes memory and processing power. Therefore, it is recommended to run *opmnctl* on this server and shutdown the management service, i.e. OC4J_EM.

If there are UNIX reboot scripts in place that start up the OMS, Agent and Database on the servers on reboot, you can leave out starting the OMS on the repository server. On this server, you need to start only the Listener, the Database and the Agent. On the other management servers, you can start the OMS and the Agent.

On Your Way to the Largest Grid Control Site

This chapter described a horizontally scalable architecture for OEM Grid Control to cater to large sites with thousands of targets that need to be managed and monitored. This architecture, using hardware load balancers and multiple management servers, has proved to be extremely powerful. The concept sits well with Oracle's Grid vision. It is possible to manage, with ease, hundreds or even thousands of Grid targets with this configuration.

In the case of the large Australian corporation which had deployed this project, they succeeded in scaling out to managing 600 to 700 target servers with multiple targets in each server with a pool of just three management servers. This was in the first phase. The next planned phase was to manage 2000 or more target servers, and this was deemed to be quite feasible because the right architecture was in place.

To scale-out further, you just need to add more low-cost Linux servers to the management service pool. Then you will be on your way to the largest Grid Control site in the world and this is no small thanks to the high-tech visionaries at Oracle Corporation. These men and women have enhanced OEM Grid Control and brought it to new heights of scalability and power at a level that has never been seen before.

Conclusion

This chapter has shown the scalable architecture that can be planned and implemented in this version of OEM Grid Control so as to enable a scale-out to thousands of targets in a corporate enterprise. This is done by using the twin concepts of management service pooling and load balancing.

Worth repeating is that it is always important to plan the OEM architecture at the outset of any implementation project so that performance does not degrade as more and more targets are added and as further features of OEM Grid Control are used by the DBAs. A failure of initial planning may lead to the failure of the Enterprise Manager project in due course. The central site also needs to be upgraded from time to time in terms of additional management services to cater to an increasing workload. Failure to upgrade the central OEM site may lead to it becoming slow and unreliable under stress and may cause DBAs to ultimately turn away from its use.

Now that the desired architecture is understood, next will be a look again at the Oracle Enterprise Manager Grid Control console, and from that point, the book will delve deeper into the advanced practical uses of Grid Control. In particular, RMAN backups, and how they can be easily configured, set up, and scheduled using Grid Control will be examined.

How Grid Control Helps in RMAN Backups

Most DBAs worth their salt know that Oracle has a powerful tool to back up and recover Oracle databases. This tool is Oracle RMAN (Recovery Manager). As has already been stated, Oracle Enterprise Manager (OEM) Grid Control is the flagship enterprise management system from Oracle. This is used to manage and monitor just about everything in the enterprise including your databases, your application servers and your hosts.

This chapter will demonstrate how today's DBA can make a very smart choice: he/she can set up and schedule RMAN backups via the modern approach of Grid Control instead of the older, more time-consuming manual method of UNIX shell scripting and cron jobs.

Command Line Issues

An increase in OEM Grid Control sites around the world is being seen. More and more DBAs are beginning to understand that they can no longer ignore the powerhouse that is Enterprise Manager like they did in the past, using the command line instead.

It does not make practical sense to use the command line anymore for the times have changed. Oracle software in the 21st century is very complex and has numerous options and products, all of which need to be managed seamlessly and on numerous instances. More sophistication and power is seen nowadays even in the core database options. If you were to use the command line only to manage these options, the task would fast become very complicated and very tedious.

As an example, take the case of Tuning Sets in 10g onwards. You could create these Tuning Sets via PL/SQL commands issued on the SQL*Plus command line. You could also call the Tuning Advisor, and other new Advisors in 10g and 11g, from the command line.

However, does it really make sense to do this?

It would mean you have to write and execute numerous SQL and PL/SQL commands. You would have to learn the correct syntax for calling all the new Database Advisors, and you would have to recall that syntax especially in times of extreme stress when the database is not performing as expected and your users are screaming.

A savvy DBA might write diagnostic and tuning scripts for this purpose, or similar scripts can be bought from tuning companies on the Internet. But in the opinion of many, there is a flaw in this approach: such scripts have to be tested initially to make sure they do their expected work. They also have to be maintained indefinitely in the future since they may not work with new database releases. When Grid Control can easily be used, why go for either the manual approach or the scripted approach?

For example, you can use the graphical interface of Grid Control to find the busiest periods of time in your production database. You can then drill down and find the top statements that are impacting the database. You can easily select these statements and create a Tuning Set, then run the Tuning Advisor.

Things are that effortless and the DBA can easily save on the manual effort of typing the commands. There is also no need for the continuous maintenance of any customized scripts with every new database release. As and when Oracle releases new versions of the database, future OEM Grid Control patches would automatically cater to the new release and the special features in that release. Script maintenance would, therefore, be totally avoided and the onus is on Oracle to provide the new features in Grid Control.

It is not that surprising that the use of OEM Grid Control is strongly recommended by Oracle for management of many of its powerful options like Real Application Clusters (RAC), which is the active-active clustered database option. Grid Control is very useful, for example, in analyzing the performance of the Oracle RAC database in a very straightforward and convenient manner. This is done via using the Diagnostic and Tuning Packs, available as license options. The numerous packs available in Grid Control will be described in later chapters of this book including more details on the popular Diagnostic and Tuning Packs.

It is quite possible to install Oracle RAC and manage it using the command line interface alone. However, the latest technology does need the latest management tools, and that is where OEM Grid Control is very important; otherwise, you may not be able to realize the full potential of Oracle RAC for your company.

This is the crux of what management should really understand. Needless to say, when a RAC project is started in the company, Grid Control with its multiple Management Packs should always be included as the management tool for the day–to-day monitoring and management of RAC. Similarly, OEM can be used to handle Oracle Recovery Manager (RMAN). Even though this technology is not as complicated as Oracle RAC, it will be used in this chapter as an example to convince the readers of the importance and many benefits of this approach.

The traditional way to set up RMAN backups, using manual shell scripts and the UNIX *cron* utility for the scheduling, will be demonstrated now. This will then be compared to the OEM method, which will continue onto the next chapter.

Early Days of Database Backups

All that has been described here has been seen in practice over the last 10-15 years in actual production – real life experience in a large company that spans an entire continent is the inspiration behind this chapter. For a number of years in this company, Oracle databases were backed up cold (offline). This then progressed to hot (online). As the years went on, RMAN started being used to back up databases, but this was still using UNIX shell scripts and the UNIX *cron* utility as had been done before.

In the early 2000s, as Grid Control started to be used in the company, database teams began performing their RMAN backups using Grid Control. Immense benefits were immediately realized. This move from manual backups to scripting, then to RMAN scripting and finally to Grid Control, was likewise being observed around the world.

The very early database backups were offline (cold) backups. The database was shut down manually by the DBA who then created an OS file copy of all the database files. This OS copy was the database backup, and would be stored either on tape or disk – more so on tape in those days when disk space was expensive.

Not long after the very early manual days, UNIX shell scripts started being written by the DBAs to do the nitty gritty work. The database would be shut down, the database files copied to the backup location or tape using OS file copy commands, then the scripts would start up the database.

Scheduling was achieved via the UNIX scheduler utility *cron*, and this was set up in the Oracle user's *crontab* file. The *crontab* executed the backup script at the appropriate time. This achieved a level of automation, but there was still the manual effort of writing, implementing, and testing the scripts. The scripts also needed to be maintained if there were system changes in the future.

What would happen if a different tape drive was used or a different backup location? What if the database name was changed? What if more databases were installed on the same server and they all needed to be backed up to the same backup location on tape or disk? In all these scenarios, the DBA would have to maintain and change the backup scripts, followed by testing them again and redeploying them, and debugging the scripts again if there were any issues.

Oracle Database Version 6 introduced online (hot) backups. In such backups, which were a very new technology at the time, the database could stay open at the same time the backup was being performed and keep on processing transactions. But before the OS file copy could take place, each tablespace had to be placed in a special backup mode. This was via the command *alter tablespace <tablespace name> begin backup*. When this was done, the checkpoint SCN in all datafile headers for that tablespace was frozen, but extra redo was also generated by the database to aid in recovering fractured blocks, i.e. blocks that were in the process of being changed when being backed up by the OS utility.

The DBA scripting team swung into action again. The scripts were made more complex; they were rewritten to connect to the database, and a list of all the tablespaces was obtained. The script would then put all the tablespaces in the special backup mode suggested by Oracle, and the OS file copy to tape or disk would then be performed. After the copy was complete, the script would take the tablespaces off the backup mode.

RMAN Enters the Fray

Oracle 8 introduced RMAN as a new backup method for Oracle databases, and it came with a strong recommendation from Oracle. Technically, this was superior to the online backup method since there was no longer any need to put the tablespaces in backup mode. RMAN understood when any block was fractured and came back to re-read it. This generated less redo and placed less strain on the database.

Even with these technical benefits, many DBAs resisted using RMAN and it took a long time to convert them. But why? Probably, this was due to Oracle's concept of a separate catalog database to be used along with RMAN to hold the backup history.

To many DBAs who were first introduced to this RMAN technology, including the writer of this book, it just did not make sense to create a new database in order to back up an existing database. The question that begged an answer was how would the new catalog database then be backed up? By RMAN again, creating a new catalog database in the process, or would it be backed up via a logical backup such as Oracle's export and import database utilities?

Oracle astutely observed that RMAN uptake was not as widespread as expected, and very soon understood the DBA mindset. Later versions of RMAN in Oracle 8i, 9i and 10g increased the power of the control file of the database to itself functioning as the RMAN catalog, thus making it less necessary to create a separate catalog database.

This made perfect sense: backup a database using RMAN and retain the history of the backups in the control file. Of course, a limited history could be held in the control file, but it was always possible to restore an older control file if you wanted an older history.

Ultimately, the enhanced RMAN control file method of database backups started to gain acceptance in the mainstream, and DBAs started to use RMAN to backup their production databases in increasing numbers.

History Repeats Itself

But RMAN still had inherited the history of the *cron* and UNIX shell scripts for these had been used since time immemorial to perform offline or online database backups. The DBAs simply modified the scripts to connect to RMAN and perform the backup using the RMAN commands. The tablespaces no longer needed to be placed in backup mode, so those commands were removed. Mostly everything else stayed the same, including the use of the UNIX *crontab*.

This carried on for the next decade. Oracle's enhanced RMAN utility, with all its powerful features that increased over the years, was still being called exactly as in the early years of backups; with *cron* and shell scripts. Sort of like taking a futuristic voice-activated car and trying to get it to start by pushing it with a horse cart.

The fact is, there are many large companies even today that use shell scripts to perform RMAN backups. This may seem outmoded in today's age of powerful enterprise management tools such as OEM Grid Control, but it is really so. In fact, some companies further mystify the situation by having their shell scripts call layers of shell scripts to perform a single database backup, all in the name of so-called script standardization and security. This is plainly ridiculous.

Oracle has simplified the RMAN command language so that it is extremely easy and English-like to perform database backup and recovery. However, this aim of simplified use is defeated by the scripting layers in these companies, the actual RMAN commands being lost under the tons of debris of these scripts.

Pity the new DBA who starts to work in these companies, even if experienced. He or she would know how to work with RMAN, but would take a few days at least to understand how the customized layers of scripts function to perform a single database backup. This would impair the productivity of such a DBA considerably.

Think of a debugging scenario and having to go through the debris of old scripts. Think of modification to these scripts to cover new backup requirements. Add all this up to extremely high maintenance costs, and all because of the dogheaded adherence to the scripting approach.

The point needs to be driven home once and for all, and the doubters in the DBA world need to be convinced. So the plan is to demonstrate a setup of RMAN backups just like was used to being done in the past using shell scripts and *crontab* – the manual approach. This will then be compared to the OEM approach where you can achieve the same results very easily, without any script writing or maintenance, by simply using OEM Grid Control.

Immense timesavings are achieved in the tasks of setting up, testing and day-to-day maintenance when this approach is used, and manual scripting is eliminated. This fact is more or less enough to convince higher management that OEM Grid Control is indeed the best choice for managing the company databases.

Shell Scripts (How It Was Done in the Old Days)

The production server to be used in this demonstration is proddb001, and this has an Oracle database PRD1FIN which is used by the financial team for their customized application. The management has asked the DBA to set up and schedule RMAN backups for the PRD1FIN database. An appropriate backup strategy is to be used as decided by the DBA.

The first step for the DBA is to write the shell scripts to generate the RMAN backup, and then to install them on the database server by following the setup steps mentioned below. The DBA would need to use similar but slightly modified steps for every database server requiring RMAN backups for its databases. In the case of an active-passive cluster such as HP-Serviceguard or SUN-HA, this would have to be done for each of the active-passive servers in the cluster.

- Step 1: Log in as Root. Edit the file */etc/cron.d/cron.allow* and add the line "oracle". This enables the Oracle UNIX user to make use of the UNIX cron scheduler.

- Step 2: Log in as the Oracle UNIX user. Edit the *crontab* of this login to include the following schedule line:

```
30 22 * * * dba/storescripts/bkp_db_via_rman.sh PRD1FIN
```

Every day at 22:30 hours, the *bkp_db_via_rman.sh* script will be executed as per this inserted line, and the PRD1FIN database will be backed up. The database name is an argument to the script.

- Step 3: Use Oracle SQL*Plus and connect as a DBA to database PRD1FIN. Create an externally identified user as follows:

```
create user ops$oracle identified externally;
```

As a result of this command, the Oracle UNIX user can log on to SQL*Plus as the Oracle database user. Since the database user is identified externally, there is no need to specify the password. The user is using operating system authentication.

It should be noted here that for RMAN backups, the OS account needs to have SYSDBA privileges and this is done via membership in the dba group in UNIX, or in the ORA_DBA group when Windows is being used.

Scripts that require SYSDBA rights, such as for database-level backups, can use this kind of OS authentication technique for connecting to the database. This avoids the hard coding of database passwords in scripts which is not advisable, since UNIX files can be read by any UNIX login if the file permissions are not made secure. It is safer to have the externally identified Oracle UNIX user login as the DBA and perform the backup.

Netapps Filer Mounts

- Step 4: The RMAN backups will be stored on a filer volume. At the server level, the backup volume should be mounted as */U777* as per the company database standards. Examine the */etc/vfstab* file and confirm that there is an entry for the mount point */U777* as follows:

```
syd-datacenter-netappsfiler-tier3:/vol/vol1/backuparea - /U777 nfs -  yes
hard,vers=3,intr,suid,proto=udp,rsize=32768,wsize=32768
```

You can refer to Netapps Manuals for details on the mount options to be used. These are different for Solaris, Aix, HP-UX and Linux. They also differ as per the filer versions. In case the entry for the mount point does not exist, the storage team must be requested to allocate a volume to the server, and the UNIX administrator must then add it to this file. Having such an entry in the */etc/vfstab* file ensures that the mount point will be mounted every time the server is rebooted.

The only other option is to mount it manually using the *mount* command as the root UNIX user, but this is not recommended. This can be done as follows:

```
mkdir  /U777
mount  /U777
```

- Step 5: Log in as root and execute the *chown* command:

```
chown -R oracle:dba   /U777
```

The *chown* command with the *–R* argument ensures that the */U777* backup mount point and all the sub-directories under this mount point are owned by the Oracle UNIX user and dba UNIX group. This enables RMAN to create backup pieces under this mount point.

- Step 6: Log in as oracle. Supposing */home/oracle* is the Oracle UNIX user's home directory, execute the following commands:

```
mkdir /home/oracle/dba
mkdir /home/oracle/dba/storescripts
mkdir /home/oracle/dba/logs
mkdir /home/oracle/dba/work
mkdir /U777/PRD1FIN
mkdir /U777/PRD1FIN/rmancmd
mkdir /U777/PRD1FIN/log
```

The *mkdir* commands create the sub-directories where the shell script will be stored, the logs will be written to, the temporary work files will be created, and also where the generated RMAN command script and RMAN log file will be stored.

RMAN Backup Shell Script

- Step 7: Change directory to */home/oracle/dba/storescripts*. Create the *bkp_db_via_rman.sh shell* script in this directory.

This file may need to be appropriately modified for every different server it is installed on.

🖫 bkp_db_via_rman.sh (partial)

```
#!/bin/ksh
#
#       bkp_db_via_rman.sh
#
#       Purpose:     Backup Database using Oracle RMAN
#       Senior DBA:  Porus Homi Havewala
#
#       Created on 30/08/2009 by Porus HH
#
```

```
# derive job name from basename of script file name
jobname="$0"
job=`basename $jobname`

# specify the dbkit directory
dbkit=$home/dba/storescripts

# specify oratab
oratab=/var/opt/oracle/oratab

# create the error message if required
errmsg="
    $job: `date '+%h:%m:%s'` you have specified an invalid parameter. the
correct syntax is:
    $job <dbname>
"

# if there is an argument, set the dbname to the argument
if [ "$1" ]
then dbname=$1
# otherwise show error message with correct syntax and exit
else echo $errmsg
     exit ${error}
fi

# Assign the first argument to the Oracle Sid
ORACLE_SID=$1

# The following is set so that the oraenv script from
# Oracle executes without interaction

ORAENV_ASK=NO; export ORAENV_ASK

# Execute oraenv which is the script supplied by
# Oracle to set the environment variables specific to Oracle

. oraenv

# Test for success, otherwise show error and exit
if [ $? -ne 0 ]; then
    echo "$JOB: `date '+%H:%M:%S'` Failed to set oracle environment
variables. Aborting.."
    exit ${ERROR}
fi

# This code can be used if in an active-passive
# cluster and running on passive node

echo "Now database $ORACLE_SID is being verified"

# Test if Oracle SID is a valid entry in the oratab file
if grep -c $ORACLE_SID $ORATAB > /dev/null ; then

    # Test if Oracle database background process PMON is running
    pmon=`ps -ef | egrep pmon_$ORACLE_SID  | grep -v grep`

      if [ "$pmon" != "" ];
```

```
        then
                echo "\n"
        else
                echo "\n******* POSSIBLY THE PASSIVE NODE*****"
                echo "\n******* ORACLE_SID NOT RUNNING *********"
                exit 0
        fi

else
        echo "\n******* $THERE IS NO ORACLE_SID ON THIS SYSTEM *******\n"
        exit 1
fi

# Define the backup directoy, exit if the directory does not exist

backuplocation=/u777/$dbname
if [ ! -d $backuplocation ]; then
    echo "$job: `date '+%h:%m:%s'` could not find $backuplocation directory.
aborting.."
    exit ${error}
fi

# define the log directory and the name of the rman command file

script=`basename $0`
logdir="$home/dba/logs"
cmdfile="${backuplocation}/rmancmd/rman_${dbname}.cmd"
nodename=`hostname`

# the backup logfile is defined under the backup location
# therefore will be backed up in any file-level backup
# also include the node name in the logfile name
# this is due to the 2 active-passive nodes

logfile="${backuplocation}/log/${script}_${nodename}_${dbname}_`date
'+%d%m%y-%h:%m'`.log"
```

Each day at the specified time set in the *crontab*, the *bkp_db_via_rman.sh* shell script will be executed. The script will generate the RMAN command file */U777/PRD1FIN/rmancmd/rman_PRD1FIN.cmd*:

```
#
#       Created                         Porus Homi Havewala     30/08/2009
#

# Configure RMAN settings
configure retention policy to recovery window of 3 days;
configure controlfile autobackup on;
configure controlfile autobackup format for device type disk to
'$backuplocation/cf_%f';
configure backup optimization on;
configure device type disk parallelism 3;
configure default device type to disk;
configure channel 1 device type disk format '$backuplocation/b_%u';
configure channel 2 device type disk format '$backuplocation/b_%u';
```

```
configure channel 3 device type disk format '$backuplocation/b_%u';
configure snapshot controlfile name to '$backuplocation/snapcf_${dbname}.f';

# create backup of database and archivelogs
# delete archivelogs that are backed up

backup database plus archivelog delete input;

# Maintainance commands for crosschecks
# Also delete expired backups

allocate channel for maintenance device type disk;
crosscheck backup;
delete noprompt expired backup;
delete noprompt obsolete device type disk;
crosscheck archivelog all;
delete noprompt expired archivelog all;

# End of RMAN command script
```

What the Steps Mean

The RMAN configuration commands specify a recovery window of three days as the RMAN retention policy. As per the policy, all backups required to recover up to the last three days will be retained.

However, depending on the size of the database and the free space available in the backup mount point */U777*, at any point this setting may need to be changed. The free space needs to be closely monitored by the DBA and the recovery window changed if necessary.

Controlfile autobackup has also been configured. This means the control file will be automatically backed up along with every database or archivelog backup. Since you are using the nocatalog mode of RMAN, it is of utmost importance to ensure the safety of the control file and make certain it is backed up since the history of all the backups is contained in the control file.

Three RMAN channels will be used to create the backup pieces because a parallelism setting of three has been configured. Using such a setting will increase the speed of the backup, but this will also depend on the disk subsystem structure. The RMAN commands that follow perform a full backup of the database and the archivelogs. The archivelogs are deleted immediately after their backup, as specified by the delete input clause.

Maintenance commands are executed after the backups are completed. These crosscheck the existing backups and archivelogs, ensuring that they are present on disk; otherwise, marking them as expired. After the crosschecks, all the expired (not found) and obsolete (as decided by the retention policy) database, archivelog and controlfile backup entries are deleted from the controlfile records, as are also expired (not found) archivelog entries.

- Step 8: Set the file permissions of the *bkp_db_via_rman.sh* script to make it user executable at the UNIX level:

```
cd /home/oracle/dba/storescripts
chmod u+x bkp_db_via_rman.sh
```

- Step 9: Before the cron scheduler swings into action and calls the *bkp_db_via_rman.sh* script, test it manually by calling it from the UNIX prompt to make sure it works as expected:

```
cd /home/oracle/dba/storescripts
./bkp_db_via_rman.sh PRD1FIN
```

This will execute the RMAN command script on the PRD1FIN database, performing a full database backup and archivelog backup. When the backup is complete, ensure that there are no errors by inspecting the generated RMAN log file. Verify that the RMAN backup pieces have been created successfully in the backup directory */U777/PRD1FIN*.

- Step 10: The last task is to ensure that the cron scheduler performs its task of calling the backup script at the right time, and the scheduled backup has completed successfully. Monitor this over the next day and for some days. If this is not the case, there may be something wrong in the *crontab* entry and it may need correction. Also make sure the backup maintenance works as expected.

Issues with Manual Steps

As can be seen, the traditional approach consists of a number of manual steps. The estimates supplied by the DBA implementation team range from three to four hours to perform these steps, including customizing the backup script and testing out the backup script for each installation. This would have to be done on every new server that is provisioned in the company.

Compressing this time frame is possible, but a rush job could potentially introduce human error. The management finally decides on an average time component of three hours per server so as to allow sufficient time for the DBA team. However, even three hours adds up to a lot if there are a number of RMAN deployments happening on projects every week in a large-sized company. DBAs are quite expensive and their time costs a lot to the business, and this approach would potentially cost a lot of expensive DBA dollars.

Besides these factors, management must also consider the maintenance cost aspect of the UNIX shell scripts. DBAs familiar with UNIX shell scripting need to be hired and retained, or if Perl has been used as the scripting language, then perl-literate resources are required. Other sites may use other scripting languages, and since there are no scripting standards in place, scripts may be written in totally different ways to do the same job. There may be little or no comments in the code and little or no documentation.

After the initial author of the scripts has moved on to bigger and better things in his career, other new DBAs inherit the scripts. The newcomers spend a lot of time, first of all, understanding the code and logic of the scripts and when they feel confident, they try their own enhancements or code fixes.

The scripts start to grow exponentially with every new DBA that comes on as more and more maintenance work gets done, until finally these initially simple scripts start to resemble a multi-headed monster. Sound familiar? The very aim of OEM is to eliminate such issues. In the next section, you will go on to set up and schedule RMAN backups without handwritten or borrowed scripts, and without the use of *cron*. This will be done by using OEM Grid Control.

The result is considerable timesavings for all these tasks such as writing the scripts, setting up and scheduling the backups, testing the backups and continued maintenance of the scripts. The dependence on homegrown scripts would virtually be eliminated; therefore, it would be no longer necessary to hire specialists in shell scripting.

Debugging of errors would also be made a lot easier if using OEM since there are no shell scripts to be debugged line by line. Only the RMAN commands would need to be checked and modified if necessary. The future maintenance of the RMAN backups of your database would also be simplified.

If you were to compare and demonstrate both the traditional and OEM approaches in this way based on real-world scenarios, a number of large companies would immediately be convinced of the fact that using OEM Grid Control is the best way for many DBA tasks for all of their databases. Seeing is believing!

The Enterprise Manager Way

The database to be used is PRD1FIN, which is used by the Accounting department in production. The departmental DBA team has been asked to set up and schedule RMAN backups for the database using the Grid Control approach. The central database team has already set up and manages a central Grid Control site in the company. The Accounting department's DBA team, along with other DBA teams all across the company, has access to this site on the company intranet.

They use the central site to monitor and manage all the databases and hosts for which their teams have the responsibility. Each team can only see and administer the databases and hosts that have been allocated to them. This makes sense rather than each team using their own Grid Control install for their own department, which would defeat the purpose of a centralized Grid Control.

When the departmental DBAs log in to Grid Control, the Console Home Page is the first thing visible on the screen (Figure 3.1).

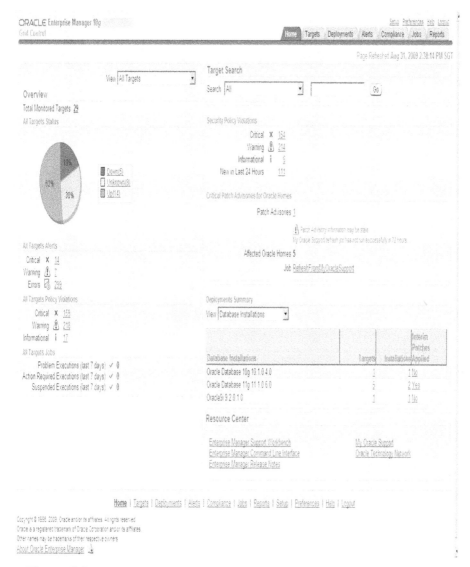

Figure 3.1: *Grid Control Console*

You should ensure that the central Grid Control site has been deployed using scalable architecture and best practices. The idea is for it to be able to handle the monitoring as well as the management of multiple database servers around the company. The database management tasks are known to be intensive, such as Dataguard setup and monitoring, database cloning, and RMAN backups besides many others which may be run multiple times over multiple databases.

If you want an idea of the appropriate architecture, please refer to the previous chapter of this book titled, "Scalable Architecture for Large Sites". This chapter explains the scenario of a massive Grid Control site monitoring and managing many hundreds of database, server and listener targets. The latest version of OEM Grid Control is strongly recommended to be deployed at such a central site. It is easy to find the version of Grid Control that is installed by going to the Console Home page and clicking on the About Oracle Enterprise Manager link at the lower end of the page as seen in Figure 3.1.

The version is clearly visible as *Oracle Enterprise Manager 10g Release 5 Grid Control 10.2.0.5.0,* which is the latest available at the time this book was written (Figure 3.2).

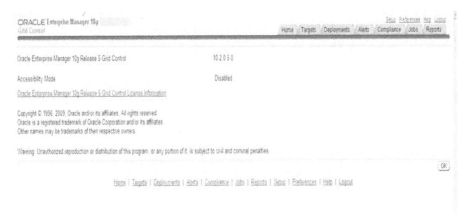

Figure 3.2: *Grid Control Version Screen*

Security Concerns

Security teams often voice their concerns when they are informed about a central management site being set up in their company. They fear that database administrators will be able to access any databases which are not in their domain. However, this fear is unfounded. Just the fact that Grid Control is a central site does not mean everything is accessible to everyone.

Grid Control imposes full security via the creation of Target Groups whose rights can be assigned to different Grid Control administrators. So when disparate database teams log in to the Grid Control console, they have access only to their own Target Groups in which the databases, listeners, hosts and application servers managed by that particular team have been placed. The access to the targets can also be controlled – full management rights or only view access.

Since the Accounting department DBA team is responsible for the PRD1FIN database and its listener, they would be assigned their own Target Group and a new Administrator login to Grid Control. When any of this team would log on to the console, the PRD1FIN database and associated targets would be available to them, but not any of the targets handled by the other DBA teams.

Pre-Install Steps

A new filer volume will be used to store the RMAN backups.

At the UNIX server level, the backup volume from the filer must be mounted as /U777 since this is as per the database standards enforced in the company. However, for the purpose of the demonstration, you will use D:\flash_recovery_area as the backup volume in Windows.

Ensure that the backup volume is mounted automatically on server reboot by placing an entry for the mount point in /etc/vfstab. As a result, when df –k (disk free space shown in kilobytes) is executed at the UNIX prompt, the backup mount point /U777 should appear in the list of filesystems displayed. This mount point should be owned by oracle:dba (UNIX user:group). If this is not the case, change the permissions via the command:

```
chown -R oracle:dba   /U777
```

The command recursively changes the ownership of the /U777 backup mount point and all its sub-directories to be owned by oracle:dba. This enables the powerful Oracle RMAN utility to create and modify backup pieces at this location.

You must also install the OEM Agent on every database server that is to be accessed via Grid Control. As covered in an earlier chapter, this is easily done via a modified *AgentDownload* script and Wget which work in conjunction to pull down the Agent installation files from the central Grid Control OMS server, and the script then automatically installs the Agent on the target host. As such, this method is called the Pull method. Wget is free, being part of the GNU project, and can be downloaded for almost any platform.

The Agent can alternatively be installed using a Push method, or of course, you could use the cd or software downloaded from the Oracle Technology Network (OTN) to perform a traditional GUI install directly on the target host.

Install the Agent in its own Home with at least two GB of space allocated. Once the Agent is installed, it commences immediately to upload target information and metric data in the form of *xml* files to the central OMS. In the matter of some minutes, information about the targets on the host is now available in the central repository of Grid Control.

Using a Separate Group and Administrator

A Target Group is a collection of related targets in OEM Grid Control. Groups can be used for bringing together targets belonging to a certain application, department, or a database administration team and are very useful in the world of Grid Control.

Target Groups can be homogenous or heterogeneous. The advantage is that you can effectively manage many as one, meaning you can run jobs collectively on members in a group. Another advantage is that alerts for members are displayed together. Also, security policies can be applied at the group level instead of the individual target level.

The SYSMAN administrator, who is the repository owner of Grid Control, has created a target group called FINANCE_GROUP for the Accounting department DBA team. This target group consists of the PRD1FIN database, the associated listener and the host as can be seen in Figure 3.3.

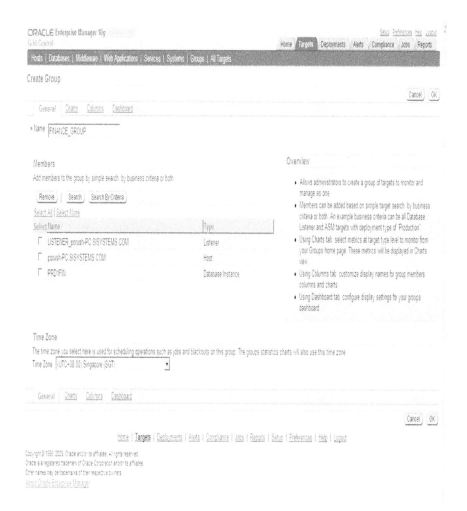

Figure 3.3: *Creating the Target Group FINANCE_GROUP*

SYSMAN, normally a DBA from the central database team, has also created a brand new Grid Control Administrator FINANCE_ADMIN. The new administrator has been assigned full management rights over the entire target group FINANCE_GROUP, as can be seen in Figure 3.4.

Properties Roles System Privileges Target Privileges Review

Create Administrator FINANCE_ADMIN: Review

Cancel Back Step 5 of 5 Finish

Properties

Name FINANCE_ADMIN
Password Profile DEFAULT
Prevent password change No
Expire password now No
E-mail Address finmgr@company.com
Description Financial Administrator
Super Administrator No

Roles

Name	Description
PUBLIC	

System Privileges

Name	Description
No system privileges are granted	

Target Privileges

Name	Type	Privilege
FINANCE_GROUP	Group	Group Administration

Cancel Back Step 5 of 5 Finish

Home | Targets | Deployments | Alerts | Compliance | Jobs | Reports | Setup | Preferences | Help | Logout

Figure 3.4: *Creating the Administrator FINANCE_ADMIN*

The DBA must now complete the following steps for the database requiring RMAN backups.

For a database on an active-passive cluster, such as HP-Serviceguard or SUN-HA, the Grid Control console would display the active-passive nodes as two different targets. Since the database is potentially able to run on any one of these nodes, the setup of the targets and their failover in Grid Control becomes slightly more complex. This is explained sufficiently in the *Oracle Enterprise Manager Advanced Configuration Guide for 10g Release 5 (10.2.0.5).* See Chapter 4 in this guide titled, "Configuring Oracle Enterprise Manager for Active and Passive Environments".

A virtual host name must be used for installation in this case. From version 10.2.0.5 onwards, a single OEM Agent running on each node in the cluster can monitor targets in an active-passive cluster. When the database is failed over, the *em cli relocate_targets* command can be used to relocate the targets, but only with 10.2.0.5 (and higher) Agents. For further details on the setup and failover mechanisms, refer to the Advanced Configuration Guide.

Once the active-passive cluster targets are configured in this way in Grid Control, the setup of the database backup will need to follow the same steps as for the single database server. The Grid Control setup is slightly complex and somewhat manual, as in the case of targets running on active-passive clusters. However, when using the more modern Oracle active-active clustering technology, i.e. Real Application Cluster (RAC), there would be only one database accessed by two or more nodes with an instance on each of the nodes.

The instance targets are handled seamlessly by Grid Control which is well integrated with RAC and there is no need for any manual failover activities using EM CLI commands. This is yet another reason to use the modern technology of Oracle RAC over the older methods of active-passive failover.

In the case of RAC, there would also need to be only one database backup job to be set up in Grid Control. In fact, the use of RMAN to backup the database is highly recommended in the case of a RAC database since it automatically understands the components to be backed up across nodes.

Configuring the Backup in Grid Control

Use the FINANCE_ADMIN login to the Grid Control console. Select Targets..All Targets. The list of targets that appears are those that have been assigned to the target group FINANCE_GROUP as can be seen in Figure 3.5.

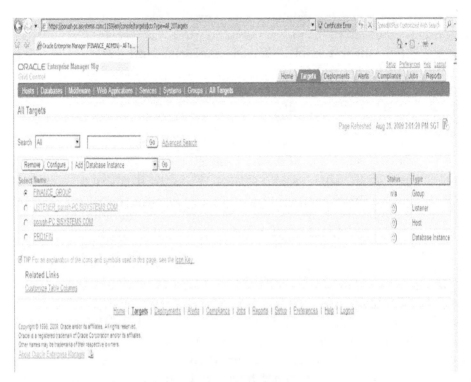

Figure 3.5: *All Targets for FINANCE_ADMIN*

Under the Targets tab, select Databases. In this list, you can see the PRD1FIN database. Click on this database to display the database home page for PRD1FIN. If you wish to check what user name you have used to log in to the console, you can see this (Figure 3.6) in the browser bar as Oracle Enterprise Manager (FINANCE_ADMIN) – Database Instance PRD1FIN.

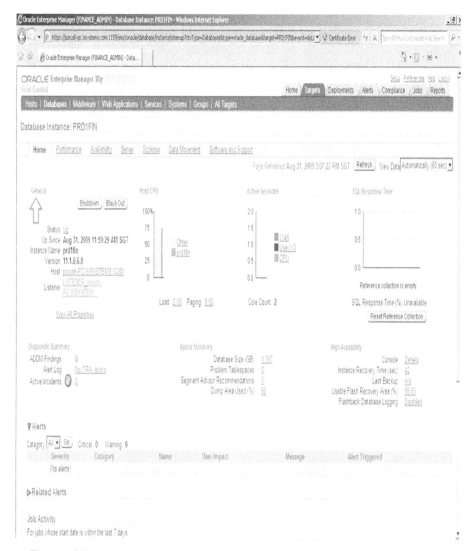

Figure 3.6: *PRD1FIN Database Instance Home Page*

If you are using Grid Control 10.2.0.4 or earlier, go to the Maintenance tab. Here, under High Availability, you can see options like Backup/Recovery, Backup/Recovery Settings, Oracle Secure Backup, and Data Guard. Select Backup Settings under Backup/Recovery Settings. In the latest Grid Control version 10.2.0.5, there is a change. Select the Availability tab. There is a

Backup/Recovery section, which has Setup and Manage sub-sections. Backup Settings is under Setup (Figure 3.7). You can select this.

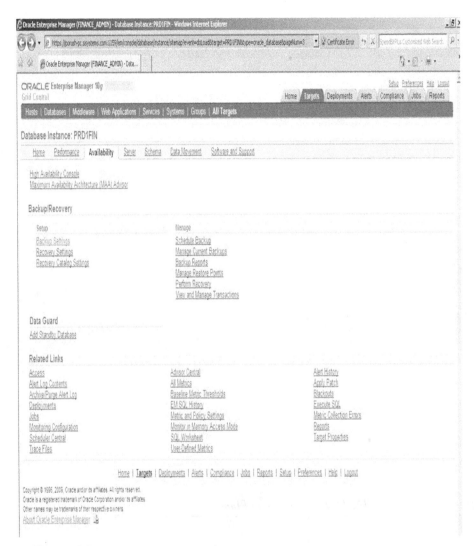

Figure 3.7: *Database Instance - Availability Tab*

When you select Backup Settings, you are now asked to log in to the database itself. At the start, you had logged in to the Grid Control console as FINANCE_ADMIN, but not to the database itself.

The database login is triggered at certain points such as clicking on Backup Settings, or even if you select the Performance tab which is seen as one of the tabs in Figure 3.7. You must log in as a user with DBA privileges since you will be setting up and scheduling the RMAN backup. Connect as normal since SYSDBA or SYSOPER rights are required only if you want to start up or shut down the database or if database recovery is to be performed, the archivelog mode is to be changed, or similar other tasks.

Make sure Save as Preferred Credential is not selected. If this is done, the password is saved in the Grid Control repository and the next time FINANCE_ADMIN logs on to the console, he/she would be able to log on to the database without supplying a password. This is potentially dangerous since the second level of database-level security is superseded by the saved database password.

This has demonstrated quite clearly that Grid Control has two levels of security: the console login, followed by the database login.

Backup Settings

On the Backup Settings page, three tabs are displayed. These are the Device, Backup Set and Policy tabs seen in Figure 3.8.

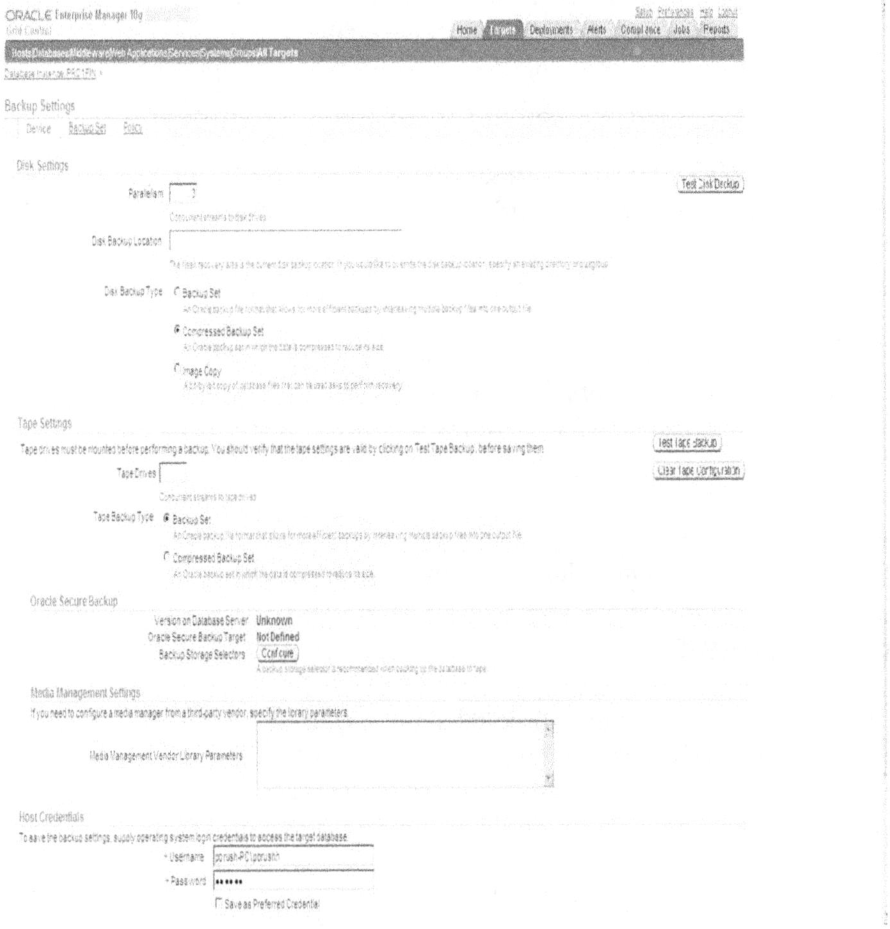

Figure 3.8: *Database Instance Backup Settings*

In the Device tab, under Disk Settings, the Parallelism is explained on the screen as Concurrent Streams to Disk Drives. Set this to 3, signifying that three RMAN channels will work in tandem to create the backup pieces. Using concurrent RMAN streams increases the speed of the database backup, but this depends to a great extent on the disk subsystem.

Do not specify the Disk Backup Location. This will then use the flash recovery area set up at the database level, and the database will be created in this area.

This would be the */U777* directory as per the company database standards for the UNIX systems, and *D:\flash_recovery_area* in the case of Windows.

Disk Backup Type allows you to select from three radio buttons. The options are to create a Backup Set, a Compressed Backup Set, or an Image Copy. Select the Compressed RMAN Backups option for the best use of the backup space.

This sort of compression of backups was introduced in Oracle 10g and was welcomed by DBAs.

Oracle Secure Backup: The Welcome Alternative

Note the Oracle Secure Backup section on this page (Figure 3.8). Oracle Secure Backup (OSB), now on version 10.3, is an   integrated secure tape backup management system from Oracle. It is a welcome alternative to third-party tape backup solutions that are highly priced and are not tightly integrated with Oracle.

Oracle Secure Backup protects not just the Oracle 9i, 10g and 11g databases, but also the entire environment including heterogeneous application filesystems from OSB 10.2 onwards. It is the fastest backup for Oracle databases, at least 25-40% faster than the competition. The low cost single component pricing (per tape drive) ensures it is attractively priced. There are no licenses payable for any media servers, backup servers or any database agent licenses.

Most importantly, Oracle Secure Backup is the only media management software that is fully integrated with OEM, which can now manage tape backup administrative tasks such as managing volumes (tapes) and tape devices. OSB can perform offline backups of 3rd party databases as part of a file system backup operation. Or the 3rd party databases can perform an online backup using their own backup utilities to disk, and OSB can backup their backup files.

The other advantage is that OSB encrypts data before it leaves the database. The database engine handles the encryption, so the data never leaves the database in unencrypted format. The encryption keys are transparently managed by the database.

As the other types of encryption options available, OSB provides native, host-based encryption or hardware (LTO-4 drive) encryption options in addition to RMAN backup encryption. The latter is performed within the database. Host-based encryption occurs on the database server outside of the database. Hardware encryption is performed on the LTO-4 tape drive.

In OSB 10.3, Oracle9i onwards is supported for backup encryption at the host or hardware level. RMAN backup encryption is supported in 10g R2 onwards. There are two other great advantages to OSB: the built-in Oracle factor and the single-vendor support.

There is also an Express version of OSB available, and this is bundled with the Oracle Database. OSB Express is free with the database for protecting one server with one attached tape drive. There is no encryption possible with the Express version.

Configure Oracle Secure Backup

The Devices tab allows you to set up OSB for your database. You can register an OSB setup and configure the administrative servers, media server hosts, and client hosts. You can also manage device and media configurations.

The OSB section displays the version on Database Server, Administrative Server, and the Backup Storage Selectors. At least one backup storage selector is required if you wish to back up the database to tape. Click on the Configure button to use OSB.

Entering and Testing Host Credentials

The Host Credentials can be entered on the lower part of the Devices tab. Select Save as Preferred Credential. Use the Oracle UNIX user if the database is on a UNIX host. Use <hostname>\<username> to log on in the case of Windows. It was observed that the logon credentials in Windows do not work every time, even after using <hostname>\<username>.

As per Metalink note 109188.1, the fix was to add the "Logon as a Batch Job" privilege to the Windows user in the Windows Control Panel..Administrative Tools..Local Security Policy..Local policies..User rights assignment..Login as a

Batch Job. At that point in the Windows menu path, you can add the Windows user specified in the Host Credentials. Please note that the menu path described here is specific to Windows XP Professional, as such, and could be different in other versions of Windows.

You can ensure that the Host Credentials work as expected by selecting Test Disk Backup on the screen. This starts and completes a physical backup test using RMAN (Figure 3.9). The purpose of the test is to verify that the backup can be physically created at the disk backup location.

Figure 3.9: *Test Backup in Progress*

When successfully completed, the message Disk Backup Test Successful! is seen at the top of the Backup Settings..Device tab.

Select the Backup Set tab, which displays the Maximum Backup Piece (File) Size along with other settings such as Copies of Datafile and Archivelog backups. These settings are not changed (Figure 3.10).

Figure 3.10: *Backup Settings - Backup Set*

Note the Compression Algorithm section in Figure 3.10.

In this section, specify the compression algorithm that will be used for both the disk and tape compressed backups. There are two possibilities:

- The BZIP2 compression algorithm, optimized for maximum compression. This type of compression will consume more CPU resources; however, more compact backups are normally produced.

- The ZLIB compression algorithm, optimized for CPU efficiency. For this kind of compression, set the *compatible* initialization parameter to 11.0.0 or higher. Also note that using this compression algorithm requires the license for the Oracle Advanced Compression option to be purchased.

Backup Policy

Select the Policy tab. The Backup Policy is specified at this point. The backup policy is an important aspect of RMAN backups (Figure 3.11). Select "Automatically backup the control file and server parameter file (SPFILE) with every backup and database structural change" to set the controlfile and SPFILE autobackup.

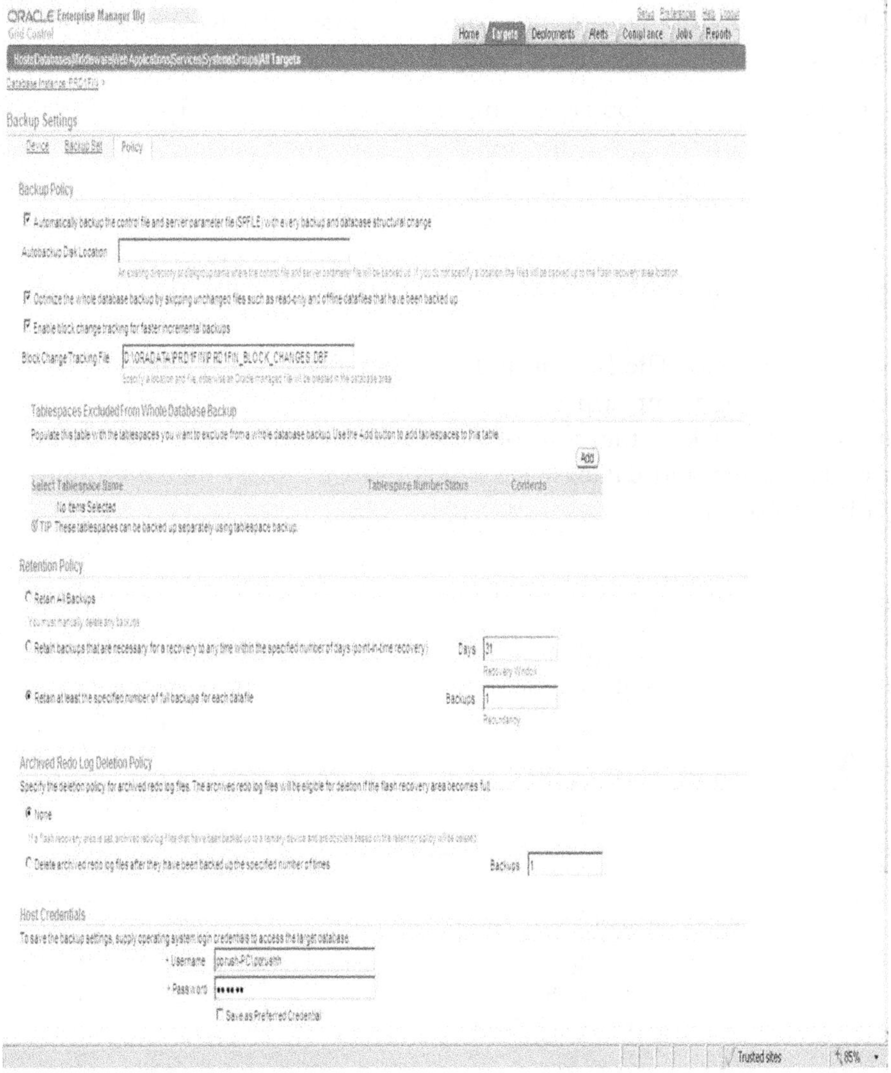

Figure 3.11: *Backup Settings – Policy*

The location of the autobackup can either be specified or it can be left as blank to default to the database flash recovery area.

It is highly recommended to turn on the autobackup, since as a result of this, the control file and SPFILE will be automatically backed up along with every database or archivelog backup. The nocatalog mode of RMAN is being used, so this is of even greater importance. The history of the backups is retained in the control file which must be definitely backed up every time, and what better way to do it than an autobackup.

The SPFILE is also backed up by RMAN, thus explaining why the binary SPFILE is recommended instead of using a text PFILE for the database. Next, select "Optimize the whole database backup by skipping unchanged files such as read-only and offline datafiles that have been backed up which is the technique known as Backup Optimization".

You can also select "Enable block change tracking for faster incremental backups". RMAN in 10g has introduced this feature known as block change tracking. If this feature is turned on, it keeps track of all changed blocks in a small file, about 11 MB in size. As a result, when incremental database backups are taken, the incremental backup does not scan the whole database for block changes. Such full scanning took place during incremental backups in 9i; as a result, the incremental backups were much slower in that version. This is no longer true in 10g onwards.

Incremental backups are much faster with block change tracking; yet another reason to upgrade to 11g from 9i. Note that the PRD1FIN database does not use Oracle managed files. As a result, the database area is not set via the initialization parameter *db_create_file_dest*. Hence, you need to specify the fully qualified file name for the block change tracking file, for example:

```
d:\oradata\prd1fin\prd1fin_block_changes.dbf
```

If the database area had been set and the file name was not specified, then an Oracle managed file would have been created in the database area.

Redundancy or Recovery Window

In the Retention Policy section under this page, you will choose a retention policy based on redundancy instead of a recovery window. To do this, select "Retain at least the specified number of full backups for each datafile", and enter 1 as the number of backups to retain at any one time; this then is your redundancy. This means that when a new backup is taken, the older backup will be marked as obsolete since only one backup is to be retained at any time.

Obsolete backups can be deleted by the RMAN maintenance commands such as:

```
delete noprompt obsolete device type disk;
```

If using the recovery window, this must be specified in terms of days. This would signify that backups would be retained so as to allow recovery of the database up to the specified number of days in the recovery window. Consider that the RMAN retention policy is specified as a recovery window of three days. This indicates that database backups will be retained so as to enable recovery up to the last three days.

However, retaining more than one database backup on disk may have space repercussions. The total size of the database needs to be considered, the types of backups taken each day (full or incremental), the amount of archive logs generated each day (since archive log backups are also included) and also the amount of space allocated to the database's flash recovery area.

The DBA needs to keep all these factors in mind and closely monitor the database backup and space available over the next few weeks, adjusting the recovery window if required or perhaps changing the retention policy to redundancy instead of a recovery window.

Archived Redo Log Deletion Policy

A new section, Archived Redo Log Deletion Policy, is displayed from Grid Control 10.2.0.5 onwards on the page shown in Figure 3.11.

In this section, the deletion policy for archived redo logs can be specified, and they can be made eligible for deletion when the flash recovery area becomes full. There are two options. If you select None, this will disable the archived redo log deletion policy. Assuming that the flash recovery area is set, then the archived redo logs that have been backed up and are obsolete as per the retention policy will be deleted by the RMAN maintenance commands examined previously.

If you select "Delete archived redo logs after they have been backed up the specified number of times", you need to specify the number of backups to a tertiary device after which the archived redo logs will be deleted. If the

PRD1FIN database is a primary database in an Oracle Data Guard configuration, then more options appear on this page. The options are different for a primary database and a standby database.

In the case of a primary database, besides the two options above, there is one more option: Delete archived redo log files. This option has two sub-options:

1. After they have been applied to all standby databases

2. After they have been shipped to all standby databases

Choosing "Delete archived redo log files" with the first sub-option means that archived redo logs will be deleted after being applied or consumed on all remote destinations. The destinations may or may not be mandatory.

Choosing "Delete archived redo log files" with the second sub-option means that archived redo logs will be deleted after transfer to all remote destinations. The destinations may or may not be mandatory. It is also possible to select both "Delete archived redo log files" and "Delete archived redo logs after they have been backed up the specified number of times". This has the effect of deleting the archived redo logs that have been applied or shipped to all remote destinations, and also after taking into consideration whether the specified number of archived log backups have been backed up to a tertiary device.

The options available for a primary database have been covered. On the other hand, in the case of a standby database, there are three main options:

1. None

2. Delete archived redo log files after they have been applied to the standby database

3. Delete archived redo logs after they have been backed up the specified number of times

Control File Configuration Settings

At this point, you can select the OK button. The backup settings will be saved in the control file of the database. Note that you are not using an RMAN catalog database. You can confirm the changed settings by logging into RMAN at the command prompt. Execute the *show all* command which displays the RMAN configuration:

```
-- Set the Oracle Sid in Windows
C:\>set ORACLE_SID=PRD1FIN

-- Move to the 11g Oracle Home
C:\>cd C:\app\porushh\product\11.1.0\db_1\BIN

-- Start RMAN in the nocatalog mode connecting to the database specified in
the Oracle Sid

C:\app\porushh\product\11.1.0\db_1\BIN>rman target=/ nocatalog

Recovery Manager: Release 11.1.0.6.0 - Production on Mon Aug 31 16:22:04
2009
Copyright (c) 1982, 2007, Oracle.  All rights reserved.
connected to target database: PRD1FIN (DBID=4147668305)
using target database control file instead of recovery catalog

RMAN> show all;

RMAN configuration parameters for database with db_unique_name PRD1FIN are:
configure retention policy to redundancy 1; # default
configure backup optimization on;
configure default device type to disk; # default
configure controlfile autobackup on;
configure controlfile autobackup format for device type disk to '%F'; #
default
configure device type disk backup type to compressed backupset parallelism
3;
configure datafile backup copies for device type disk to 1; # default
configure archivelog backup copies for device type disk to 1; # default
configure maxsetsize to unlimited; # default
configure encryption for database off; # default
configure encryption algorithm 'aes128'; # default
configure compression algorithm 'bzip2'; # default
configure archivelog deletion policy to none; # default
configure snapshot controlfile name to
'c:\app\porushh\product\11.1.0\db_1\datab
ase\sncfprd1fin.ora'; # default
```

You can see that your modifications in the Backup Settings pages of Grid
Control have been saved as the configuration settings in RMAN. These are
stored in the control file of the PRD1FIN database.

The # *default* comment shows the unchanged configuration settings.
Conversely, the settings without this comment are the ones that have been
modified. The setting for the backup optimization is ON, controlfile
autobackup is ON, and there is a parallelism of 3 using a backupset that is
compressed. These are all the settings that you had changed in the preceding
pages.

Conclusion

In this chapter, you looked into the use of Grid Control for a very common and repetitive DBA task: the set up of Oracle database backups. First, there was an examination on the history of offline and online backups, and the introduction of Oracle RMAN.

Noting how RMAN backups had also retained their scripting historical roots, it was decided to go step-by-step and set up and schedule an RMAN backup in the traditional way by using UNIX shell scripts and the *cron* scheduler utility, noting all the steps required.

This was then followed by a step-by-step setup of a database backup with the Grid Control screens using the multi-level security for the Accounting department DBA team: log in to the console first and then to the database. Oracle Secure Backup (OSB), Oracle's powerful tape management solution, was also introduced in this chapter. The RMAN configuration of the database was set up using Grid Control.

In the next chapter, this process will be continued. The RMAN database backup will be scheduled and tested, all without using shell scripts or cron jobs, vastly reducing the time of deployment, testing and maintenance. Also, the benefits of using Grid Control for RMAN backups will be made very evident for all to see.

Database Backup
Strategies Using Grid
Control

In the previous chapter, the RMAN configuration was set up using Oracle Enterprise Manager Grid Control. At the RMAN command line, the configuration was also verified as stored in the control file of the database. You can now proceed to schedule the database backup.

Schedule the Backup

In the Grid Control console, move to the Availability tab of the PRD1FIN database. Select Schedule Backup in the Backup/Recovery section. The screen in Figure 4.1 appears.

In the Schedule Backup screen, select Whole Database in the Customized Backup section. Then click on Schedule Customized Backup. The Customized Backup section also allows you to backup individual tablespaces, datafiles, or only the archivelogs. The final option on this page is to backup All Recovery Files on Disk. Selecting this option enables you to backup the flash recovery area of the database to tape.

You can only create the flash recovery area in a 10g database or later version because it is not possible in older versions of Oracle databases. This area is where all the RMAN backup pieces, image copies, and archive logs are stored. Hence, backing up the flash recovery area is effectively a backup of your backup.

Figure 4.1: *Schedule Backup*

The recommendation from Oracle is to backup the database to a less expensive disk, i.e. not your tier 1 or even tier 2 disk, instead of tape so that at least one database backup exists on disk. This backup location on disk is the flash recovery area.

This then allows the DBA to perform a fast recovery from the available disk-based backup in case of any production issues rather than spend time waiting for the tape to be located and then the tape backup to be restored to the disk. Oracle's practical concept of disk-based recovery is certainly instrumental in reducing expensive outage to the business in the event of any such required database restores.

The flash recovery area, which contains the disk-based database backups, can then be backed up to tape once a week, thereby allowing offsite tape backups as well as onsite disk backups. This would be a suitable Oracle backup strategy.

The Schedule Customized Backup: Options page now appears. As the Backup Type on this page, select Full Backup. The backup mode should be Online Backup (Figure 4.2).

Figure 4.2: *Schedule Customized Backup - Options*

In the Advanced section on this page, select the option "Also back up all archived logs on disk" and also select the option "Delete all archived logs from disk after they are successfully backed up". Selecting these options configures the backup to include all archive logs with the full database backup and deletes the archive logs from disk after they are backed up. The option Delete obsolete backups should also be selected so that backups marked as obsolete will be deleted since these are no longer required as per the retention policy.

Expand the Encryption icon on this page by clicking on it. The Encryption fields that are applicable to your target database version are displayed. Backup Encryption was first introduced in Oracle 10g Release 2 and is available for all later versions such as Oracle 11g Release 1 and Oracle 11g Release 2.

Note that Oracle's Advanced Security Option is required if you wish to create encrypted backups on disk with RMAN. You must make sure you are licensed to use this option because being licensed for the Oracle Database Enterprise Edition (EE) does not automatically mean you are licensed to use the Advanced Security Option.

The other alternative is to use Oracle Secure Backup (OSB) to create encrypted backups on tape as explained in the previous chapter. Again, you must make sure you are licensed to use this product. Oracle Secure Backup must be installed separately.

Select Use Recovery Manager Encryption, and as the Encryption mode, select encryption using the Oracle Wallet as well as encryption using the password. Specify the password in the field below and confirm. This will encrypt the backup using both these methods. Also, there will be greater flexibility since you can use either the wallet or the password when the RMAN backup needs to be restored.

AES256 has been selected as the Encryption Algorithm. Move to the next page. The Disk Backup Location is displayed as the flash recovery area (Figure 4.3). On the Windows platform, this is configured in your case as *D:\flash_Recovery_area*.

Figure 4.3: *Schedule Customized Backup - Settings*

Move to the next page, which is the Scheduling screen (Figure 4.4). This is where you set the day and time you want your backup to run.

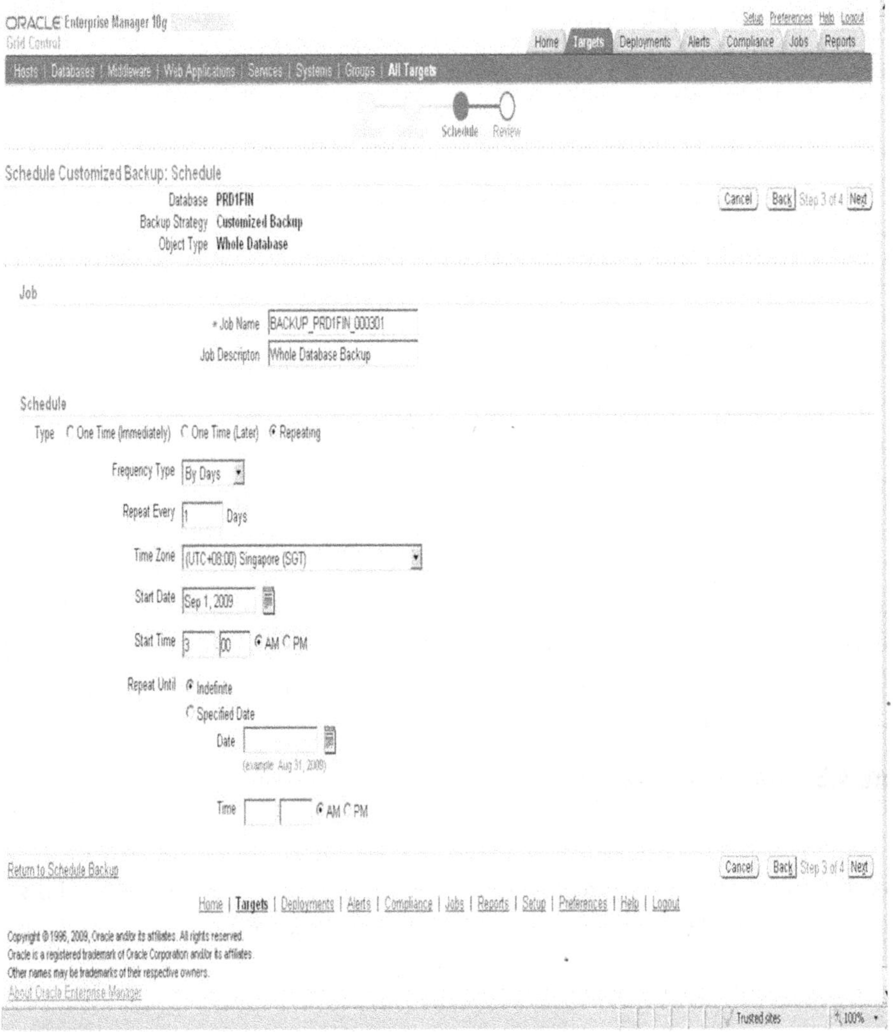

Figure 4.4: *Schedule Customized Backup - Schedule*

There are three options. You can schedule the backup to run once either immediately, at a later time or repeatedly at a schedule you define. The one time later and repeating options both allow you to specify the start date and time you wish the back up to run and the time zone associated with the time you specify. The repeating option also lets you select the frequency type, such as days or weeks, and the frequency. For example, if you select days as the

Oracle Enterprise Manager Grid Control

frequency type and 1 as the frequency, the back up will run once every day at the time you have specified. In addition, whatever frequency type and frequency you select, you can repeat it either indefinitely or until a specified date and time.

The current time is shown as the suggested setting for the backup. 3:00 AM the following morning is chosen so that the backup will start at this time of low activity. The Frequency Type is selected as Days and Repeat Every is selected as 1 Day since the management required a full database backup to be performed each day.

Select the Repeat until Indefinite radio button, which means that the backup schedule will be continued indefinitely with no end date or time.

Review of Backup Job

Click on Next. This is the Scheduled Customized Backup: Review screen (Figure 4.5). This displays the following job parameters.

```
Destination   Disk
Backup Type   Full Backup
Backup Mode   Online Backup
Encryption Algorithm   AES256
Encryption Mode   Oracle Encryption Wallet, Password
Flash Recovery Area   D:\flash_recovery_area
Disk Parallelism   3
```

Grid Control has generated the RMAN script which will be used in the backup based on the input criteria you identified in the previous screens. This is also shown on the Review screen as:

```
set encryption on for all tablespaces algorithm 'AES256' identified by
'%PASSWORD';
backup device type disk tag '%TAG' database;
backup device type disk tag '%TAG' archivelog all not backed up delete all
input;
allocate channel for maintenance type disk;
delete noprompt obsolete device type disk;
release channel;
```

The RMAN commands set encryption on for all tablespaces, followed by a full database and archivelog backup. The archive logs are deleted after backup. After this, the maintenance commands that delete obsolete disk backups are executed. These actions are derived from what has been previously specified in the Grid Control backup setup, and backup schedule wizard pages.

Figure 4.5: *Schedule Customized Backup - Review*

Editing the Generated Script

Selecting Edit RMAN Script allows you to make modifications to the generated script and then submit it. Note that once modifications are made, it is not possible to return to the previous pages of the Wizard. Nevertheless, you may want to change the RMAN script to include maintenance commands which will crosscheck backups and archivelogs, and delete the backups and archivelogs that have expired.

The changed script with the extra maintenance commands appears as follows:

```
set encryption on for all tablespaces algorithm 'AES256' identified by
'%PASSWORD';
backup device type disk tag '%TAG' database;
backup device type disk tag '%TAG' archivelog all not backed up delete all
input;
allocate channel for maintenance device type disk;
crosscheck backup;
delete noprompt expired backup;
delete noprompt obsolete device type disk;
crosscheck archivelog all;
delete noprompt expired archivelog all;
release channel;
```

Select Submit Job. After the job is submitted successfully, you can then select View Job. This will display the status and the progress of the job.

Now go to the Jobs tab of Grid Control where the job is visible under Job Activity. It is displayed as a Scheduled job. (Figure 4.6)

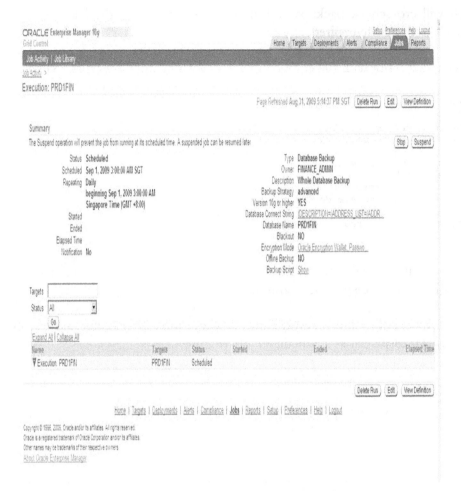

Figure 4.6: *Job Activity - Job Summary*

You can now select Backup Script...Show which displays the contents of the backup script. The RMAN script is wrapped in Perl and appears as follows:

```
$rman_script="set encryption on for all tablespaces algorithm 'AES256'
identified by '%PASSWORD';
backup device type disk tag '%TAG' database;
backup device type disk tag '%TAG' archivelog all not backed up delete all
input;
allocate channel for maintenance device type disk;
crosscheck backup;
delete noprompt expired backup;
delete noprompt obsolete device type disk;
```

```
crosscheck archivelog all;
delete noprompt expired archivelog all;
release channel;
";
&br_save_agent_env();
&br_prebackup($l_db_connect_string, $l_is_cold_backup, $l_use_rcvcat,
$l_db_10_or_higher, $l_backup_strategy, "FALSE");
my $result = &br_backup();
exit($result);
```

When the job appears in the list of scheduled jobs, it can be edited at this
point, but only the Schedule, Credentials, or the Access can be changed
(Figure 4.7). Any other changes require you to delete the scheduled job and
create a new job. This is not a problem because recreating the job is very
straightforward and quickly completed.

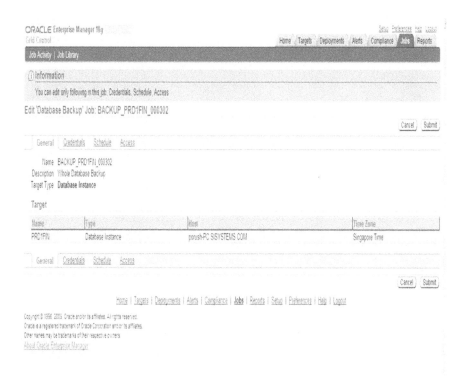

Figure 4.7: *Edit Database Backup Job - General*

When changing the Access of the job, it is possible to allocate Access levels of
View or Full to different Grid Control administrators (Figure 4.8).

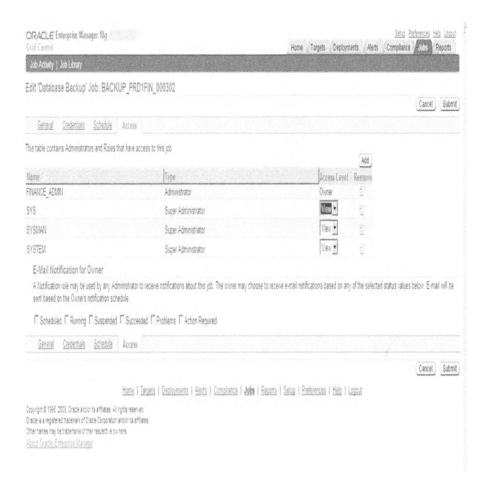

Figure 4.8: *Edit Database Backup Job - Access*

The owner of the job on this page is identified as FINANCE_ADMIN, which is the administrator login for the target group FINANCE_GROUP. This ownership is due to the fact that the job was created after logging in as FINANCE_ADMIN. You can set the Preferred Credentials for the database and host.

The credentials allow the backup job to log in and execute its tasks seamlessly without the host or database password needing to be specified each time such a job is created. Select the Preferences link on the upper part of the Grid

Control console, and then the Preferred Credentials link, which is visible on the side of the page (Figure 4.9).

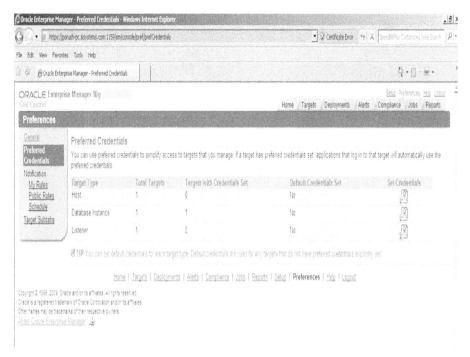

Figure 4.9: *Preferred Credentials Main Page*

On this page, you can choose to set the login name and password for the database as well as the host.

Select Test to verify the username and password. This logs on to the server using the credentials you specify, but errors out if the username or password is wrong. After the verification has succeeded, you can Apply the changes (Figure 4.10).

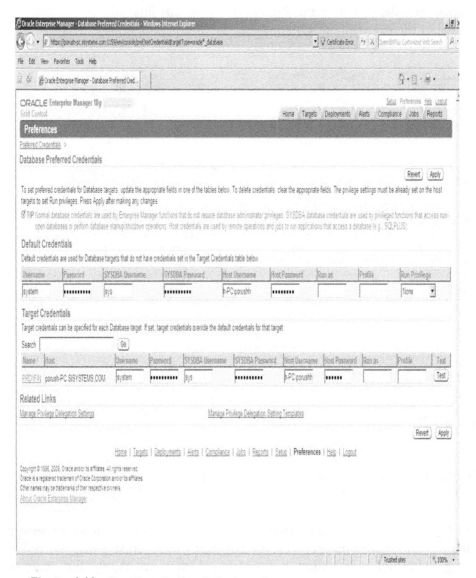

Figure 4.10: *Database Preferred Credentials*

When you have completed setting up the Preferred Credentials, select the Jobs Tab of the Grid Control console. The scheduled RMAN backup job is displayed (Figure 4.11).

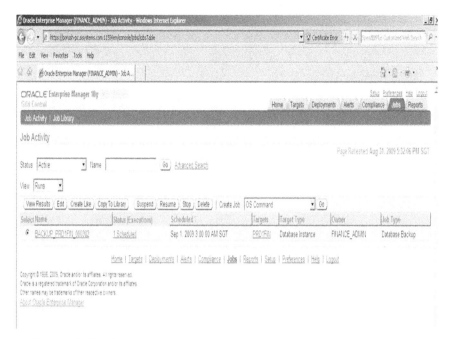

Figure 4.11: *Job Activity - List*

If you wish to test the backup job at this point, you can do so by editing it. Simply change the schedule of the job so that it will run immediately (Figure 4.12).

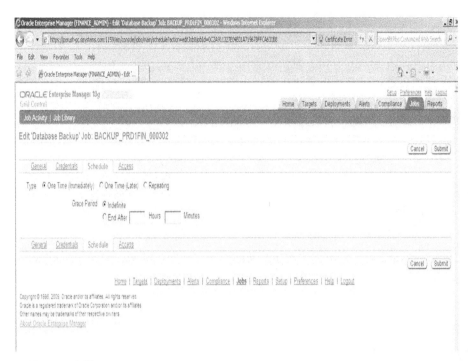

Figure 4.12: *Changing the Schedule*

The schedule is changed to an immediate run and the job is submitted. It is now displayed with the status Running. Press F5 every few seconds to refresh your browser and enable you to follow the progress of the job (Figure 4.13).

Oracle Enterprise Manager Grid Control

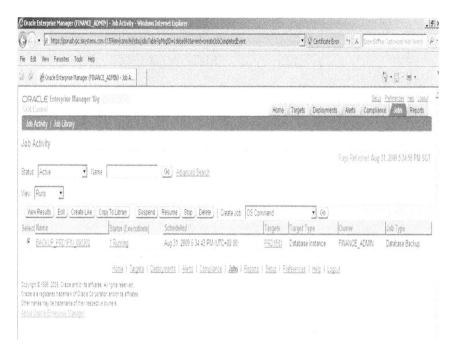

Figure 4.13: *Job Activity - Running*

Initial Issues

The Job Activity screen shows that the job has disappeared. Select the Status as All, and then click on Go. All jobs are now displayed, including jobs that have not completed successfully due to some problem occurring. One of the problem jobs is seen as the PRD1FIN Backup job (Figure 4.14).

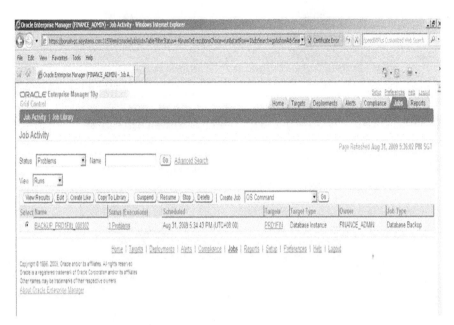

Figure 4.14: *Job Activity - Problems*

Select the Problem link. This displays the job steps, which enables you to pinpoint exactly where the job has had a problem (Figure 4.15).

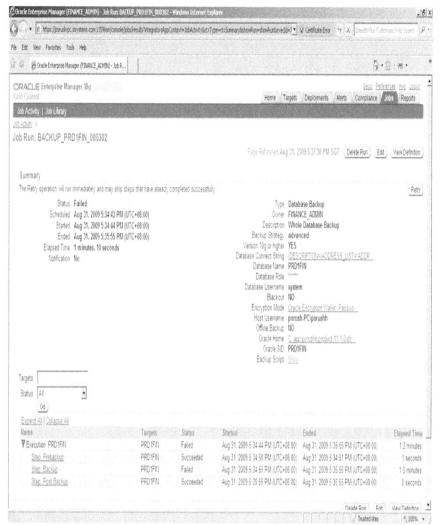

Figure 4.15: *Job Activity - Problems*

It can be seen that the Prebackup and PostBackup steps have succeeded, but the Backup step has obviously failed. Select the failed step. This will display the entire RMAN output. The cause of the error is quickly apparent from the output, which will now be explained.

```
Output Log

Recovery Manager: Release 11.1.0.6.0 - Production on Mon Aug 31 17:35:00
2009

Copyright (c) 1982, 2007, Oracle.  All rights reserved.

RMAN>
connected to target database: PRD1FIN (DBID=4147668305)
using target database control file instead of recovery catalog

RMAN>
echo set on

RMAN> set command id to 'BACKUP_PRD1FIN_000_083109053445';
executing command: SET COMMAND ID

RMAN> set encryption on for all tablespaces algorithm 'AES256' identified by
*;

executing command: SET encryption

RMAN> backup device type disk tag 'BACKUP_PRD1FIN_000_083109053445'
database;

Starting backup at 31-AUG-09
allocated channel: ORA_DISK_1
channel ORA_DISK_1: SID=170 device type=DISK
allocated channel: ORA_DISK_2
channel ORA_DISK_2: SID=126 device type=DISK
allocated channel: ORA_DISK_3
channel ORA_DISK_3: SID=124 device type=DISK
channel ORA_DISK_1: starting compressed full datafile backup set
channel ORA_DISK_1: specifying datafile(s) in backup set

input datafile file number=00001 name=D:\ORADATA\PRD1FIN\SYSTEM01.DBF

channel ORA_DISK_1: starting piece 1 at 31-AUG-09
channel ORA_DISK_2: starting compressed full datafile backup set
channel ORA_DISK_2: specifying datafile(s) in backup set

input datafile file number=00002 name=D:\ORADATA\PRD1FIN\SYSAUX01.DBF
input datafile file number=00004 name=D:\ORADATA\PRD1FIN\USERS01.DBF
channel ORA_DISK_2: starting piece 1 at 31-AUG-09
channel ORA_DISK_3: starting compressed full datafile backup set
channel ORA_DISK_3: specifying datafile(s) in backup set
input datafile file number=00005 name=D:\ORADATA\PRD1FIN\EXAMPLE01.DBF
input datafile file number=00003 name=D:\ORADATA\PRD1FIN\UNDOTBS01.DBF

channel ORA_DISK_3: starting piece 1 at 31-AUG-09
RMAN-03009: failure of backup command on ORA_DISK_1 channel at 08/31/2009
17:35:25

ORA-19914: unable to encrypt backup
ORA-28365: wallet is not open

continuing other job steps, job failed will not be re-run
```

Oracle Enterprise Manager Grid Control

```
RMAN-03009: failure of backup command on ORA_DISK_2 channel at 08/31/2009
17:35:26

ORA-19914: unable to encrypt backup
ORA-28365: wallet is not open

continuing other job steps, job failed will not be re-run

RMAN-00571: ===========================================================

RMAN-00569: =============== ERROR MESSAGE STACK FOLLOWS ===============

RMAN-00571: ===========================================================

RMAN-03009: failure of backup command on ORA_DISK_3 channel at 08/31/2009
17:35:27

ORA-19914: unable to encrypt backup
ORA-28365: wallet is not open


RMAN> backup device type disk tag 'BACKUP_PRD1FIN_000_083109053445'
archivelog all not backed up delete all input;

Starting backup at 31-AUG-09
current log archived
using channel ORA_DISK_1
using channel ORA_DISK_2
using channel ORA_DISK_3

channel ORA_DISK_1: starting compressed archived log backup set
channel ORA_DISK_1: specifying archived log(s) in backup set
input archived log thread=1 sequence=2 RECID=2 STAMP=696344559
channel ORA_DISK_1: starting piece 1 at 31-AUG-09
channel ORA_DISK_2: starting compressed archived log backup set
channel ORA_DISK_2: specifying archived log(s) in backup set
input archived log thread=1 sequence=3 RECID=4 STAMP=696360933
channel ORA_DISK_2: starting piece 1 at 31-AUG-09

RMAN-03009: failure of backup command on ORA_DISK_1 channel at 08/31/2009
17:35:37

ORA-19914: unable to encrypt backup
ORA-28365: wallet is not open

continuing other job steps, job failed will not be re-run

RMAN-00571: ===========================================================

RMAN-00569: =============== ERROR MESSAGE STACK FOLLOWS ===============

RMAN-00571: ===========================================================

RMAN-03009: failure of backup command on ORA_DISK_2 channel at 08/31/2009
17:35:37
```

Schedule the Backup   **119**

```
ORA-19914: unable to encrypt backup
ORA-28365: wallet is not open
```

Encryption Wallet

There are several channels backing up the database and the archive logs. All these channels have failed. The error message "wallet is not open" is indicative of the fact that the Oracle wallet is not open or has not been created for the database. This has caused the failure.

Therefore, you need to create the encryption wallet for the PRD1FIN database for the backup encryption to work. This is done via the following steps.

1. Add these lines to the *sqlnet.ora* file on the database server:

```
encryption_wallet_location=
        (source=(method=file)(method_data=
            (directory=c:\app\porushh\product\11.1.0\db_1)))
```

2. Stop and restart the listener for the database to affect the changes in the previous step.

3. Issue the following command to generate a new master key:

```
C:\app\porushh\product\11.1.0\db_1\BIN>sqlplus / as sysdba

SQL*Plus: Release 11.1.0.6.0 - Production on Mon Aug 31 18:05:02 2009

Copyright (c) 1982, 2007, Oracle.  All rights reserved.

Connected to:
Oracle Database 11g Enterprise Edition Release 11.1.0.6.0 - Production
With the Partitioning, Oracle Label Security, OLAP, Data Mining,
Oracle Database Vault and Real Application Testing options

SQL>
alter
 system set encryption key identified by <password>;

System altered.
```

You can now encrypt your RMAN backups. You can also use features such as Transparent Data Encryption (TDE) to encrypt the database data.

Job Success

Select the failed job and click on the Retry button on the Job page. This will rerun the backup job and the job will now complete successfully (Figure 4.16).

Figure 4.16: *Job Activity - Success*

Select the successful Step Backup. This will display the RMAN output and you will be able to verify the successful completion of all the backup commands issued on the database.

🖫 connecting to target database (partial)

```
Output Log

Recovery Manager: Release 11.1.0.6.0 - Production on Mon Aug 31 18:06:01
2009

Copyright (c) 1982, 2007, Oracle.  All rights reserved.

RMAN>
connected to target database: PRD1FIN (DBID=4147668305)
using target database control file instead of recovery catalog

RMAN>
echo set on

RMAN> set command id to 'BACKUP_PRD1FIN_000_083109060547';
executing command: SET COMMAND ID

RMAN> set encryption on for all tablespaces algorithm 'AES256' identified by
*;

executing command: SET encryption

RMAN> backup device type disk tag 'BACKUP_PRD1FIN_000_083109060547' database
not backed up since time "TO_DATE('083109053444', 'MMDDYYHHMISS')";

Starting backup at 31-AUG-09
allocated channel: ORA_DISK_1
channel ORA_DISK_1: SID=128 device type=DISK
allocated channel: ORA_DISK_2
channel ORA_DISK_2: SID=137 device type=DISK
allocated channel: ORA_DISK_3
channel ORA_DISK_3: SID=126 device type=DISK
channel ORA_DISK_1: starting compressed full datafile backup set
channel ORA_DISK_1: specifying datafile(s) in backup set
input datafile file number=00001 name=D:\ORADATA\PRD1FIN\SYSTEM01.DBF

channel ORA_DISK_1: starting piece 1 at 31-AUG-09
channel ORA_DISK_2: starting compressed full datafile backup set
channel ORA_DISK_2: specifying datafile(s) in backup set
input datafile file number=00002 name=D:\ORADATA\PRD1FIN\SYSAUX01.DBF
input datafile file number=00004 name=D:\ORADATA\PRD1FIN\USERS01.DBF

channel ORA_DISK_2: starting piece 1 at 31-AUG-09
channel ORA_DISK_3: starting compressed full datafile backup set
channel ORA_DISK_3: specifying datafile(s) in backup set
input datafile file number=00005 name=D:\ORADATA\PRD1FIN\EXAMPLE01.DBF
input datafile file number=00003 name=D:\ORADATA\PRD1FIN\UNDOTBS01.DBF

channel ORA_DISK_3: starting piece 1 at 31-AUG-09
channel ORA_DISK_3: finished piece 1 at 31-AUG-09
piece
handle=D:\flash_recovery_area\PRD1FIN\backupset\2009_08_31\O1_MF_NNNDF_BACKU
P_PRD1FIN_000_0_59Q853B8_.BKP tag=BACKUP_PRD1FIN_000_083109060547
comment=NONE

channel ORA_DISK_3: backup set complete, elapsed time: 00:01:16
channel ORA_DISK_2: finished piece 1 at 31-AUG-09
```

```
piece
handle=D:\flash_recovery_area\PRD1FIN\backupset\2009_08_31\O1_MF_NNNDF_BACKU
P_PRD1FIN_000_0_59Q84X0H_.BKP tag=BACKUP_PRD1FIN_000_083109060547
comment=NONE

channel ORA_DISK_2: backup set complete, elapsed time: 00:02:01
channel ORA_DISK_1: finished piece 1 at 31-AUG-09

piece
handle=D:\flash_recovery_area\PRD1FIN\backupset\2009_08_31\O1_MF_NNNDF_BACKU
P_PRD1FIN_000_0_59Q84OF5_.BKP tag=BACKUP_PRD1FIN_000_083109060547
comment=NONE

channel ORA_DISK_1: backup set complete, elapsed time: 00:02:42

Finished backup at 31-AUG-09
```

Understanding RMAN Output

On studying the RMAN output, you can gain a clear understanding of the entire sequence of events that occur during the backup job. First of all, encryption is set on for all tablespaces in the database using the *aes256* algorithm. A compressed full backup set for the database is created.

After this database backup is completed, a control file and SPFILE autobackup are also created because you identified earlier that you wanted these files to be automatically backed up with each backup. A compressed archived log backup set is then created to backup the archive logs. After successful backup due to the included DELETE INPUT clause, RMAN deletes the archivelogs from their disk location.

But what if you require any of these deleted archive logs during a database recovery? Oracle, during such a recovery, complete or incomplete, uses the archive logs to apply all the changes so as to restore the database to any point in time, which is the main purpose of archive logging.

So some or all of the archive logs may be needed by the recovery. To achieve this in the past, DBAs used to perform a manual restore of the archive logs from their compressed UNIX tar archives and then place the restored archive logs in a directory accessible by the Oracle-controlled recovery. DBAs had to do all the searches for the necessary archive log files manually.

This kind of manual searching and restoring of the archive logs is no longer needed in the case of RMAN. This powerful utility from Oracle automatically locates the archive log backup sets needed and extracts the archive logs that are required for the recovery. Fantastic! Yet another tremendous benefit of using RMAN as your Oracle database backup mechanism of choice.

When the backup is completed, it is seen that the database backups, archivelogs backups, control file and SPFILE autobackups, all comprising of RMAN backup pieces, are created in the appropriate sub-directories in the flash recovery area as follows:

```
<Flash Recovery Area>\PRD1FIN\backupset\2009_08_31\

<Flash Recovery Area>\PRD1FIN\autobackup\2009_08_31\
```

Because the database is using the flash recovery area, Oracle automatically handles the creation of the directory structure using the database name PRD1FIN and creates subdirectories for the backupset and autobackup. A further subdirectory is also created for the date the backups have taken place. This happens every time a backup is taken and if the directory structure up to the day level does not exist, it is created.

As shown in the RMAN output, another control file and SPFILE autobackup takes place after the archive logs backup. Once configured, these autobackups will automatically occur after any RMAN database backup or archive logs backup completes.

The maintenance actions are next.

Importance of Maintenance

The names of the backup files and archive log files have been catalogued by RMAN and exist as entries in the control file records. During the RMAN maintenance activities that are started by the maintenance commands you included, these entries are crosschecked to verify that they physically exist on disk. If the file does not physically exist, the corresponding entry is marked as expired, i.e. not found.

In a similar manner, since the database backup, archive log backup, and the autobackup in this job have succeeded, the entries of the previous backup and autobackup files are checked to see if they still need to be retained as per the retention policy. If they are no longer required, they are marked as obsolete.

After this, the *delete noprompt expired* … and *delete noprompt obsolete* … commands are used one after the other to delete all the expired or obsolete database backup, archivelog backup, controlfile backup entries and also the archivelog file entries from the controlfile records. In the case of obsolete records, the actual physical backup files are also deleted from the disk.

The maintenance commands are obviously very important for space management.

Reopening the Wallet

What happens if the database is restarted? The RMAN backup fails with these errors:

```
ORA-19914: unable to encrypt backup
ORA-28365: wallet is not open
```

It is obvious that the wallet must be reopened whenever the database is restarted; an important consideration to bear in mind for reboots. Open the wallet with the following command:

```
alter system set wallet open identified by <password>;
```

You have now looked at the RMAN output in detail and hopefully understood each step. It has also been verified that the backup job has been completely successful.

Select the Jobs tab in the Grid Control console. On this tab, keep the Status as All, then select Go. This will display the job in the output job list.

Scheduling the Job for Each Day

Select Edit on this job. Since the job has already executed, you may only change the Access. The Schedule cannot be changed (Figure 4.17).

Figure 4.17: *Edit Database Backup Job*

The only option, in this case, is to recreate the job using the backup job wizard. Schedule the job to run this time in the early morning and use a repeating schedule that is repeated each day indefinitely. The job will now appear in the Jobs tab of the Grid Control console with the status of Scheduled (as was seen in Figure 4.11).

The backup job will execute each day and the RMAN output log from each run, regardless of whether the job completed successfully or not, will be stored in the Grid Control repository. It is, therefore, possible for the DBA to examine the status of all RMAN backup jobs for all databases using the central Grid Control console. Corrective action, if necessary, can be taken immediately. The failure of any job can also be set up to trigger an email notification to the DBA.

DBCA and Automatic Backups

Oracle now facilitates setting up and scheduling database backups as soon as a database is created via the Database Configuration Assistant (DBCA). Even if there is no central OEM Grid Control environment in the company, this backup can be accomplished via Grid Control's little brother, Database Control, which manages only a single database. Database Control is normally configured at the time a single 10g or 11g database is installed. However, it can be configured later if required. The DBCA screen (Figure 4.18) allows you to configure a new database with either OEM Grid Control or OEM Database Control.

You can choose if an existing Grid Control installation is to be used to manage and monitor this new database. However, the management agent corresponding to that Grid Control installation must be installed and running on the server on which you are creating the new database. Otherwise, you can choose to use the single-database-specific Database Control for database management.

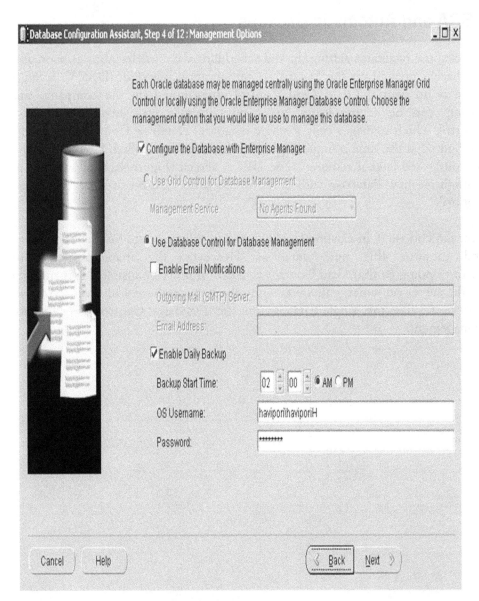

Each Oracle database may be managed centrally using the Oracle Enterprise Manager Grid Control or locally using the Oracle Enterprise Manager Database Control. Choose the management option that you would like to use to manage this database.

☑ Configure the Database with Enterprise Manager

○ Use Grid Control for Database Management

Management Service ___No Agents Found___

● Use Database Control for Database Management

☐ Enable Email Notifications

Outgoing Mail (SMTP) Server: _____

Email Address: _____

☑ Enable Daily Backup

Backup Start Time: 02 00 ● AM ○ PM

OS Username: haviporihaviporiH

Password: ********

Cancel   Help   ‹ Back   Next ›

Figure 4.18: *Database Configuration Assistant*

At this step in DBCA, you can Enable Email Notifications for any database alerts if you specify an SMTP server for outgoing mail.

What is of interest is that you can also enable daily backups on this DBCA screen by simply specifying the backup start time and the OS username and password. It is that simple. When the database is created in this manner, Database Control is automatically configured by DBCA.

In Windows, a service called OracleDBConsolePRD1FIN is created and has its startup type as Automatic. The new service can be seen immediately in the Windows services list. The database creation completes and provides the information on how to access Database Control (Figure 4.19).

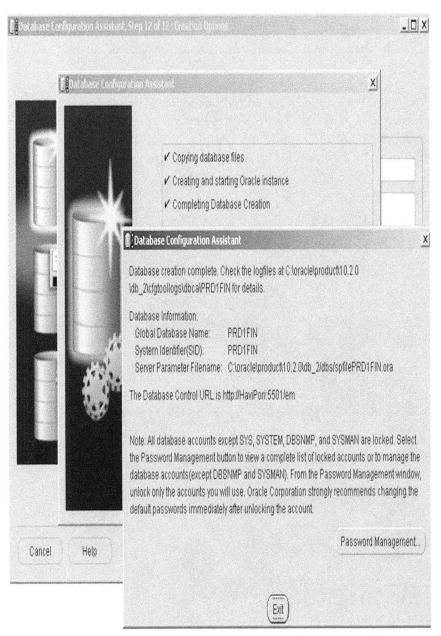

Figure 4.19: *Database Control Configured by DBCA*

Oracle Enterprise Manager Grid Control

The Database Control URL is displayed as the following: http://HaviPori:5501/em. Accessing this URL takes you to the OEM 10g Database Control Home Page (Figure 4.20). Log in as SYS user with SYSDBA rights.

Figure 4.20: *Database Console Home Page*

As can be seen from the Console Home page, the Job Activity shows a scheduled execution. Click on the link for the execution displayed as 1. The screen that is displayed is the Job Activity screen (Figure 4.21).

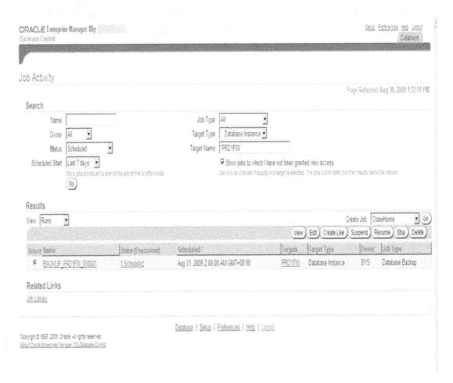

Figure 4.21: *Job Activity - Scheduled*

As can be seen, there is a backup job scheduled for the coming night at 2:00 AM. The job is owned by SYS and it is named BACKUP_PRD1FIN_000001. Drilling down on the job shows that it is using a backup script (Figure 4.22).

Figure 4.22: *Database Backup Job Summary*

Clicking on the Daily Backup Script will enable you to examine the code of the script (Figure 4.23).

Figure 4.23: *Daily Backup Script*

The RMAN script line is seen as follows:

```
run { allocate channel oem_disk_backup device type disk; recover copy of
database with tag 'ORA\$OEM_LEVEL_0'; backup incremental level 1 cumulative
copies=1 for recover of copy with tag 'ORA\$OEM_LEVEL_0' database;}
```

This is an Oracle suggested backup. Using this automatically generated script, RMAN will perform a full database copy on the first backup. This will create datafile copies rather than RMAN backup pieces. Consequently, every day an incremental cumulative backup will be performed that updates the datafile copies with all the changes.

This means the datafile copy backup will always be up-to-date with production. The advantage is that you can easily switch over to this backup and use it as a production database in the case of an emergency without any restore of the backup or recovery of the database. This new concept dramatically reduces recovery time and is one of the many advanced features of Oracle Recovery Manager (RMAN) in 10g onwards.

Now attempt to edit the job. However, you find that it will not allow you to change the script or method of RMAN backup. Only general information about the job can be edited (Figure 4.24)

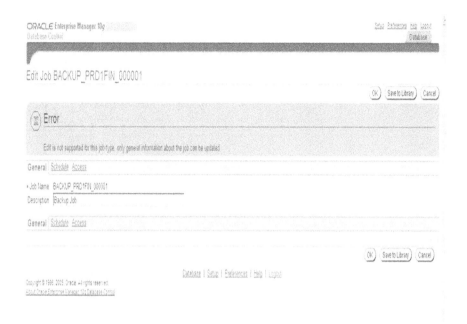

Figure 4.24: *Editing the Database Control Job*

In this case, only the Schedule and the Access can be changed for the job. Move to the Schedule tab and change the schedule as required (Figure 4.25).

Figure 4.25: *Editing the Schedule*

Next, move to the Access tab (Figure 4.26). On this screen, SYS, SYSMAN and SYSTEM all appear as OEM Super Administrators. By default, SYSMAN and SYSTEM users only have view access to this job instead of the full access granted to SYS, the user that is also the owner of the job.

Edit Job BACKUP_PRD1FIN_000001 : Access

OK   Save to Library   Cancel

General Schedule Access

This table contains Administrators and Roles that have access to this job

Add

New	Name	Type	Access Level	Remove
	SYS	Administrator	Owner	
	SYS	Super Administrator	Full ▾	
	SYSMAN	Super Administrator	View ▾	
	SYSTEM	Super Administrator	View ▾	

TIP The Full access level can be granted to an administrator only if that administrator has at least view access to all targets

General Schedule Access

OK   Save to Library   Cancel

Database | Setup | Preferences | Help | Logout

Figure 4.26: *Editing the Access*

Suppose you are not happy with the Oracle recommended backup strategy and want to create your own backup using RMAN backup pieces. Since you cannot edit the automatically created backup job, you can create your own backup strategy as before by moving to the Maintenance tab in Grid Control (Figure 4.27).

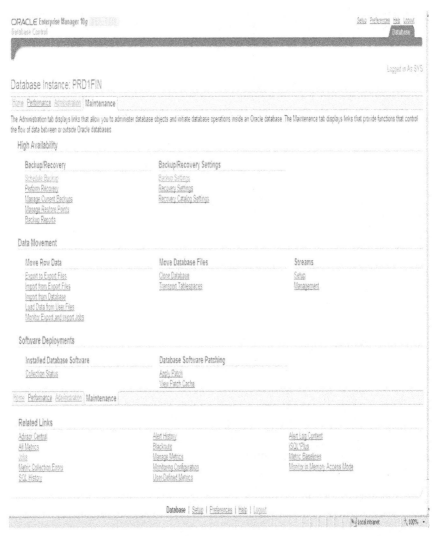

Figure 4.27: *Database Control Maintenance Tab*

Selecting Schedule Backup gives you a warning about the currently scheduled backup job (Figure 4.28). But from there on, you can proceed as before like you did in Grid Control and set up backup jobs as you please for full and incremental backups.

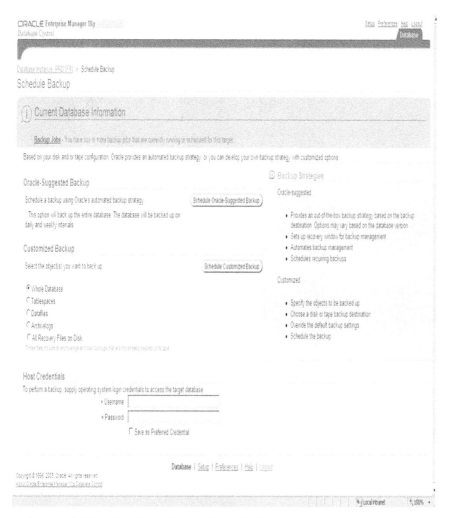

Figure 4.28: *Database Control Schedule Backup*

Since you have decided to set up your own backup strategy, it will be necessary to disable the automatically created backup job. This is done by first stopping all executions of the job (Figure 4.29).

Figure 4.29: *Stopping Executions*

Then delete it from the Job Activity screen (Figure 4.30).

Figure 4.30: *Deleting All Runs*

Backup Strategy

Executing a full database backup every night is fine for small or medium-sized databases and no one complains about the small amount of disk space the back up requires or why the backup executes in a very short time. However, when the database size is more than 200 GB, it is time to rethink your backup strategy.

In most of the real world database scenarios, having a proper and validated backup strategy is very important, even for small databases. Remember, regular testing of your RMAN backup of all your databases is one of the DBA's mandatory responsibilities.

Consider a larger database with a total of 500 GB of database files. Obviously, it will not be appropriate to take a full database backup each day. You can adopt a better backup strategy by taking a full database backup once a week on a Sunday and then an incremental database backup Monday through Saturday.

This will enable you to recover the database to any point in time during the previous week by first restoring Sunday's full database backup and then applying the appropriate incremental backups. You will now see how to set this up in Oracle Enterprise Manager. For the purpose of this illustration, Database Control has been used.

Creating a Level 0 Backup

Log on to the Database Control console as a user with DBA rights and access the Maintenance tab of the PRD1FIN database. Select Schedule Backup in the Backup/Recovery section. In the Schedule Backup screen, select Whole Database in the Customized Backup section. Then click on Schedule Customized Backup.

The Options page appears. Select Full Backup and click on "Use as the base of an incremental backup strategy" (Figure 4.31). This backup of the database you create as part of an incremental strategy is called a Level 0 backup.

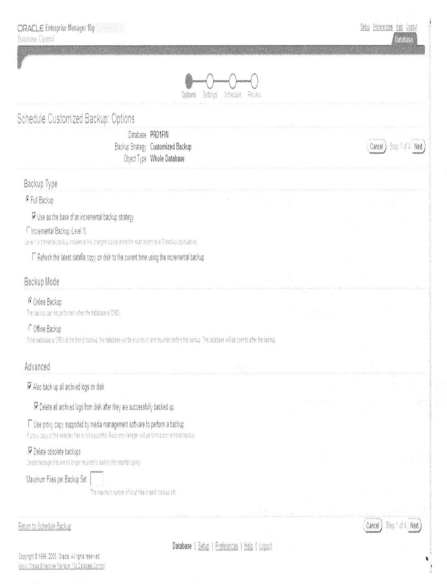

Options   Settings   Schedule   Review

Schedule Customized Backup: Options

Database PRD1FIN
Backup Strategy Customized Backup
Object Type Whole Database

Cancel   Step 1 of 4   Next

Backup Type

⦿ Full Backup

☑ Use as the base of an incremental backup strategy

○ Incremental Backup (Level 1)
Level 1 incremental backup includes all the changed blocks since the most recent level 0 backup (cumulative).

☐ Refresh the latest datafile copy on disk to the current time using the incremental backup

Backup Mode

⦿ Online Backup
The backup can be performed when the database is OPEN.

○ Offline Backup
If the database is OPEN at the time of backup, the database will be shut down and mounted before the backup. The database will be opened after the backup.

Advanced

☑ Also back up all archived logs on disk

☑ Delete all archived logs from disk after they are successfully backed up

☐ Use proxy copy supported by media management software to perform a backup
If proxy copy of the selected files is not supported, Recovery Manager will perform a conventional backup.

☑ Delete obsolete backups
Delete backups that are no longer required to satisfy the retention policy.

Maximum Files per Backup Set [   ]
The maximum number of input files in each backup set.

Return to Schedule Backup

Cancel   Step 1 of 4   Next

Database | Setup | Preferences | Help | Logout

Copyright © 1996, 2005, Oracle. All rights reserved.
About Oracle Enterprise Manager 10g Database Control

Figure 4.31: *Full Backup with Incremental Strategy*

Select the other options on this page, such as backup all archived logs, delete all archived logs after backup, delete obsolete backups and so on as before. Move on to the next pages.

On the scheduler page, set the full backup to start on a Sunday at 2:00 AM, allowing time for the database backup to complete before the database is required by application users. Set the repeat interval to be once each week and repeat until indefinitely (Figure 4.32). This will set up the full backup, which is the base of the incremental strategy, to repeat once a week on Sunday morning.

Figure 4.32: *Scheduling Full Backup on Sundays*

Move on to the next screen. The Review screen now appears (Figure 4.33). This shows the following information:

```
Database:  PRD1FIN
Backup Strategy:  Customized Backup
Object Type:  Whole Database

Destination : Disk
Backup Type:  Use as the base of an incremental backup strategy
Backup Mode:  Online Backup
Flash Recovery Area:  D:\flash_recovery_area
Disk Parallelism:  3
```

Figure 4.33: *Review of Sunday Full Backup*

The RMAN script is generated as follows:

```
backup incremental level 0 cumulative device type disk tag '%TAG' database;
backup device type disk tag '%TAG' archivelog all not backed up delete all
input;
allocate channel for maintenance type disk;
delete noprompt obsolete device type disk;
release channel;
```

The *backup incremental level 0 cumulative* command indicates that it is a level 0 incremental backup. This is physically identical to a full backup except that the only difference is that the level 0 backup will be used as the parent for a level 1 incremental backup; thus, forming your incremental strategy. A plain full backup cannot be used in this way. Also, the *cumulative* word in the RMAN command signifies that this will be a cumulative backup that will back up all blocks that have been modified after the most recent level 0 incremental backup.

The alternative to this is a differential backup, which backs up all blocks modified after the latest level 1 or 0 incremental backup. As an example, a cumulative backup on Tuesday will include all blocks changed on both the Monday and Tuesday. A differential backup on Tuesday will include only the blocks modified on Tuesday, provided a previous differential backup was taken on the previous Monday to back up the blocks modified on that Monday.

At this point, proceed and submit the Level 0 incremental backup job, which is immediately scheduled at the selected time on Sunday morning.

Creating a Level 1 Backup

You can now set up the level 1 incremental backup for every weekday. Select Schedule Backup in the Backup/Recovery section. In the Schedule Backup screen, select Whole Database in the Customized Backup section. Then click on Schedule Customized Backup. The Options page appears. Select Incremental Backup (Level 1). All the other options are the same as before (Figure 4.34).

Figure 4.34: *Incremental Backup (Level 1)*

Proceed to the following pages. On the scheduler page, set the incremental backup to start on a Monday at 5:00 AM. Set the repeat interval to be once every day to repeat indefinitely (Figure 4.35). This will set up the incremental level 1 backup to be repeated every day of the week.

Figure 4.35: *Scheduling Weekday Incremental Backup*

However, note that the scheduler in OEM 10g Database Control does not allow you to specifically identify Monday to Friday in the schedule.

Since the repeat interval is set to once every day, all the days in the week are selected (including Sunday, the day of the Level 0 backup).

No need to press the panic button. This is fine because you have set the time of the Level 0 backup on Sunday morning to be 2:00 AM, and the incremental

Level 1 backup on the same day will be at 5:00 AM. If necessary, you can adjust the schedules of the jobs to increase the time gap between the two scheduled times.

Another option is to set up five separate incremental backup jobs, one for each weekday, Monday to Friday, and then repeat these jobs each week. In effect, you will have one Sunday job repeating every Sunday and each weekday job repeating one week later on the same day of the week. Although this is one option, you will have six separate backup jobs for one database, which is more difficult to manage.

Scheduling Monday to Friday

Any hope for the future? Yes. In Oracle Enterprise Manager 11g Database Control, this issue is avoided since the scheduler in this 11g version allows you to schedule exactly what you want: only the Monday to Friday weekdays.

On the Schedule screen, there is a new frequency type called Weekly. If you select this type, you can select the days of the week by ticking the box that corresponds to each day (see Figure 4.36). Please note that this is for illustration purposes only, since for this exercise, you are using OEM 10g and not 11g.

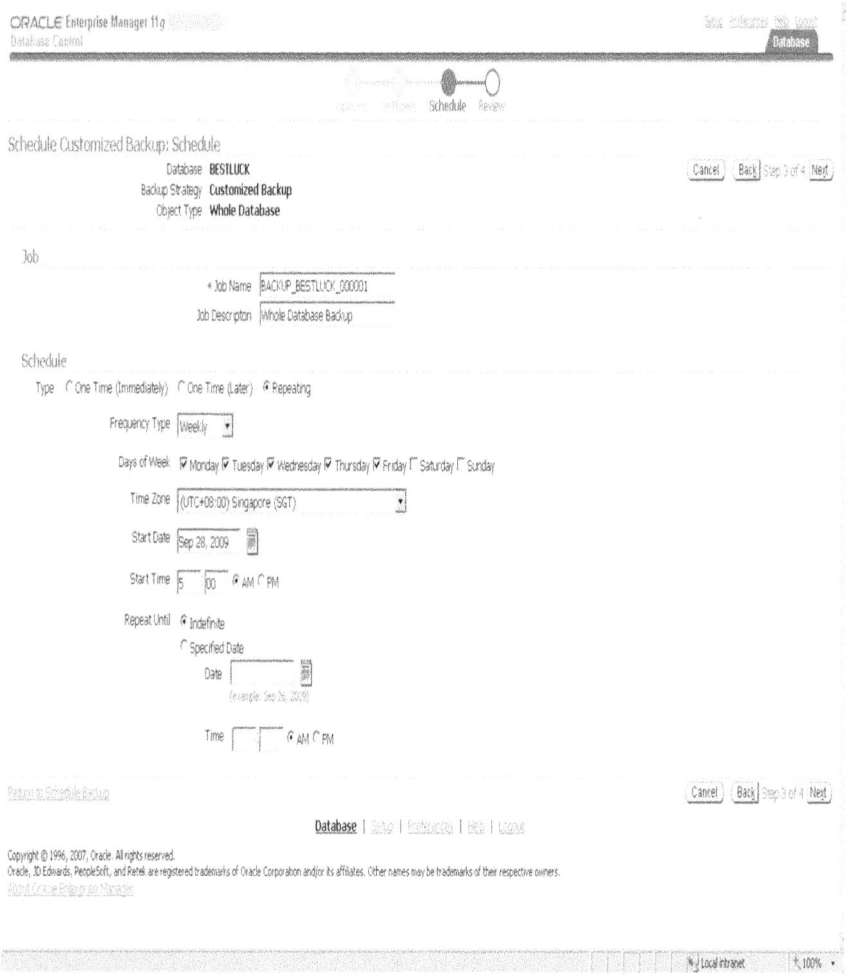

Figure 4.36: *Scheduling Monday to Friday in DB Control 11g*

This demonstrates how Oracle features are truly advancing in newer versions and how Oracle listens to its user community and the issues they experience, resolving any such issues in subsequent releases. Oracle has a great connection to the user community and is seriously involved with its users.

Upgrading is a Good Idea

As an aside, there is another very significant reason to upgrade your corporate database to the latest version of 11g Release 2. You should do this if you want the best support from Oracle at the best possible price. Extended support for Oracle 9i ended on July 31st, 2010. Even the 10g version went to extended support after this date.

So, if you are upgrading today from 9i, it does not make sense to upgrade to 10g. Go straight to 11g Release 2. The Oracle support fee officially increases to 20% after the first year of extended support. It is always advisable to plan for an upgrade in advance.

Coming back to the incremental backup job, the Review screen now appears (Figure 4.37). The following information can be seen on this screen:

```
Database: PRD1FIN
Backup Strategy:  Customized Backup
Object Type:  Whole Database

Destination:  Disk
Backup Type:  Incremental Backup (Level 1)
Backup Mode:  Online Backup
Flash Recovery Area:  D:\flash_recovery_area
Disk Parallelism:  3
```

Figure 4.37: *Review Incremental Backup Level 1*

The RMAN script generated is as follows:

```
backup incremental level 1 cumulative device type disk tag '%TAG' database;
backup device type disk tag '%TAG' archivelog all not backed up delete all
input;
allocate channel for maintenance type disk;
delete noprompt obsolete device type disk;
release channel;
```

The command *backup incremental level 1 cumulative … database* is responsible for creating the incremental level 1 backup of the database via RMAN.

Examining the Backup Jobs List

In OEM 10g Database Control, the Jobs link is located within the Related Links section at the lower end of any of the database tabs. See Figure 4.38.

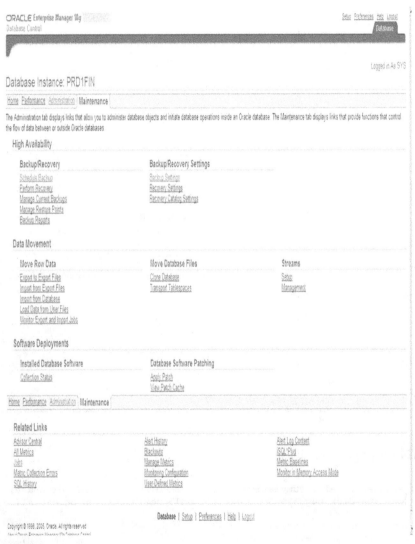

Figure 4.38: *Related Links - Jobs*

Click on the Jobs link. The two backup jobs that have been set up can be seen in the Job list (Figure 4.39). These are the Level 0 and Level 1 incremental jobs that comprise your backup strategy.

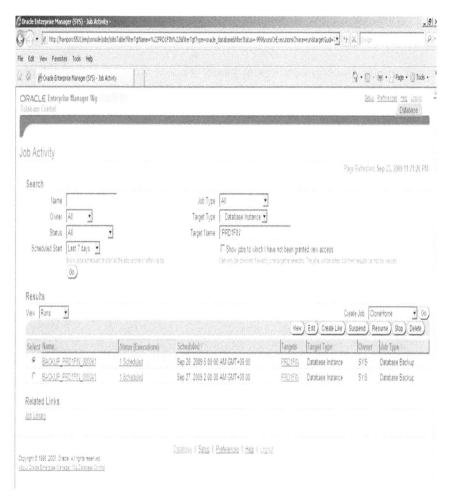

Figure 4.39: *Job Activity - Level 0 and Level 1 jobs*

Creating an Image Copy Backup

How can you make an image copy backup? Very easily indeed with OEM 10g. Select Backup Settings. This is on the Maintenance tab if using Grid Control 10.2.0.4 or earlier, or on the Availability tab if using the latest Grid Control version 10.2.0.5.

The first tab of the Backup Settings appears. This is the Device tab (Figure 4.40). On this page, select Image Copy as the Disk Backup Type. Save this by clicking on the OK button. This is an RMAN configuration setting, which is now saved in the control file of the database.

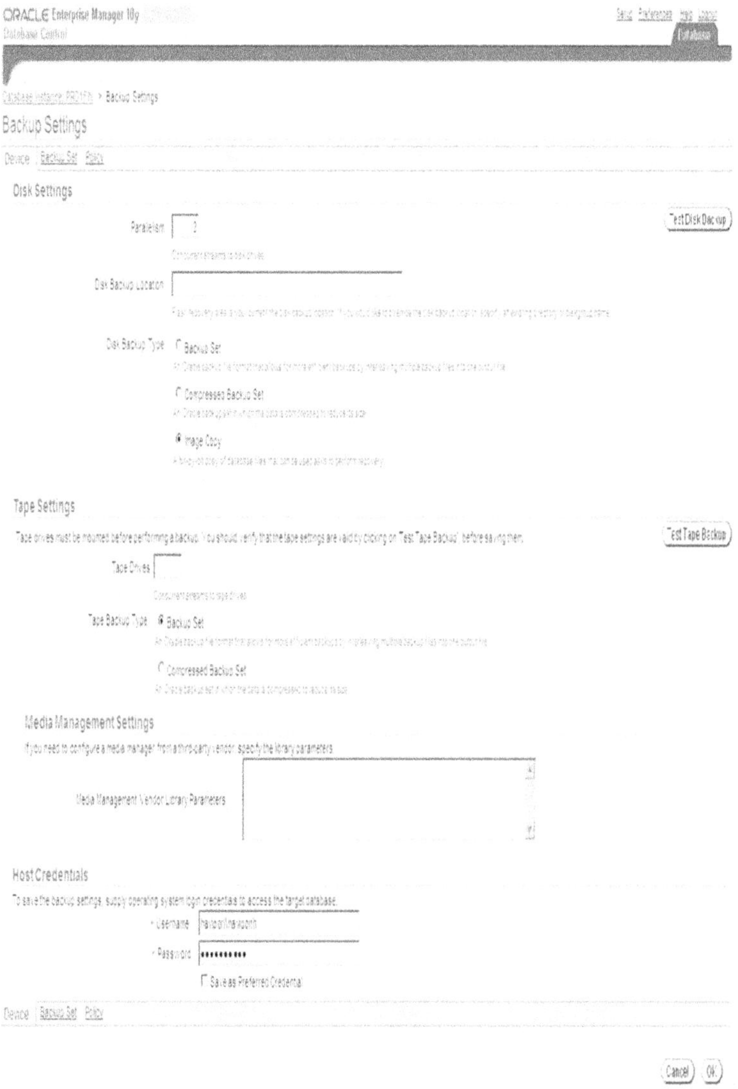

Figure 4.40: *Image Copy Disk Backup Type*

To schedule the image copy backup, select Schedule Backup in the Backup/Recovery section. Then select Whole Database in the Customized Backup section, and click on Schedule Customized Backup.

The Options page appears. Select Full Backup and "Use as the base of an incremental backup strategy". All the other options such as choosing an online backup, backup all archived logs on disk, delete archived logs after backing up and such are set just like before (Figure 4.41).

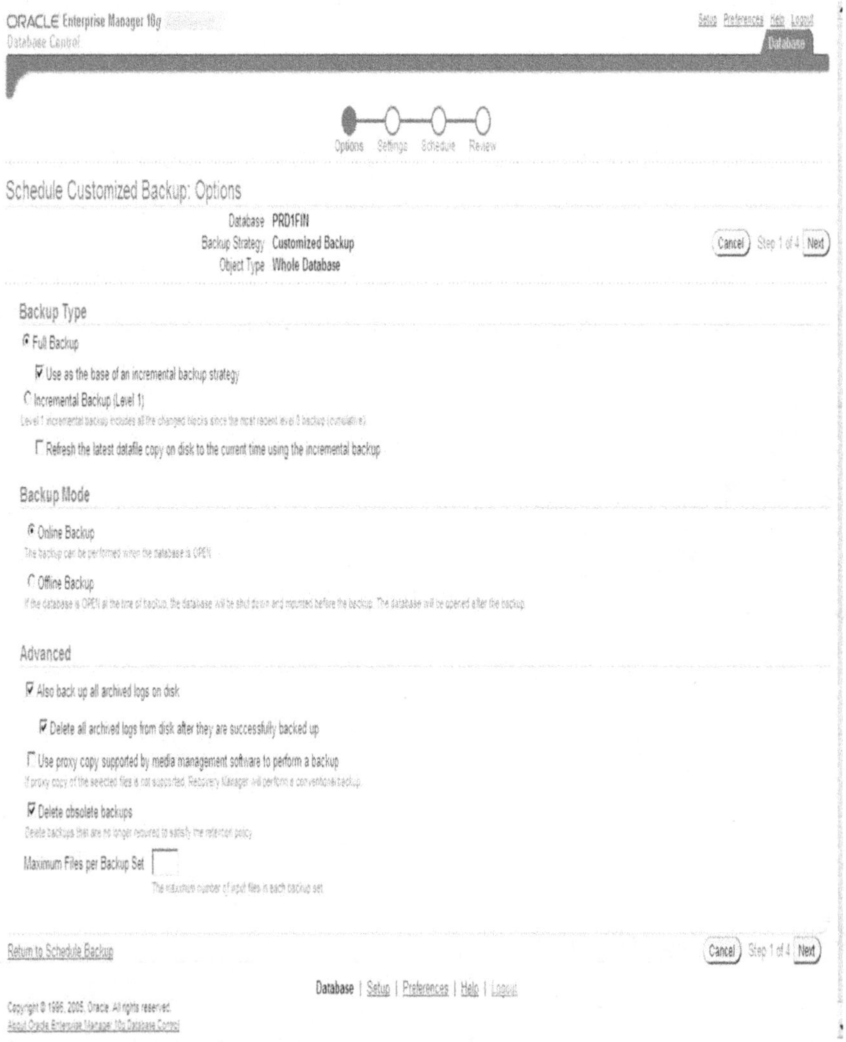

Figure 4.41: *Schedule Customized Backup - Options*

However, moving to the next page shows a validation error on the screen (Figure 4.42). This is because an incremental backup strategy is not supported if you are using an image copy to disk as the backup type.

Figure 4.42: *Validation Error*

To correct the validation error, you must move back to the previous screen and remove the selection of "Use as the base of an incremental backup strategy". You can then proceed without an error, and generate the RMAN script shown here:

```
backup device type disk tag '%TAG' database;
backup device type disk archivelog all not backed up delete all input;
```

```
allocate channel for maintenance type disk;
delete noprompt obsolete device type disk;
release channel;
```

As can be seen, the script command *backup device type disk ... database* is no
different from the first full backup that was scheduled. The only difference, in
this case, is the RMAN configuration setting of the backup type is *image copy to
disk* compared to the *compressed backup set* used previously. This means that
when the backup runs, image copies of the database files will be created on
disk rather than backup sets being generated by RMAN.

These image copies will be created in the *datafile* subdirectory under the flash
recovery   area.   In   your   case,   this   is
D:\flash_recovery_area\PRD1FIN\DATAFILE. A sample of the RMAN
output producing the image copies is shown below:

```
RMAN> backup device type disk tag 'BACKUP_PRD1FIN_000_092709123353'
database;

Starting backup at 27-SEP-09
allocated channel: ORA_DISK_1
channel ORA_DISK_1: sid=128 devtype=DISK
...
channel ORA_DISK_1: starting datafile copy
input datafile fno=00001 name=d:\oradata\prd1fin\system01.dbf
channel ora_disk_2: starting datafile copy
input datafile fno=00003 name=d:\oradata\prd1fin\sysaux01.dbf
...
output
filename=d:\flash_recovery_area\prd1fin\datafile\o1_mf_example_5cwjnfqg_.dbf
tag=backup_prd1fin_000_092709123353 recid=7 stamp=698632491

channel ora_disk_1: datafile copy complete, elapsed time: 00:02:08
channel ora_disk_2: datafile copy complete, elapsed time: 00:00:48
...
finished backup at 27-sep-09
```

Refreshing the Image Copy

Oracle 10g offers an extremely useful facility in RMAN, which is not known to
many DBAs. You can take an image copy of all the datafiles of a database once
in awhile, and then take an incremental backup each day that will actually
refresh the image copy of the database with all the incremental changes. Does
that sound good?

The datafile copies become the same as in production since they are being brought up-to-date each day when the incremental backup is run. This is extremely useful for large databases since they will always have the latest refreshed datafile copies in the flash recovery area to fall over to in the case of an emergency.

The datafile copies actually become the production database in this case. Technically, you have managed a recovery of the database without performing a restore of the files from backup, and this makes the entire recovery faster and simpler. If you use a backup strategy like this, which is based on incrementally updated backups, it can help minimize the media recovery time of your database.

If the refresh of the datafile copies is done daily, then at recovery time you never have more than one day of redo (archived or online) to apply. This facility is visible and easily understandable if OEM is used to schedule RMAN backups. New features such as these, enhanced for every version of the databases, are displayed and explained clearly in OEM, thereby playing an important role in DBA education.

You can now set up the level 1 incremental backup for every weekday as before, but with this refreshing of the image copy as well to keep it up-to-date with your production database. To do this, select Schedule Backup in the Backup/Recovery section.

In the Schedule Backup screen, select Whole Database in the Customized Backup section. Then click on Schedule Customized Backup. The Options page appears. Select Incremental Backup (Level 1). Also, tick the option "Refresh the latest datafile copy on disk to the current time using the incremental backup".

All the other options are the same as before (Figure 4.43).

Figure 4.43: *Refresh the Latest Datafile Copy on Disk*

Proceed to the following screens. The Review screen appears (Figure 4.44).

Figure 4.44: *Review of Refresh Datafile Copy*

The RMAN script generated in this case is as follows:

```
backup incremental level 1 cumulative device type disk tag '%TAG' database;
recover copy of database;
```

```
backup device type disk tag '%TAG' archivelog all not backed up delete all
input;
allocate channel for maintenance type disk;
delete noprompt obsolete device type disk;
release channel;
```

The command *recover copy of database* is responsible for refreshing the datafile
copies on disk. This RMAN command applies any available incremental level 1
backups to a set of datafile copies. Part of the output of this command is
shown below.

```
RMAN> recover copy of database;
```

```
Starting recover at 27-SEP-09
using channel ORA_DISK_1
…
channel ORA_DISK_1: starting incremental datafile backupset restore
channel ORA_DISK_1: specifying datafile copies to recover

recovering datafile copy fno=00002
name=D:\flash_recovery_area\prd1fin\datafile\o1_mf_undotbs1_5cwjqbws_.dbf
…
channel ORA_DISK_1: reading from backup piece
D:\flash_recovery_area\prd1fin\backupset\2009_09_27\o1_mf_nnnd1_backup_prd1f
in_000_0_5cygbc98_.bkp
…
channel ORA_DISK_1: restored backup piece 1

piece
handle=D:\flash_recovery_area\prd1fin\backupset\2009_09_27\o1_mf_nnnd1_backu
p_prd1fin_000_0_5cygbc98_.bkp tag=backup_prd1fin_000_092709060650

channel ORA_DISK_1: restore complete, elapsed time: 00:00:16
…
Finished recover at 27-SEP-09
```

On the disk, you can see that the datafile copies in
D:\flash_recovery_area\PRD1FIN\DATAFILE have been refreshed and are
now current as of the date of the incremental backup, i.e. 27-Sep-09.

```
D:\>dir /od D:\flash_recovery_area\PRD1FIN\datafile
 volume in drive d is acerdata
 Volume Serial Number is 010A-D4B9

 Directory of D:\flash_recovery_area\PRD1FIN\DATAFILE

09/23/2009  11:36 pm    <dir>           ..
09/23/2009  11:36 pm    <dir>           .
09/27/2009  06:08 pm         5,251,072 o1_mf_users_5cwjqdmk_.dbf
09/27/2009  06:08 pm        36,708,352 o1_mf_undotbs1_5cwjqbws_.dbf
09/27/2009  06:08 pm       104,865,792 o1_mf_example_5cwjnfqg_.dbf
09/27/2009  06:08 pm       251,666,432 o1_mf_sysaux_5cwjn71g_.dbf
```

```
09/27/2009  06:08 pm        503,324,672 o1_mf_system_5cwjn6vt_.dbf
              5 file(s)     901,816,320 bytes
```

Looking back at this strategy, it seems it is similar to the Oracle-suggested strategy seen earlier. When the daily backup had been set up using DBCA, the script automatically generated was:

```
run {
allocate channel oem_disk_backup device type disk;
recover copy of database with tag 'ORA\$OEM_LEVEL_0';
backup incremental level 1 cumulative copies=1 for recover of copy with tag
'ORA\$OEM_LEVEL_0' database;
}
```

It is now possible to understand, in a detailed sense, how the Oracle-suggested backup works.

If no level 0 image copy backup of a datafile exists, then executing the *backup incremental level 1 .. for recover of copy with tag ..* command immediately creates an image copy of the datafile on disk with the specified tag and the level 1 backup is not created. This means that the first time the script runs, it will create the image copy of the datafile and this copy is used to begin the cycle of incremental updates. All subsequent runs of the script produce level 1 incremental backups of the datafile.

The *recover copy of database with tag* command applies the incremental level 1 backup to the set of datafile copies with the named tag.

Backing Up the Flash Recovery Area

The strategy suggested in the previous pages has almost always been a disk-based backup strategy. All the backup files, including the RMAN backup pieces for the database and the archive log backups, as well as the datafile copies, are located in the flash recovery area. This disk-based strategy makes it easy for the DBA to restore and recover the database and even block-level recovery can be performed easily. However, the disk backups must sooner or later be transferred to good old tape.

So Oracle allows making a backup of the entire flash recovery area to tape. This can be done in the Schedule Backups screen. Under the Customized

Backup section, select All Recovery Files on Disk and click on Schedule Customized Backup (Figure 4.45).

Figure 4.45: *Back Up the Flash Recovery Area*

In the pages that follow, only the tape backup option is displayed and the disk backup sections cannot be selected.

This is seen in Figure 4.46; since the tape device has not been configured in this case, a validation error appears as follows:

```
Error - You must configure a tape device in order to backup to tape. Cancel
the wizard, configure a tape device in Backup Settings, then restart the
Schedule Backup wizard.
```

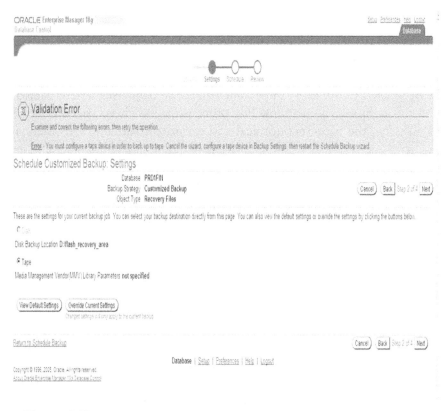

Figure 4.46: *Must Configure a Tape Device*

If a tape device has been configured, you can use this type of backup job in OEM to back up the entire flash recovery area to tape, perhaps once a week.

Backing Up Using Snapshots

Now look at a different type of backup and see how to set this up using OEM Grid Control. You see many databases today deployed on NAS filer storage, such as those from NetApp. This is happening even in large corporations where databases have traditionally been deployed on higher-end storage systems, such as SANs.

NAS is network-attached storage connected to servers by standard Ethernet. On the other hand, SANs (Storage Area Networks) are faster performing storage, which are more expensive to purchase and maintain. SANs have normally been used in the most important enterprise databases where database speed and throughput is important. For other projects where speed is not so much of an issue, the more economical and easier-to-maintain NAS filers are just fine.

In the case of SANs, the main backup mechanism that was used for many years was the Business Continuance Volume (BCV): a copy of the full volume. This occupied as much space as the volume itself and frequently, two or three BCV copies would be used, all this adding to the cost of the SAN storage.

An alternate and interesting technology was introduced by the NetApp filer: the snaphot. This technology allowed the storage system to take read-only copies of the file system at any time. You could do this manually or schedule the snapshot at intervals. When the need arose, you could easily restore a single file or an entire file system from the snapshot in seconds.

A very important advantage is that the snapshots are very space-effective, taking up a minimal amount of space dependent on the total number of blocks that have been modified in the file system and captured by the snapshot. So if there are major changes after the snapshot was taken, the snapshot would grow in size.

When databases started being placed on these filers, the DBAs could now use the new snapshot technology to take database backups with the tablespaces put in backup mode just before the snapshot was taken.

A database on a NAS filer could also be backed up using Oracle Recovery Manager (RMAN) without using snapshots. The advantage of using pure RMAN is that the backup mode, which places a strain on the database because it generates more redo information, is not needed, and mainframe-like block-level recovery is possible from RMAN backups. However, the benefit of a filer snapshot is faster speed and the ability to store multiple snapshots without sacrificing the large amount of space required to store multiple traditional backups on disk.

The actual snapshot creation takes place in the background after the command to create the snapshot is issued, so there is no need to keep the database in backup mode for a long period of time. And if the database is large in size, say half a terabyte, then a snapshot may occupy far less space than even a compressed RMAN backup. Therefore, the snapshot technology is excellent for larger sized databases.

RMAN can, of course, still be used for smaller databases due to the technical benefits it offers, such as block-level recovery. It is simply not possible to recover to the block level in snapshots. If you would like the best of both worlds, then you could perform the snapshot backups as the primary method of database backup, and then also have RMAN backups as the secondary method of backups.

You have seen that it is possible to use OEM Grid Control to set up and schedule RMAN backups very easily and seamlessly in a fraction of the time it used to take to set up RMAN shell scripts and schedule them using crontab at the unix level. At this point, you will see if it is possible to use the Grid Control facility to set up and schedule your database backups using the filer's snapshot utility and catalogue these snapshot copies in RMAN at the same time.

Basic Snapshot Setup

NetApp filer administrators almost always schedule hourly, nightly and weekly snapshots on the filer volumes, not understanding that these snapshots are useless if the database has not been placed in backup mode. These snapshots are scheduled at the filer level and waste valuable space since snapshots grow in size as the filer blocks change. A weekly snapshot, for example, may have grown drastically in size by the time the next week comes along. If a snapshot is taken and not deleted or overwritten, it can easily fill up the storage file system. Therefore, the first step is to modify the filer snapshot schedule and make sure the hourly, nightly or weekly snapshots are not being created automatically.

Our database server itself will be provided with a new snapshot script, scheduled by OEM Grid Control. This script will log in remotely to the filer and create the snapshots at the filer level. The script will also log in to the database to place the tablespaces in backup mode before the snapshot is taken and finally catalogue the newly created snapshots in RMAN.

The game plan is to create four snapshots per database. These snapshots should be taken each day after every six hours in the following manner:

```
Snapshot Number              Time

Snapshot 0                   24:00
Snapshot 1                   06:00
Snapshot 2                   12:00
Snapshot 3                   18:00
```

The intention is not to have an unlimited number of snapshots, but to recycle them daily via the script. Each snapshot is deleted and then recreated at the time the script is executed. The script itself will be a simple shell script placed on the database server. If the database is a RAC clustered database, then you must place the script on every node within the cluster and in the same directory.

Another possibility is to place the entire script in Grid Control itself. In this way, there is no need to create the script on the database server or on any node in a RAC cluster. Grid Control simply takes the stored script and runs it when scheduled. Yet there are certain issues to this approach as you will shortly see, and this method is not recommended.

It is estimated that for this database, only about 5% of the blocks will be modified between the six-hour snapshots. This means each snapshot will take up only 5% of the volume size. If you are storing four snapshots per day, this would mean 20% of the database volume size. This will help in calculating the amount of disk required on the filer. You should always overestimate to cater for times of increased application activity.

A final thing to bear in mind is that the snapshot prevents any space that belonged to a deleted file from being reused unless the snapshot itself is deleted. As per NetApp guidelines, the storage administrator may need to cater for up to 20 percent of extra space on the database volumes to handle this kind of file deletion. If the database files are large, care should be taken to delete the snapshots after any database file has been deleted.

Setting Up Filer Snapshots in Grid Control

It is presumed, as before, that target groups and administrators with rights over the target groups have been set up in the Grid Control system. This is often done so as to handle multiple targets and DBA teams in a large corporation.

In the previous chapter, the FINANCE_GROUP target group has been mentioned along with the corresponding FINANCE_ADMIN administrator. Use this to log on to the OEM Grid Control console at this point in time.

Select the Jobs tab on the console page. On that page, you can create a new job which is an OS Command job (Figure 4.47). Select this from the dropdown list, and click on the Go button.

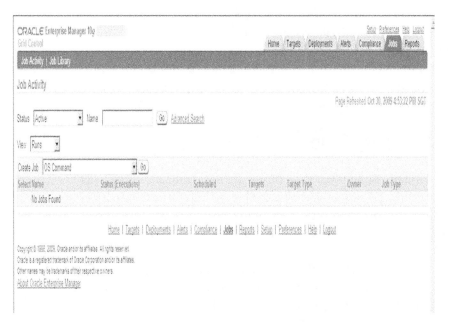

Figure 4.47: *Jobs Tab*

The Create OS Command Job..General tab appears on the screen (Figure 4.48). Here, type in the Job Name as RMANSnapShotJob. Select the target of the job as the host itself.

Figure 4.48: *Create OS Command Job..General*

Move to the Parameters tab (Figure 4.49). Select Single Operation as the Command Type. As the command itself, enter the following:

```
/bin/ksh /dba/myscripts/db_back_snap.sh
```

Figure 4.49: *Create OS Command Job..Parameters*

On the Schedule tab (Figure 4.50), you can now schedule the OS command job to execute at any of the four periods in the day with a repeating schedule for every six hours. Also specify a grace period of two hours in case the job fails to execute.

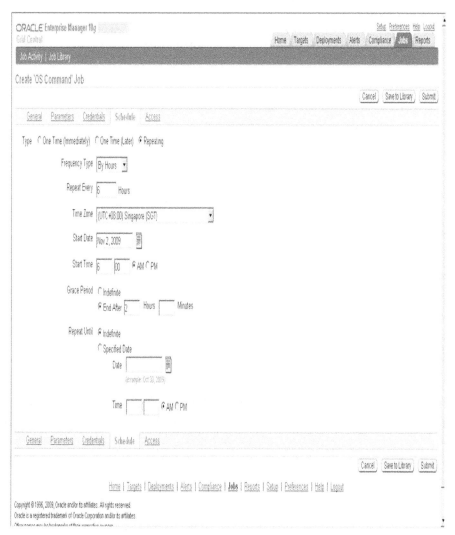

Figure 4.50: *Create OS Command Job..Schedule*

You can now submit the job. The job is created successfully and immediately appears on the Job Activity screen as a scheduled job (Figure 4.51).

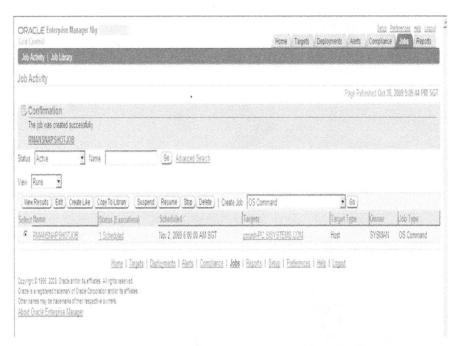

Figure 4.51: *Job Created Successfully*

Suppose you attempt to place your script in the Grid Control job. You do this by specifying the Command Type as Script in the Parameters tab, and then pasting the script in the OS Script box that is displayed. However, there is a conflict. An error message is seen (Figure 4.52) when you try to save the script.

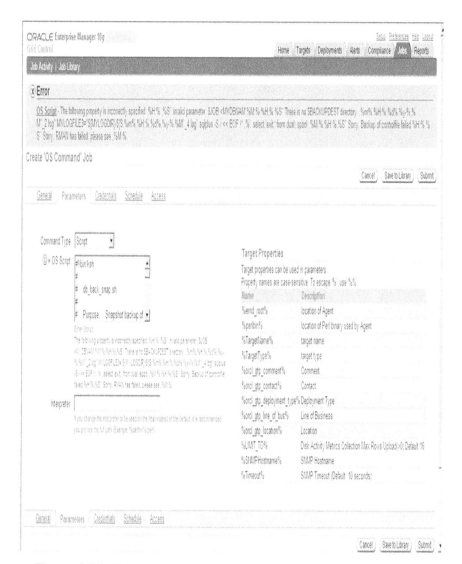

Figure 4.52: *Error Due to Script Conflict*

The conflict occurs since OEM allows target properties to be used in parameters. Examples of these target properties are *%emd_root%* for the location of Agent, *%TargetName%* for the target name, and so on. So if you have entries like *%H*, *%S* and such in your script, OEM will give an error message (as was seen in Figure 4.52) when you try to save the OS Script.

The solution to this is simply to escape % by using %%. However, that does mean modifying your shell script specifically for Grid Control. It would be nice if you could use the script as is, so decide not to store the whole script in the Grid Control job system. Less complicated scripts would be more suited to that.

The script *db_back_snap.sh* is listed below. Since you are not placing the script *db_back_snap.sh* directly in the Grid Control job, you must place it on the database server in the specified location. If the database is a RAC clustered database, place it on every node in the same directory. There is a slight modification required in the script: set the variable SIDNAME manually to the correct SID name on the node; in this case, FINP1 on node 1 and FINP2 on node 2.

The IP address of the filer must also be manually modified in the script as well as the names of the database volumes.

db_back_snap.sh (partial)

```
#!/bin/ksh
#
#     db_back_snap.sh
#
#     Purpose:      Snapshot backup of Database
#                   and catalogue backup in RMAN
#     DBA:          Porus Homi Havewala
#

# job name
jobname="$0"
job=`basename $jobname`
errmsg="
  $job: `date '+%h:%m:%s'` invalid parameter:
  $job <mydbname>
"

mydbname="finp"

# the sid must be modified manually in this script

sidname="finp1"

# set oracle home and other environment vars
. set_db_env.sh $sidname

if [ $? -ne 0 ]; then
  echo "$job: `date '+%h:%m:%s'` sorry, could not set oracle env vars. will
exit now.."
  exit ${error}
fi
```

```
# set the backup destination
backupdest=/u100/flash_recovery_area/$mydbname

if [ ! -d $backupdest ]; then
  echo "$job: `date '+%h:%m:%s'` there is no $backupdest directory. will
exit now.."
  exit ${error}
fi

# set filer details

# production filer ip
filerip="<ip_address>"
```

Script Mechanism

The script works as follows. At the start, an RMAN script is generated to uncatalog all the datafile copies that have been created in the preceding day's six-hourly snapshot that occurred at the same time, a day ago. This RMAN script is then executed.

Next, an RMAN script to back up the control file of the database is generated. This is also executed. Finally, the last RMAN script is generated and executed. This is the main script that is responsible for placing the tablespaces into hot backup mode, logging in remotely to the storage filer and deleting the snapshots that were taken at six-hour intervals the previous day. This is followed by the script, creating a new six-hour snapshot, and then taking the tablespaces out of hot backup mode. The datafile copies in the current snapshot are then catalogued by the script.

The snapshot deletion occurs asynchronously in the background, so you must make sure the snapshot has been deleted. You can do this by introducing the UNIX *sleep* command just after the snapshot is deleted. If this is not done and you proceed with the snapshot creation straight away, there is a chance it may fail if the previous snapshot has not already been deleted. Heavy activity at the storage filer level may cause this kind of situation.

Now once the Grid Control job has been created and scheduled, the filer snapshot backups will occur in the six-hour intervals you have specified. You can verify that the snapshots are being taken and all steps are successful by examining the RMAN logs.

The New Way: ACFS Snapshots

In September 2009, Oracle Database 11g Release 2 was released. This new and latest database release included Oracle Automatic Storage Management Cluster File System (Oracle ACFS). ACFS is an extension to Oracle ASM (Automatic Storage Management) that allows customer-specific non-Oracle files to be stored in a cluster file system. While ASM is used mainly for the database, ACFS can now be used to store any kind of non-database files.

The interesting thing is that along with the cluster file system, Oracle has provided the facility of ACFS snaphots for the first time, and this is exciting news. This is a read-only, point in time copy of an Oracle ACFS file system, much like the NetApp snapshots that were covered in the earlier section. Each snapshot is space-efficient and up to 63 snapshot views are supported for each file system.

The ACFS snapshots are administered using the *acfsutil snap* commands, such as *acfsutil snap create* and *acfsutil snap delete*. The Oracle ACFS snapshots can also be administered using OEM. When you log in to the console, you will notice that the ASM Home page that manages ASM now has an ASM Cluster File System tab. On this page, you can select any mount point and then move to the Snapshots tab. The Snapshots tab allows you to delete or create snapshots easily.

Therefore, it is quite possible to refer to the techniques that were described in the earlier section for NetApp snapshots and use them for Oracle ACFS snapshots instead. The only issue is that ACFS is not supported for use with actual database files. These should be placed on ASM as always. If in the future Oracle decides to allow database files to be put on ACFS as an option to ASM, then the ACFS snapshots would be a nice way to backup large databases.

Backup Strategies: Recap

This completes a solid backup strategy you could use for Oracle databases. The following is a recap of the technologies that were examined:

1. Perform a full backup of the database followed by an archivelog backup. For smaller-sized databases, this can be done every day. For medium-sized

databases over 200 GB (or any figure you feel is reasonable), perform this full backup once a week. For the full database backup, use one of the following backup types:

- Compressed backup set, OR

- Image copy

2. For the medium-sized databases, complement the full weekly backup with a daily incremental backup. Preferably, use cumulative backups so that the restore time is reduced.

   Refresh the image copy each day with the incremental backup if your full backup is an image copy.

3. Back up the entire flash recovery area to tape once every week.

4. If your database is deployed on a NetApp filer or SAN and if your database is of a large size, feel free to use the specific backup technology of the storage, such as using snaphots. You can easily tie this in with OEM via the Jobs capability of the management system.

When using the DBCA to create a new database, you can also set up and schedule a backup job at a specified date and time to back up the new database. This job uses an Oracle-suggested backup strategy to create image copies of the datafiles and refresh them daily with incremental backups.

You can keep the Oracle suggested backup or change this to your own backup strategy as described above using full database backups on every Sunday and incremental backups on each weekday, followed by a backup of the entire flash recovery area to tape every Sunday. It was shown how this can be done using either Oracle Enterprise Manager Database Control or Grid Control, the big brother.

The Numerous Advantages of Using Grid Control

The Oracle database has always required a solid database strategy. So the ability to set up and schedule database backups easily using all the modern techniques of RMAN assumes paramount importance, and this is done by OEM very easily. Does this approach actually have more steps to follow than the traditional UNIX shell script and cron approach? Maybe. But in the real world, these steps can be done very fast via the GUI wizards of OEM and all the scripts are auto-generated.

Of course, the OEM Agent needs to be installed first on every database server you want to back up. However, this task should not be included in your time comparisons since the OEM Agent is the foundation of all Grid Control activities for the server it is installed on, and RMAN backups are just one of its many uses.

Therefore, here is a summary list of the numerous advantages you can think of for using the Grid Control approach:

1. Timesavings: If you consider only the time taken in the GUI wizards, it can be immediately seen that the use of Grid Control will lead to a lot of time savings. Contrast this to the many hours required for the earlier manual approach of writing, setting up and testing script files and running them via a cron.

   The follow-on effect of this is that expensive DBA man-days can be drastically reduced. This will be very helpful in a multi-project, multi-database provisioning environment. DBA time can be used in more productive ways rather than mundane tasks such as shell script writing and setting up backups using the manual method for every new database that comes along.

2. Reduction of human error: The probability of human error is also reduced due to the RMAN backup setup being totally wizard-driven. What can you mistype if you are just selecting options?

3. Do not need rare skills any more: The need to hire and retain shell scripter skills is also largely eliminated since Grid Control generates its own RMAN scripts in Perl wrappers. No more tinkering with miles of shell scripts. At the most, you need to retain RMAN command expertise in case you need to add to the generated scripts. Also, RMAN is well known to most DBAs.

4. Easier debugging: Debugging has also become a lot simpler since there are less script lines to debug. In fact, you do not write any scripts!

5. Maintenance dream: Maintenance and future enhancements are also much easier since a new backup job can be easily created using the Grid Control console, even if any new backup requirements come up in the future or if the backup strategy needs to be changed. The previous job can be easily deleted from the job system.

6. Learn and use latest RMAN technology: When using the wizards, the latest advances in RMAN technology are available as options depending

on the version of database in use. This immediately creates awareness in the mind of the DBA of new possibilities with RMAN, and the DBA starts using these new techniques such as backup compression, encryption, block change tracking and so on.

Compare this to the scripted approach, where in many cases old 8i RMAN scripts are still being executed almost unchanged against new 9i, 10g or 11g databases without using any of the RMAN enhancements.

7. Centralized control of backups: Using Grid Control, it is possible to set up and schedule RMAN backups for all the databases in a large company, use a consistent backup strategy, and refer to all past RMAN output logs at any time since they are stored in the Grid Control repository. There is also no need to use a central RMAN catalog since information about the backups is centrally available from Grid Control.

Conclusion

Management and DBAs do not need any further arguments or proof when they finish comparing the Grid Control approach to the manual approach as has been done in this chapter. Once actually experienced, the benefits of Grid Control will be obvious to all. It is indeed a fact that over time, OEM Grid Control will become increasingly popular with companies that are looking for an easy way to provision their ever-increasing number of databases.

DBAs will understand that RMAN backups can be easily set up and scheduled for every new provisioned database in a fraction of the time taken by the manual approach.

In the next chapter, another great advantage of this product – Database Patching using Grid Control and the Patch Advisory – will be introduced.

Database Patching and the Patch Advisory

Oracle DBAs have always enjoyed the numerous and varied activities of database patching. Hang on a minute. Did we just say enjoy? And just what are these confounded patches?

Go back to the beginning. Oracle patches are nothing new and have been created and supplied by Oracle Support since the earliest days of the Oracle database. Patches are needed to apply security fixes or remedy database bugs, or they can be used to upgrade databases from one version to another. In this way, a database can be patched from 8.1.5 to 8.1.6, 9.2.0.4 to 9.2.0.6, or 10.2.0.1 to 10.2.0.4.

The Early Days

In the very early days when Internet availability was still limited to the military and certain universities, patches were sent to the DBA via floppy disks that were posted or couriered via snail mail. The floppy disk medium then changed to the medium of CDs and so patches were couriered on CDs even as late as the mid 1990s. Oracle Support was limited to phone calls or faxes of Oracle Support documents to clients to fix their issues.

Once Oracle Metalink became available on the Internet, DBAs could simply download patches from the Metalink site and apply them to the database software, which made the whole process much less complicated. DBAs could then apply the patch to the target database in a much shorter time frame and with greater convenience.

From January 2005 onwards, Oracle started publishing Critical Patch Updates (CPUs) every quarter and recommended they be applied on a regular basis. Many companies decided to make applying Oracle CPUs mandatory for their corporate databases because of stringent security policy requirements. This caused immense pressure for DBAs who had to regularly apply the CPUs against many Oracle databases without impacting production applications availability.

In August 2009, Oracle introduced Patch Set Updates (PSUs), which were proactive, cumulative patches comprised of recommended bug fixes and released on the same quarterly schedule as the Critical Patch Updates (CPU). DBAs could now use either a PSU or CPU to apply patches provided a patch had not been applied previously using a PSU. Once a patch had been applied using a PSU, all subsequent patching had to be applied using a PSU.

Complexities of Patching

Patching is necessarily more complicated in the case of the Oracle E-Business suite, a gregarious group of complex business applications that includes Financials, Manufacturing, Procurement, Supply Chain Management, CRM, ERP, and so on. The patch sets Oracle releases for its E-Business Suite are a much larger superset of normal database patch sets since they include database patches as well as the patches specific to the complex E-Business Suite application software. It can take many hours to test and apply these patch sets, and the patching may need to be restarted if any of the worker processes fail.

E-Business Suite patching was one of the first to use the innovative multiple and restartable worker processes that performed parallel patching updates to the PL/SQL programs in the database. This parallelism was a great help when applying large patches to the complicated codeset. However, this still meant long working hours for the DBA who had to apply these patches overnight and keep a close eye on the progress. The process needed to be manually restarted in the event of any failure.

There was another major advance. The release of the Oracle9i database introduced Oracle Real Application Clusters (RAC), a scalable, clustered database technology from Oracle that provided the ability to distribute database access and load across two or more nodes in a RAC cluster. Patching in this scenario was more complex because each patch had to be applied to every node in the database cluster and extra steps were required to patch the Oracle Home, the Clusterware Home, and/or to apply the patch scripts to the shared database if the patch had a database component.

Oracle9i RAC also introduced Oracle Clusterware on the Linux platform, whereas Oracle10g RAC introduced Clusterware on most of the other operating platforms, including Windows and UNIX. This added the complexities of Oracle Clusterware patching to most Oracle RAC environments.

In addition to the effort involved in the complexities and complications associated with patching, many companies expected their DBAs to administer an ever-increasing number of development, test and production databases that could number in the hundreds or even thousands. These multitudes of databases had to be patched separately at some time. The consequence was a very monotonous, repetitive process for the DBA and prone to human error because the creative human mind, being what it is, eventually rebels against machine-like, unthinking tasks such as applying patches to hundreds and thousands of databases following the same steps again and again.

The future of the DBA world was quickly becoming bogged down in an endless sea of patch applications and it was becoming apparent that there was a vital need for an automated tool to facilitate Oracle patching. Who would be better than Oracle to deliver this tool?

The Savior Arrives: Grid Control

In the early years of the Third Millennium, Oracle introduced Enterprise Manager Grid Control (Release 1) as its Flagship Enterprise Management product. Grid Control featured a freshly redesigned interface and architecture, and was primarily intended to assist DBAs with their database management and monitoring tasks. This was achieved through the streamlining and automation of day-to-day DBA activities such as performance diagnosis and tuning, setting up and scheduling RMAN database backups, and setting up and managing Oracle Data Guard.

Other capabilities included configuration management and monitoring of the server, operating system and database, and provisioning via the ability to clone Oracle software and databases to new servers. Grid Control also allowed the DBA to schedule and execute scripts at the database or operating system level.

Grid Control Release 2 (10.2.0.2) formally introduced the Provisioning Pack, which allowed the DBA to provision and deploy Oracle software and databases located on a source gold server to another server using the cloning feature within the Provisioning Pack. The Provisioning Pack was an optional, licensable feature within Grid Control and included the capability to patch Oracle databases and application servers. Later releases of Grid Control enhanced these capabilities to a high level of sophistication. The Provisioning Pack is now known as the Provisioning and Patch Automation Pack as a result.

These patching capabilities are one of the best advantages of OEM Grid Control over third-party database management tools that have very limited capabilities in this regard. Also, using Oracle patching and provisioning products to patch and provision other Oracle products is ideal because third-party vendors are not privy to the internal workings of the Oracle database machine.

It is worth mentioning at this point that the database management tasks that are performed using Grid Control may be very resource-intensive. If this is the case, the Grid Control must be installed on scalable infrastructure that satisfies the demand, as was examined in an earlier chapter of this book.

Proof of Concept: Patching via Grid Control

A few months ago, a large financial institution in Southeast Asia approached our team to conduct a Proof-of-Concept (POC). They were interested in database patch automation using Oracle's Enterprise Manager Grid Control. The main emphasis was to prove the benefits of this technology to their management and DBAs for the purpose of the patching of their many hundreds of databases. This experience will now be examined in depth.

We started the POC with an OEM 10g Grid Control installation that had been patched to Release 5 (10.2.0.5.0).

Figure 5.1 displays the Grid Control console home page.

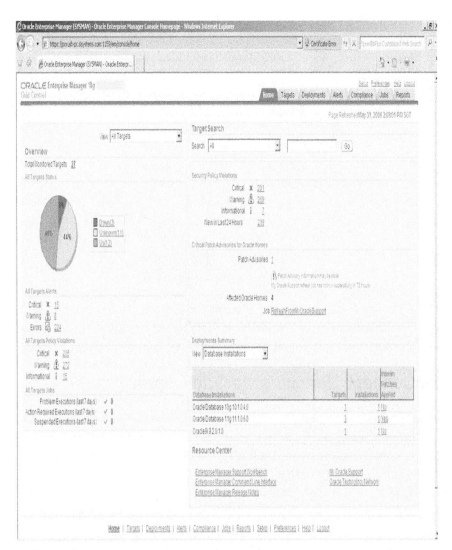

Figure 5.1: *Grid Control Console Home Page*

The informational message on the console reads as follows:

```
"The Patch Advisory information may be stale. My Oracle Support refresh job
has not run successfully in 72 hours."
```

The metadata of the latest patch advisories, products, and product versions that are available from the My Oracle Support Internet site are downloaded each day by the My Oracle Support refresh job. The job also computes the targets for the most recent Critical Patch Updates (CPU).

Once we clicked on the RefreshFromMyOracleSupport link, the Job Activity screen was displayed and showed that the job was scheduled to run once a day. As this was proof of concept, the Grid Control site had been shut down for a few days, so the My Oracle Support refresh job had not run for 72 hours. It is strongly recommended you run this job before attempting any patching with OEM Grid Control to ensure you have the latest patch advisories from Oracle.

To immediately run the job, you must first create a copy of the job. From the Job Activity page under Jobs, select Refresh From My Oracle Support and click Create Like. Name the copied job "one-time refresh from my oracle support" and submit the job to run immediately.

The job status is now displayed as running. The job connects to the My Oracle Support site over the Internet and then downloads a number of XML files into the *C:\MetalinkMetadataDump* directory whose location may be user defined. The My Oracle Support refresh job should complete successfully within minutes and the "The Patch Advisory Information may be stale" message is no longer displayed on the Grid Control console home page because the Patch Advisory information has been updated by the refresh job.

Offline Update of the Patch Advisory

Many companies restrict Internet access to production servers for security reasons. In such cases, the OEM Grid Control site will not have a direct or even proxy Internet connection to the My Oracle Support site. Conveniently, Oracle allows you to perform offline updates to overcome this restriction. The official reference on how to achieve this is provided in FAQ #8, "How can I patch if my OMS [Oracle Management Service] is Offline or Disconnected from the Internet?". This FAQ is in the Oracle Technical Network (OTN) Document "Achieving Grid Automation with Deployment Procedures". The URL is: http://www.oracle.com/technology/ products/oem/pdf/grid-automation-deployment-procedures.pdf. We tested this facility of offline updates on our site to ensure that it could be done if the company decided to restrict all connections to the Internet from production servers.

Click Setup at the top of the Grid Control console, then click on Patching Setup. Three tabs are visible as seen in Figure 5.2.

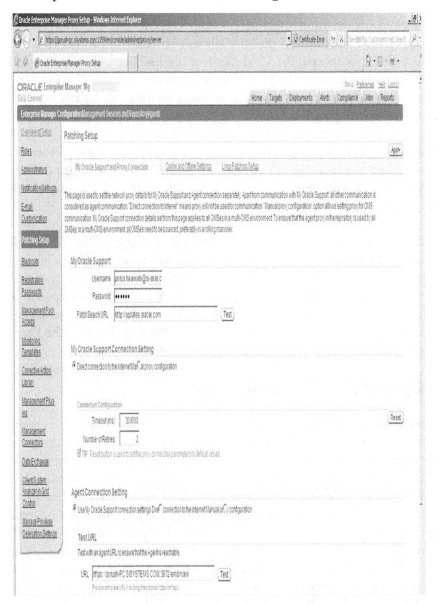

Figure 5.2: *My Oracle Support and Proxy Connection*

Enter the login details in the My Oracle Support and Proxy Connection tab to access the My Oracle Support site, and then set the Patch Search URL to http://updates.oracle.com. You can use the Test button to verify a successful login to My Oracle Support using the login details you have supplied.

You can select either a direct connection to the Internet or select Manual Proxy Configuration if you use a proxy server for Internet connections. This will enable you to specify a proxy server host for both http and https. You must provide a username and password for each server. There is another Test button under the Test URL section. Using this button, you can verify if the agent is reachable.

The second tab Online and Offline Settings (Figure 5.3) allows you to select either the online or offline mode for patch advisories.

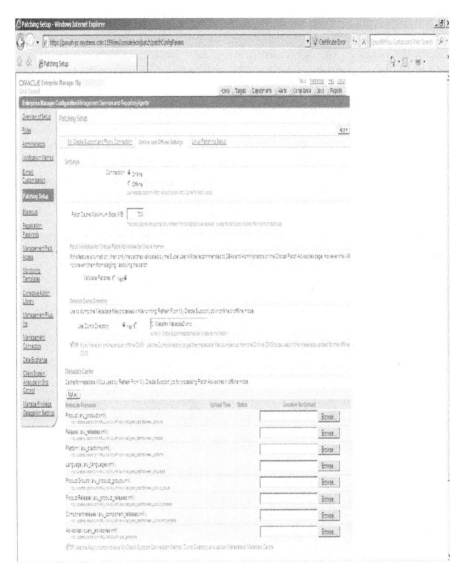

Figure 5.3: *Online and Offline Settings*

The offline mode is available in the event Grid Control servers do not have access to the Internet, either directly or via a proxy. In this case, the XML files must first be downloaded manually from the Internet onto a workstation. This is the list of XML files that are currently required (the list may change in the future).

- http://updates.oracle.com/ARULink/XMLAPI/download_seed_data?table=aru_products

- http://updates.oracle.com/ARULink/XMLAPI/download_seed_data?table=aru_platforms

- http://updates.oracle.com/ARULink/XMLAPI/download_seed_data?table=aru_languages

- http://updates.oracle.com/ARULink/XMLAPI/download_seed_data?table=aru_product_groups

- http://updates.oracle.com/ARULink/XMLAPI/download_seed_data?table=aru_product_releases

- http://updates.oracle.com/ARULink/XMLAPI/download_seed_data?table=aru_component_releases

- http://updates.oracle.com/ARULink/XMLAPI/query_advisories

- http://updates.oracle.com/ARULink/XMLAPI/download_seed_data?table=aru_releases

Once the XML files have been successfully downloaded, you can click on the Upload button to upload the files to the Oracle Management Service Metadata Cache using the Online and Offline Settings tab, which also displays the URLs in the listing above.

The Metadata Dump directory, which is also displayed in the Online and Offline Settings, now contains the XML files. These files are used when you run the RefreshFromMetalink job, which then performs the exact same actions as it would if there were a direct connection to the Internet.

Patch Advisory and Earlier CPUs

Some companies have a policy that prohibits applying the latest Oracle Critical Patch Update and only allows a patch update that has been available for a number of weeks or months. As a result, one of the essential processes we had to test and prove in our Proof-of-Concept environment at the financial institution was to use OEM Grid Control to apply an earlier CPU within the Patch Advisory.

We would like to digress here. Why do some companies prefer earlier CPUs over the latest? There is a very common misconception, particularly in companies where security policies are conservative: that CPUs that have been available for more than six months are less likely to cause problems when applied to production environments.

In reality, the reverse is true. Once you have tested the patch, the overall risk is much lower when you apply the most recent security fix to your production environment. However, this policy of only applying mature patches is very popular and often proves to be successful, so who are we to argue its merits?

When we previously tested the RefreshFromMetalink job in our POC environment, the downloaded XML files were processed immediately and contained information pertaining to the most recent CPU. Not surprisingly, the Patch Advisory recommended that we apply the latest CPU. However, we were tasked with proving that OEM could apply an earlier CPU within the Patch Advisory.

A workaround was suggested to resolve this conundrum.

The DBAs were asked to download the XML files at regular intervals over a period of time and save them in user-defined directories on a workstation or shared network directory, i.e. external to Enterprise Manager. As and when required, any one of these files could be uploaded to the Oracle Management Service. This would force the Patch Advisory to consider the CPU that was described in a specific set of XML files uploaded.

Therefore, storing XML files external to Enterprise Manager, it allowed us to apply CPUs that had been published by Oracle longer than six months ago. However, if you decide to use this workaround, you must change the setting to Offline in Online and Offline Settings under Setup -> Patching Setup.

RPM Patching at the LINUX level

Linux Patching Setup (Figure 5.4) is the final tab on this screen. This controls Red Hat Package Manager (RPM) patching for Linux servers.

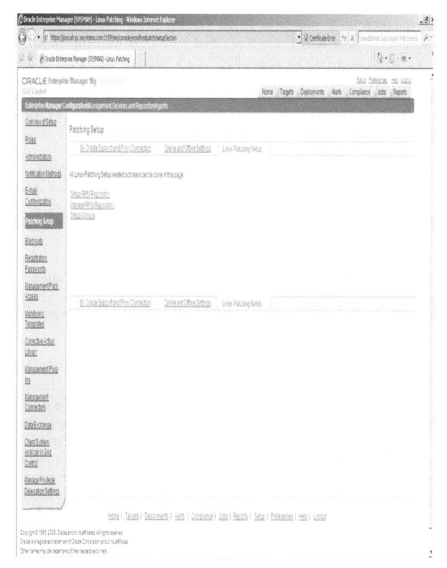

Figure 5.4: *Linux Patching Setup*

You will need to access the Oracle Unbreakable Linux Network (ULN) to perform this type of Linux patching and you must have a Customer Support Identifier (CSI) from Oracle to access the ULN.

It should be noted here that Oracle has its own brand of Linux called Oracle Enterprise Linux (OEL), which is based on Red Hat Enterprise Linux (RHEL). Both OEL and RHEL are supported by Oracle through the ULN and you are not compelled to reinstall Oracle's version of Linux to use Oracle's support. Using Oracle's ULN support has two main benefits: the lower cost of the support and only one vendor to contact for support of the OEL, Database, and Oracle Application Server as well as any other Oracle applications.

In our experience, a single vendor approach is more practical and eliminates the situation where multiple vendors might point fingers at each other when an issue has not been resolved. Not that a vendor would ever do that! It should also be said here that there are a couple of things available with the ULN support that set Oracle apart from its competitors.

The first great advantage is that Oracle's ULN highest level of enterprise support provides backports that can be applied to fix issues in Linux releases that are not current. In our experience, only Oracle provides this ability to backport and apply a fix to versions of Linux that are not current.

The second tremendous advantage is that Oracle Unbreakable Linux Basic and Premier support customers can freely use the Enterprise Manager Management Pack for Linux as well as Oracle Clusterware. The OEM Management Pack for Linux is an excellent tool in that it allows you to bare metal provision new Linux servers, collect and analyze configuration information at the Linux level, perform lights-out and ad hoc Linux operating system patching, and provides out-of-the-box availability and performance monitoring.

If the Management Pack for Linux is enabled, the Linux Patching tab (Figure 5.4) allows you to update your Linux servers with the latest Linux operating system patches, just as you would by using the *up2date* utility. We observed that the Oracle Unbreakable Linux support program delivers enterprise-class support for Linux, and with premier backports, comprehensive management (the OEM pack for Linux), indemnification, abilities for testing, i.e. the Oracle Linux Test (OLT) Kit and more, at considerably lower cost.

RefreshFromMetalink Job Success

After you have completed exploring the tabs, you will notice that the RefreshFromMetalink job completed successfully. To review the results, you can simply click the Patch Advisories link on the console's home page. Figure 5.5 displays the computational findings of the RefreshFromMetalink job.

Figure 5.5: *Patch Advisories*

The Patch Advisories tab displays the Critical Patch Update 2009. This advisory is seen to affect four distinct Oracle homes.

Selecting the Critical Patch Update link takes you directly to the My Oracle Support Internet site, where after you have provided your login details, you can view the Critical Patch Update document that is published in My Oracle Support. The Interim Patches to Apply section lists the actual patch numbers.

The patch for Oracle Database 11.1.0.6 is shown to be 8333655, derived from the Critical Patch Update April 2009 advisory. You can always verify that this is the correct patch number for the Windows platform your database resides on by looking at the My Oracle Support document for the Critical Patch Update.

The remaining tabs Affected Homes (Figure 5.6) and Remedies (Figure 5.7) are closely related to each other. You use these tabs to select any Home located in any of your Grid Control targets, then by clicking on the Show Remedies link, you display the Remedies tab where the patches applicable for that home are listed (Figure 5.7).

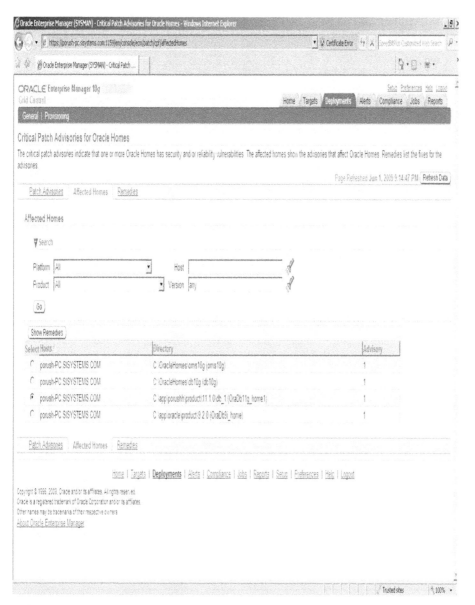

Figure 5.6: *Affected Homes*

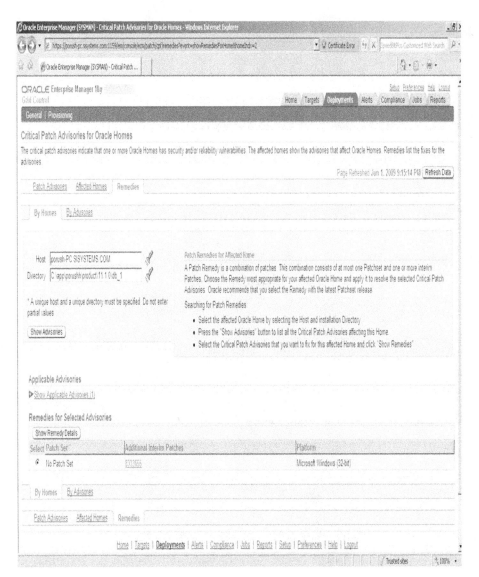

Figure 5.7: *Remedies*

Patch 8333655 is confirmed as the remedy for the 11.1.0 home. Select Show Remedy Details to display the Remedy Details page (Figure 5.8).

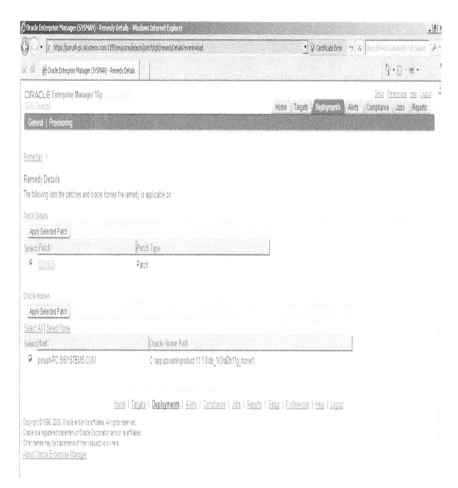

Figure 5.8: *Remedy Details*

Applying the Remedy

From the Remedy Details page, select Apply Selected Patch to commence the patch wizard (Figure 5.9). This wizard guides you through the steps to patch a specific home.

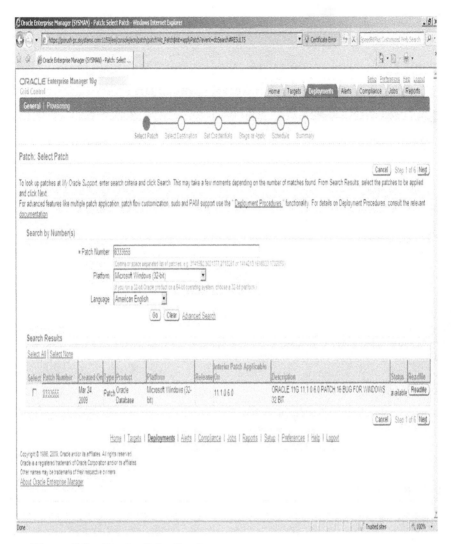

Figure 5.9: *Patch - Select Patch*

The wizard prompts you to select the patch, the destination for the patch and provide your credentials. You are then asked if you want to stage the patch by downloading it to a subdirectory of the Oracle home or if you wish to stage and apply the patch at the same time. Once you have provided this information, you can schedule the job to apply the patch. The job and its schedule details are confirmed on the summary page (Figure 5.10).

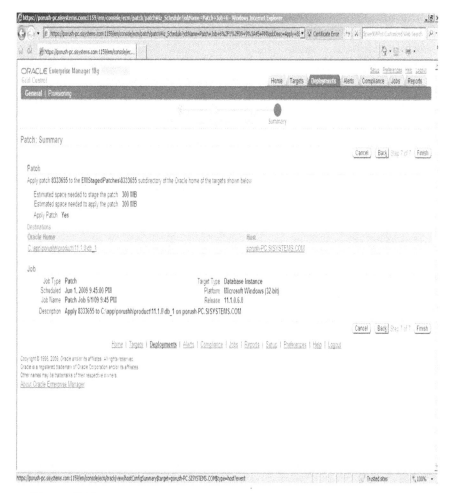

Figure 5.10: *Patch - Summary Screen*

The wizard also requests that you provide an e-mail address which can be used for informing you of any security issues in your particular database configuration. Once you have scheduled the patch job, it runs immediately or at a later time depending on what time you have scheduled the job (Figure 5.11).

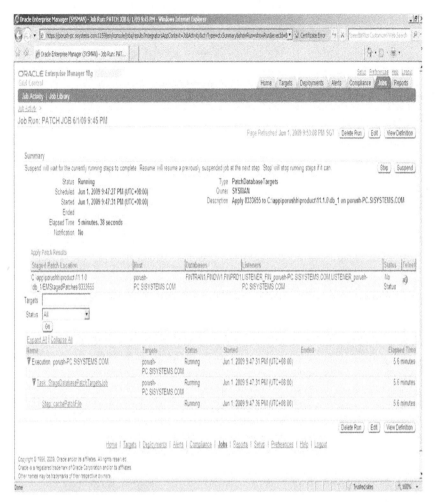

Figure 5.11: *Job Run - Patch Job*

You can click on the Jobs tab within OEM Grid Control to display the job status as either scheduled or running.

When the job executes, it downloads and caches the patch file, stages it to the database and uses the *opatch* utility to apply the patch to the database. The job shuts down the database, applies the patch and then restarts the database.

This was the first automatic patching method we tested in our POC environment and although it achieved the desired result, it is not recommended. Why? Because this method is suitable only for applying single patches on single databases and does not allow much flexibility or customizations. Another reason is that Oracle will replace this patching method very shortly.

So what can you use instead? The new and extremely powerful deployment procedures functionality, explained in the next section, in OEM Grid Control is recommended because it allows you access to a number of advanced features including multiple patch application, patch flow customization, sudo, and also pluggable authentication modules (PAM) support. These deployment procedures are based on best practices and a lot of Oracle experience over the years. The deployment procedures functionality will now be explored in more detail.

Brave New World of Deployment Procedures

Deployment procedures functionality is indeed a new world. It enables patching of multiple homes on different OEM targets using multiple patches and, most importantly, allows you to customize the steps in the deployment procedures. Because of this, the use of deployment procedures is highly recommended for the automation of day-to-day production patching scenarios, which due to their complexity, require varying degrees of customization.

To use the deployment procedures, click on the Deployments tab on the OEM Grid Control main console and then select Patching through Deployment Procedures, which is displayed under Patching (Figure 5.12).

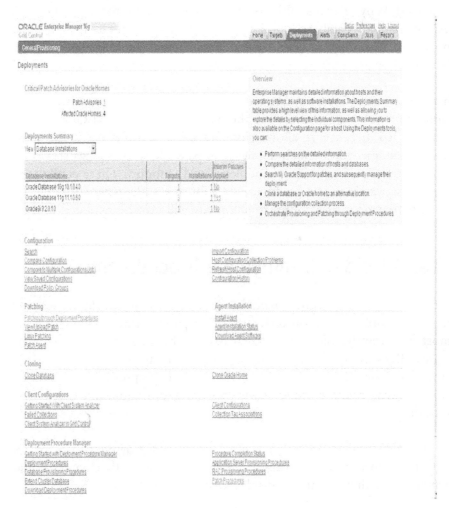

Figure 5.12: *Deployments*

You are now able to see a list of the out-of-the-box deployment procedures (Figure 5.13) Oracle provides. Any customized procedures you have created are also visible in this list. You create customized procedures by cloning any of the out-of-box procedures, and then modifying or adding to the component steps as per your customization requirements.

Figure 5.13: *Deployment Procedure Manager - Procedures*

Now look at the Patch Oracle Database procedure. Select this out-of-the-box procedure and view the steps in the deployment procedure by clicking on the View button (Figure 5.14).

Figure 5.14: *View Procedure*

The Patch Oracle Database procedure is used to patch standalone Oracle database installations with Critical Patch Updates (CPUs), interim patches, or patch sets. The procedure does not allow you to perform major database upgrades such as 10.1 to 10.2, for example.

You can see in Figure 5.14 that the deployment procedure performs the following actions in the following order:

1. Upgrade the Oracle *opatch* utility, which is the actual database-level mechanism for patching Oracle databases. This upgrade of OPatch is optional but is always recommended.

2. Stage the selected patch in a staging location.

3. Initiate a blackout for the database in Oracle Enterprise Manager. Since this downtime has been planned in advance, no alerts should be raised when the database is brought down.

4. Shut down the database.

5. Apply the database patch.

6. Execute any applicable root script.

7. Restart the database in the upgrade or migrate mode.

8. Apply any applicable SQL script in the case of a patch set or a CPU.

9. Apply a post-SQL script.

10. Shut down the database.

11. Restart the datasbase.

12. Apply additional SQL scripts as required.

13. Stop the OEM blackout for the database so that OEM can begin raising alerts again.

14. Refresh the host configuration collection.

The final step above will be examined, along with its importance, in more detail in the next chapter.

Conclusion

This chapter gave a first look at the next-generation patching capabilities of Oracle Enterprise Manager Grid Control using the Provisioning and Patch Automation Pack. The history of database patches was covered and also the growing complexities of patching.

The other factor was the ever-increasing multitude of new databases that keep on being added for new projects in the company, all adding to the DBA workload. Hence, Grid Control's ability to ease the burden of patch application is indeed welcome to many DBAs.

In the course of our Proof-of-Concept, tests were conducted on the Patch Advisory, offline updates to the Advisory, and remedy application from the Patch Advisory to apply recommended patches on vulnerable Oracle Homes. The new deployment procedures were also introduced and a glimpse was given of the source of their power: the procedure steps.

In the next chapter, the deployment procedure to patch an Oracle database will be executed in its out-of-the-box form. It will then be executed in a customized incarnation. This is when the real power of the deployment procedures will be understood.

Next Generation Deployment Procedures

It is time to test the new deployment procedure functionality of the Provisioning and Patch Automation Pack in Oracle Enterprise Manager (OEM) Grid Control. The Patch Oracle Database deployment procedure was covered in the previous chapter, and the individual steps of this procedure were presented in the view mode.

These steps involve a number of actions including Enterprise Manager blackouts, shutting down the database, applying the patch and executing patch scripts – all of which can be run in a lights-out fashion so as to fully automate patch application. Automation of patching, to as great an extent as possible, is the key word here. Next to be shown is how to execute the procedure and see it in action.

Executing the Deployment Procedure

After you select Schedule Deployment, the wizard takes you through a series of pages (Figure 6.1).

On these pages, you can specify one or more software updates you wish to apply and to where you want to deploy each update, i.e. deployment targets. Here is also where to specify the credentials required to logon to specific targets, followed by the deployment scheduling, and so on.

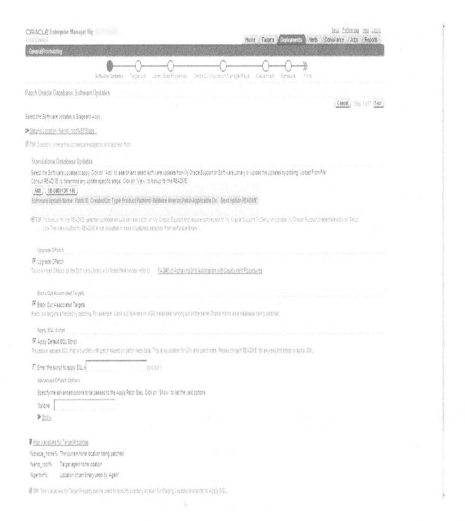

Figure 6.1: *Patch Oracle Database - Software Updates*

This initial page is used to specify the staging location set by default to *%emd_root%/EMStage*. If the target database is on Windows, the default directory for the staging location is *C:\OracleHomes\agent10g\EMStage*.

Under the Standalone Database Updates section, you can select one or more patches you want to apply. Use the Add button to display a new screen (Figure 6.2) where either Search My Oracle Support or Search Software Library can be selected.

The Search Software Library option provides you with a list of patches that have already been downloaded, either direct from My Oracle Support or via a manual process, which will be explained further in due course.

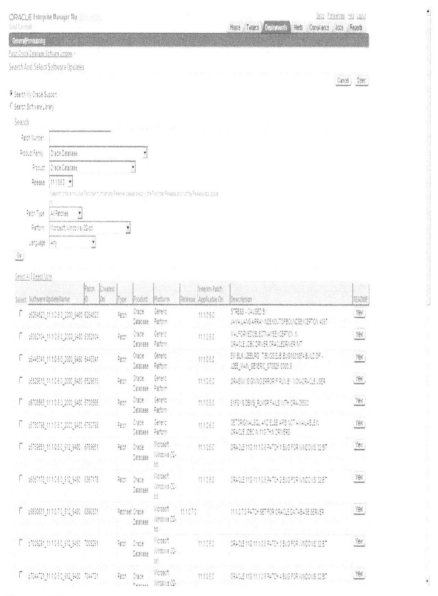

Figure 6.2: *Search And Select Software Updates*

On this page, you can choose the appropriate release and platform. Select Go to display a list of applicable patches.

This list includes the 8333655 patch, which is the Oracle 11g 11.1.0.6.0 patch 16 bug for Windows 32 b (32-bit). The patch advisory previously advised that this patch be applied. Hence, you can select this patch. The initial page now reappears. Select Upgrade OPatch so that the *opatch* utility is upgraded as part of this process. At this point, you can also choose if the default SQL script of the patch or any specific SQL scripts should be executed.

When the next page appears, select the database targets to which you would like the database patch to be applied. Either select one database target or select multiple database targets on multiple servers. This is very useful in a large site where you need to apply patches to the same level on the database targets.

On the following page, you may, or may not, specify the e-mail address where security updates and security issue information can be mailed. Also specify your My Oracle Support password at this point. Next, supply the credentials for the Oracle databases and hosts. Then schedule the deployment procedure to run either immediately or later at a specified time.

Scheduling patch updates allows you to patch several databases overnight in a lights-out operation. Of course, make sure that the entire automated patching procedure has been tested successfully, typically on a development or UAT database, before running the procedure in a production environment.

Accept the summary page when it appears. The deployment procedure is now scheduled to run at the time you have specified.

Select the procedure to display the running steps and their status (Figure 6.3).

Figure 6.3: *Procedure Status Details - Running*

To view the job at any time, select the Deployments tab, then "patching through deployment procedures", and next select Procedure Completion Status. The deployment procedure that is currently running will be displayed (Figure 6.4).

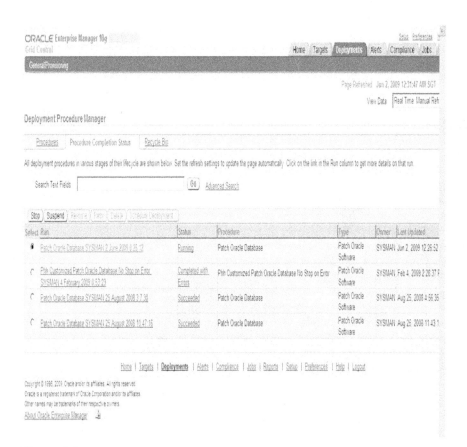

Figure 6.4: *Procedure Completion Status*

During the run of the deployment procedure, the Jobs tab of OEM Grid Control displays the individual job tasks of the procedure, which are displayed as running and completing, such as the Upgrade OPatch job task. The main deployment procedure, on the other hand, can only be seen on the Procedure Completion status screen and not on the Jobs tab.

First Attempt Results

On Linux/UNIX, the deployment procedure almost always completes successfully. However, on the platform of Windows, the very first deployment procedure run shows that certain steps have failed. Figure 6.5 shows that the "iterates over a list of hosts" step has not successfully completed.

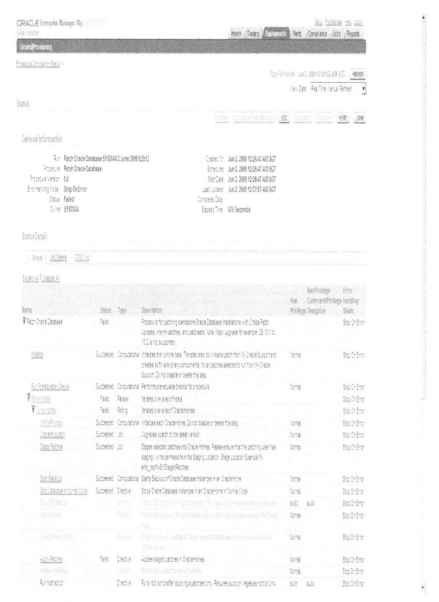

Figure 6.5: *Procedure Status Details - Step Failure*

It is also shown that the Apply Patches step has failed. Drill down on the link and scan the output sequentially to find the exact point where the failure has occurred. The output log is displayed at this step as:

```
Output Log
 Step is being run by operating system user : 'porushh'
Run privilege of the step is : Normal
This is Provisioning Executor Script(Windows)
...
Directive Type is SUB_Perl
...
The output of the directive is:
...
Tue Jun 2 00:34:40 2009 - Found the metadata files; '8333655' is an Interim
patch
...
Tue Jun 2 00:34:40 2009 - OPatch from
'C:/app/porushh/product/11.1.0/db_1/OPatch/opatch.pl' will be used to apply
the Interim Patch.
...
Tue Jun 2 00:34:57 2009 - Invoking OPatch 11.1.0.6.6
...
Following patches will be rolled back from Oracle Home on application of the
patches in the given list :
    7210195
...
Do you want to proceed? [y|n]
Y (auto-answered by -silent)
User Responded with: Y
OPatch continues with these patches:    8333655

Do you want to proceed? [y|n]
Y (auto-answered by -silent)
User Responded with: Y

Running prerequisite checks...
Prerequisite check "CheckActiveFilesAndExecutables" failed.
The details are:

Following files are active :
C:\app\porushh\product\11.1.0\db_1\bin\oci.dll
UtilSession failed: Prerequisite check "CheckActiveFilesAndExecutables"
failed.
...
OPatch failed with error code = 73
Apply of Interim Patch(es) failed
Tue Jun 2 00:34:57 2009 - Patching failed.
```

The output log shows that *opatch* has failed due to the *oci.dll* file in the 11g
database home being in a locked state, which has not allowed the *opatch* to
proceed.

Locking issues such as these are a frequent showstopper when applying
patches on the Windows platform. Shared Libraries are implemented in
Windows as DLLs (Dynamic-Link Libraries). The locking issue occurs because

Windows keeps DLL files in memory for unspecified times, mainly to augment performance.

A further complication is that the files are kept in memory, even long after the programs that were using them are no longer active.

Workaround for the Locking Issue

In this example, a Shareware utility, Process Explorer, was initially used to discover that the file was locked by svchost (Service Host). This is a generic Windows host process for the services that use DLLs.

Svchost.exe is an executable found in the Windows subdirectory *%SystemRoot%\System32*. It loads a number of services at startup. Multiple svchost processes can be active simultaneously, each having its own list of loaded services. This helps in Windows debugging.

In the Windows Task Manager, multiple svchost processes were seen to be active. *tasklist / svc* was then used in a command window to see which copy of svchost was running which service, and the copy that was running *oci.dll* that had caused the lock was found. This was good for informational purposes, but ending the process using Task Manager did not resolve the issue. The lock persisted and svchost processes kept on being respawned.

It was also found that Process Explorer itself locked other Oracle DLLs when this utility was used, so there was a need to remember to unload this utility. Finally, a workaround to this vexing locking issue was found. The free *donate ware* utility known as *Unlocker* was used to unlock *oci.dll* immediately after the databases and listeners were shut down by the deployment procedure. Below were the steps that were followed to make sure the patch was applied when the *oci.dll* file was locked:

1. Schedule the deployment procedure called Patch Oracle Database.

2. Open Windows Explorer and open the Oracle *home/bin* subdirectory for the Oracle 11g home.

3. Locate the file *oci.dll* in this subdirectory. Keep this window open.

4. In the Enterprise Manager window, observe the deployment procedure running step-by-step.

5. When the deployment procedure reaches the step of stopping the database, proceed with the following actions.

6. Right-click on *oci.dll* using the mouse. Since the *Unlocker* utility has been installed, you are able to unlock the lock of scvhost on this file by selecting Unlock from the right-click menu.

7. The file is not locked anymore, and therefore patching continues and is finally successful.

However, automation was cleared stated at the start of this chapter. Surely this is the main aim of the deployment procedures. The above procedure is certainly not automated since it requires human intervention to perform the manual step of the unlocking. These issues are known on the Windows platform. How can they be circumvented to fully automate this patching?

Herein lies the power of the deployment procedure due to its flexibility. You can customize any of the deployment procedures and either add new steps or modify the existing steps.

This is very useful in certain cases, such as when you need to insert customer-supplied steps, send an e-mail message before or after any step, or complete a database backup before the patch is applied. You could also start an OS level job to perform a concurrent task at any point in the process, or perhaps a workaround is needed to handle known issues during patch application. All these would be handled by customizing the deployment procedures.

Remember that in most cases, there may be no need for you to develop custom procedures and a normal out-of-the-box deployment procedure can be used. Now it is time to examine how the deployment procedure can be customized to work around the issue of Windows locking the DLL file so that full automation is achieved once again.

Deployment Procedures: Customization

Deployment procedures are offered by the Provisioning and Patch Automation Pack of OEM Grid Control as the new way – the next generation per se – to patch Oracle products such as databases. Inherently highly flexible, these procedures are used to patch one or more Oracle databases with one or more patches, and allow full customization of the patch flow.

In the previous section, it was found that the Patch Oracle Database deployment procedure had failed at the Apply Patches step. This was because the *oci.dll* file in the Oracle home's *bin* subdirectory had been locked by the Operating System (Windows). This file needs to be unlocked before the Apply Patches step is executed.

On the command line, *oci.dll* can be unlocked by the *Unlocker* utility as follows:

```
cmd -c "c:; "\Program Files\Unlocker"\Unlocker
C:\app\porushh\product\11.1.0\db_1\bin\oci.dll -S"
```

This manual step must be added to the patching flow. To do this, select Deployments -> Patching through Deployment Procedures. Locate the Patch Oracle Database procedure in the list of procedures under Deployment Procedure Manager.

Select it and then select Create Like. This creates a copy of the procedure which you can then customize. You can modify the copy of the procedure. It is possible to modify various settings, such as:

- What status of the procedure will trigger notifications

- The error handling mode of each step of the procedure - whether to stop on error, or continue on error

- Insert new steps into the customized procedure or delete existing steps

Click the Insert button after you select the Apply Patches step. This allows you to add the "Unlock oci.dll in Windows" step to execute the *unlocker* command (Figure 6.6).

Figure 6.6: *Edit Host Command Step - Review*

Select Save and you now have a new customized deployment procedure, which can be scheduled as before.

You observe that the new procedure runs successfully to apply the patch (Figure 6.7). OS level locks have not interfered this time. Success is seen in both the *unlock oci.dll* in Windows and the Apply Patches steps.

Figure 6.7: *Successful Run*

Raw Power of Deployment Procedures

This has been a good demonstration of the raw power of deployment procedures in OEM Grid Control, provided you are licensed to use the Provisioning and Patch Automation Pack. Due to the capabilities of customization in these deployment procedures, known issues such as Windows DLL locking can be worked around and resolved.

Various other related steps can also be integrated into the patching workflow, and this furthers the general automation of business tasks, which is what all software is ultimately working towards. The concept of deployment procedures that are customizable surely makes Grid Control a very powerful tool for the purpose of corporate automation.

If you now run *opatch* on the command line in the Oracle home, you can confirm that the Oracle inventory has registered the patch that was recently applied:

```
C:\>set ORACLE_HOME=C:\app\porushh\product\11.1.0\db_1
C:\>set ORACLE_SID=FINPRD1

C:\>cd C:\app\porushh\product\11.1.0\db_1\BIN

C:\app\porushh\product\11.1.0\db_1\BIN>opatch lsinventory

Invoking OPatch 11.1.0.6.0

Oracle Interim Patch Installer version 11.1.0.6.0
Copyright (c) 2007, Oracle Corporation. All rights reserved.
….
Installed Top-level Products (1):
Oracle Database 11g
11.1.0.6.0
There are 1 products installed in this Oracle Home.
Interim patches (1) :
Patch 8333655      : applied on Tue Jun 02 16:25:33 SGT 2009
   Created on 20 Mar 2009, 12:29:01 hrs US/Pacific
   Bugs fixed:
…..

OPatch succeeded.
```

Manually Download Patches

As was noted before, the security policies in a number of financial institutions prohibit direct connection of the OEM Grid Control installation to the My Oracle Support site on the Internet, thereby effectively stopping Grid Control from downloading the actual patches.

To cater for this scenario, Oracle has provided an option to manually download the required patch to an individual workstation, and then such a patch can be uploaded to the Grid Control software library and patch cache. FAQ #8, "How can I patch if my OMS is Offline or Disconnected from Internet?", which is contained in the OTN document *Achieving Grid Automation with Deployment Procedures*, also explains this procedure. The URL is: http://www.oracle.com /technology/products/oem/pdf/grid-automation-deployment-procedures.pdf.

Use the Deployments tab on the Grid Control console. Then select View/Upload Patch in the Patching section. The Patch Cache screen that appears displays a list of patches – these patches have either been uploaded manually, or else downloaded from the My Oracle Support site. If the patch you require is not found, you can manually upload the patch. Click Upload Patch.

Next, fill in the details of the patch manually on the screen that appears (Figure 6.8). Select Oracle System Management Products for the Product Family field or Universal Installer for the Product field if you are uploading a patch for *opatch*.

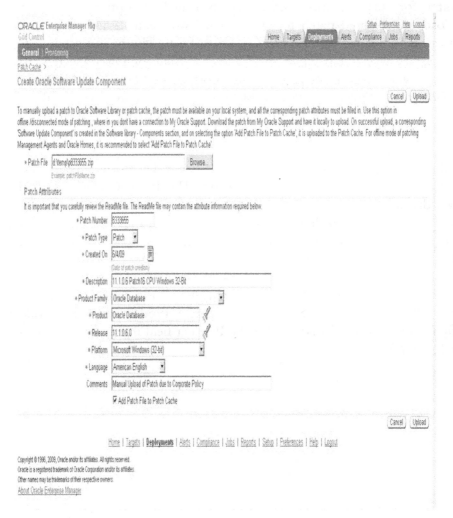

Figure 6.8: *Create Oracle Software Update Component*

FAQ #6, "What does Upgrade OPatch mean?" in the OTN *Achieving Grid Automation with Deployment Procedures* document explains this in further detail. The URL for this document was supplied in the previous pages.

If your intention is to manually upload a database patch, select Oracle Database for both Product Family and Product. Select the Upload button when complete. This results in the patch being uploaded.

The software library and the patch cache list (Figure 6.9) now display the patch.

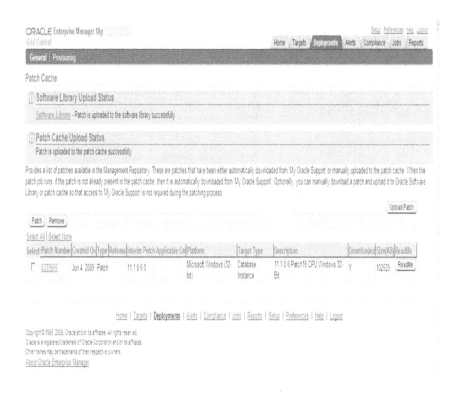

Figure 6.9: *Patch Cache - Upload Status*

From this point onwards, whenever a deployment procedure is scheduled, it is possible to select any of the manually uploaded patches – these will now appear in the software library on searching.

The same effect is achieved as with a direct connection to the My Oracle Support internet site, albeit with some extra steps. The plus point is that the corporate security rules have been followed.

Patch Deletion

Deletion of an existing patch is achieved by first removing it from the patch cache list (Figure 6.9), and then from the software library. The software library is accessed by going to Deployments and then selecting the Provisioning subtab on the blue bar at the top of the screen.

Expand Oracle Software Updates to see the patch component. First select the component, and then click on Delete (Figure 6.10).

Figure 6.10: *Provisioning - Components*

The component must also be purged from the repository. The Purge facility is on the Administration tab. This is done so that the binary files will not occupy space on the file system.

ITIL Compatibility

ITIL (Information Technology Infrastructure Library) is a leading framework of information technology best practices with concepts and policies that any company can adapt to its needs to standardize their IT services and processes, improve application performance and the quality of service, and also reduce operational costs.

In September 2008, Oracle announced that the Oracle IT Service Management Suite – comprised of Oracle Enterprise Manager, Oracle's Siebel CRM HelpDesk, and Oracle Business Intelligence Suite Enterprise Edition Plus – had been certified as ITIL compatible through the PinkVERIFY IT Service Management (ITSM) certification program. The certification was achieved by Oracle for six core ITIL processes: Incident, Problem, Change, Configuration, Release and Service Level Management. This was after an objective and vigorous assessment conducted by Pink Elephant, an IT management best practices global leader.

The software library is used extensively in Enterprise Manager Patch Automation where it is used to store the patches for mass deployment in the corporate world. The software library is also used in provisioning scenarios to store Gold images of software to be pushed out to the enterprise.

ITIL mandates the use of software libraries; it has the concept of a Definitive Software Library (DSL) in which all definitive authorized versions of software to use in the company are stored and protected, and any additions to the library are controlled. Enterprise Manager, with the software library in the Provisioning and Patch Automation Pack, does exactly that. Here is one example of how Enterprise Manager is ITIL compliant.

Report on Applied Interim Patches

There is an extensive set of reports offered by OEM Grid Control relating to database patching. Click on the Reports tab and search for the Oracle Home Patch Advisories section. One of the reports seen in this section is the

Applied Interim Patches report which shows the interim patches applied on Oracle homes across all the host targets. This also includes the CPU patch that was applied during the testing. The Applied Interim Patches report is based on the Grid Control *mgmt$applied_patches* repository view, which is in the repository database.

One of the observations in the testing is that during the execution of the deployment procedure, the Grid Control *mgmt$applied_patches* repository view is not updated with the applied patch even if the Apply Patches step has been completed. It is found that this view is updated only after the completion of the entire deployment procedure.

The effect of this end-point update is that, even if a later step in the deployment procedure has failed, the entire job will be marked as failed. As a result, the Grid Control repository *applied patches* view will not be updated even if the database has already been patched.

Running *opatch lsinventory* at the operating system prompt can verify the patch in the database. Whether the view should be updated as soon as the patching step is completed, or the update should take place during the last step of the deployment procedure, was a matter of initial debate among the testing team. Ultimately, when the working of the deployment procedure and the way it interacts with the view was properly understood, this question was resolved. The explanation follows.

These four tables in the repository: *mgmt_inv_container con, mgmt_ecm_snapshot snap, mgmt_inv_patch patch,* and *mgmt_targets tgt* – are in the *mgmt$applied_patches* view, which is defined as follows:

```
create or replace force view
"sysman"."mgmt$applied_patches"
("patch", "bugs", "installation_time",
 "host", "home_location",
 "home_name", "container_guid",
 "target_guid")
 as
select
to_char(patch.id) as patch,
ecm_util.concat_col('distinct BUG_NUMBER',
'mgmt_inv_patch_fixed_bug', 'PATCH_GUID = ''' || patch.patch_guid ||
'''',',') as bugs,
patch.timestamp as installation_time,
tgt.target_name as host,
con.container_location as home_location,
```

```
con.container_name as home_name,
con.container_guid, tgt.target_guid
from
mgmt_inv_container con,
mgmt_ecm_snapshot snap,
mgmt_inv_patch patch,
mgmt_targets tgt
where
con.snapshot_guid = snap.snapshot_guid AND
snap.is_current = 'Y' AND
snap.snapshot_type = 'host_configuration' AND
con.container_guid = patch.container_guid AND
tgt.target_name = snap.target_name
WITH READ ONLY;
```

The WHERE clause seen in the view includes *snap.is_current* = 'Y' AND *snap.snapshot_type* = 'host_configuration'. This helps to understand why the patch information was not updated.

Host configuration collection is the last step in the deployment procedure, and this refreshes the host configuration with the latest patch information. However, this last step is not reachable if any one of the earlier steps fails, thereby stopping the entire deployment procedure. The default of each step in the procedure is "stop on error", so the solution is to customize the later steps to "continue on error."

It is possible to manually refresh the host configuration via Deployments -> Refresh Host Configuration. If a manual refresh is not done, then an automatic refresh takes place every 24 hours.

What if the *opatch* utility is used to apply a database patch manually outside Grid Control at the operating system prompt? In such a case, the Refresh Host Configuration job must be run manually in order to update the view with immediate effect. Otherwise, the view will be updated only after 24 hours with the new patch information.

Patch Advisory Smarts

The company where the Proof-of-Concept (POC) was conducted had a very interesting test for the Patch Advisory. They wanted to see "if the Patch Advisory was smart enough to tell that a 9.2.0.1 database has to be upgraded to a later patch set such as 9.2.0.8, before the current Critical Patch Update can be applied."

The DBAs wanted to see what would happen when a CPU (interim patch) was recommended by the Patch Advisory. The test was a check to see if the Advisory would simply advise the latest CPU it found or if it would also advise whether other patches needed to be applied in addition, such as the latest patch set 9.2.0.8 for that platform, if the original patch level of the target database was lower, like 9.2.0.1 or 9.2.0.2. Would it say that the upgrade to 9.2.0.8 was necessary? Or would it simply advise the DBA to apply the CPU, and leave it at that?

The test commenced. Oracle Enterprise Edition 9.2.0.1 was installed by the testing team in a new Oracle home on the testing server. A 9.2 database was created using this Oracle home, and the database was added as a target in OEM Grid Control. Next, the Refresh From Metalink job was run so that the Patch Advisory was up-to-date with the latest CPU information. It proceeded like this:

On the Grid Control console home page, under Critical Patch Advisories for Oracle Homes, select Patch Advisories. Next, select Affected Homes, and find the applicable Oracle 9.2.0.1 home. Click on Show Remedies. A new screen (Figure 6.11) appears with the relevant information.

Figure 6.11: *Critical Patch Advisories - Remedies*

Two patches, 9.2.0.8 (4547809) and 8300340, are displayed in the section Remedies for Selected Advisories. When the first patch is selected, you can see it is the 9.2.0.8 patch set which was created by Oracle Support on August

21, 2006. The second patch reveals that it was created on the much later date of April 8, 2009. This patch is part of the CPU released in April by Oracle Support.

Therefore, the conclusion is that the proper recommendation is being made by the Patch Advisory. It recommends an upgrade to the latest patch set 9.2.0.8 before the April CPU is applied.

The Patch Advisory turned out to be definitely smarter than the team thought it was. The team marked the result of this test as successful.

Patch Reports Customization

The Proof-of-Concept also requires the production of a mandatory report on the patching activities on the databases. The report is required to display a list of the applied interim patches on any database which are a target in OEM Grid Control. The database could be on any server in the entire company due to the proliferation of Grid Control all over the place.

Under the Reports tab, the Oracle Home Patch Advisories section has a number of out-of-the-box reports. A few reports from this section are tested, and one particular report is found to display the patches applied on all the Oracle homes on any server. However, this is not satisfactory for the purposes of the POC. The out-of-the-box reports in general display the patch, fixed bugs, installation time, host, home directory, and the platform, but do not show the databases.

The logical explanation is that the patch is not applied at each database level, but it is actually applied at the Oracle home level and each Oracle home can have multiple databases. Once the patch is applied at the Oracle home, it can be applied on each database if there is a database component. This is why the out-of-box reports for interim patches did not show the databases.

However, the required report does need the database name. Therefore, the decision is to create a customized report to satisfy the requirement of the POC. Customization of reports is one of the other many capabilities of the Grid Control system. The report can be modified easily: create a copy and include the database name in the SQL statement.

First, examine the SQL statement that is used by the Applied Interim Patches report in the following code listing:

```
select
distinct patch as PATCH,
                bugs as BUGS,
                installation_time as TIMESTAMP,
                host as HOST,
                home_location as HOME_DIRECTORY,
                platform as PLATFORM
from
     mgmt$applied_patches patch,
     mgmt$em_homes_platform  home,
     mgmt$target tgt
where
home.HOME_ID = patch.CONTAINER_GUID
and patch.target_guid = tgt.target_guid
and patch.installation_time>
MGMT_VIEW_UTIL.ADJUST_TZ(??EMIP_BIND_START_DATE??,
??EMIP_BIND_TIMEZONE_REGION??,tgt.TIMEZONE_REGION)
and patch.installation_time<=
MGMT_VIEW_UTIL.ADJUST_TZ(??EMIP_BIND_END_DATE??,
??EMIP_BIND_TIMEZONE_REGION??,tgt.TIMEZONE_REGION)
```

You can add one more JOIN to the *mgmt$target_components* view. This would have the same Oracle home as the *mgmt$applied_patches* home. You could then easily select the database targets contained in this home.

A new Grid Control customized report is, therefore, created as Applied Interim Patches (Customized - Database Level). This uses the following SQL statement:

```
select
 distinct  patch as "Applied Interim Patch",
                installation_time as "Time Applied",
                tgtcomp.target_name as "Database Target Name",
                patch.home_location as "Oracle Home Directory",
                patch.home_name as "Oracle Home Name",
                host as Host
from
 mgmt$applied_patches patch,
     mgmt$em_homes_platform  home,
     mgmt$target tgt,
     mgmt$target_components tgtcomp
where
     home.HOME_ID = patch.CONTAINER_GUID
and
 patch.target_guid = tgt.target_guid
and
 tgtcomp.home_name = patch.home_name
and
```

```
  tgtcomp.target_type = 'oracle_database'
and
  patch.installation_time>
MGMT_VIEW_UTIL.ADJUST_TZ(??EMIP_BIND_START_DATE??,
??EMIP_BIND_TIMEZONE_REGION??,tgt.TIMEZONE_REGION)
and
  patch.installation_time<= MGMT_VIEW_UTIL.ADJUST_TZ(??EMIP_BIND_END_DATE??,
??EMIP_BIND_TIMEZONE_REGION??,tgt.TIMEZONE_REGION)
order by
  installation_time desc
```

The column headings are changed in the new report. The report definition *styled text* is also modified from *instr_applied_patches_all_hosts* to the following:

```
"The report shows the interim patches applied on Oracle Databases across all
the hosts in the last 31 days. Use the time period selector to view the
interim patches applied within a time-period. Thanks."
```

This customized report displays the output in Figure 6.12. In this output, you can see the interim patches applied to each database. This clearly satisfies the requirement of the Proof-of-Concept and also demonstrates the power of customized reports in Grid Control.

Figure 6.12: *Applied Interim Patches (Customized – Database Level)*

More Sophisticated Customization

A second customized report, "Applied Interim Patches (Customized - Database Level and Select which Database)" is also created by the testing team. This enables the selection of any one particular database for the report rather than all databases. It uses the following SQL:

```
select
distinct  patch as "Applied Interim Patch",
                installation_time as "Time Applied",
                tgtcomp.target_name
                    as "Database Target Name",
                patch.home_location
                    as "Oracle Home Directory",
                patch.home_name as "Oracle Home Name",
                host as Host
from
    mgmt$applied_patches patch,
    mgmt$em_homes_platform  home,
    mgmt$target tgt,
    mgmt$target_components tgtcomp
where
    home.HOME_ID = patch.CONTAINER_GUID
and
 patch.target_guid = tgt.target_guid
and
 tgtcomp.home_name = patch.home_name
and
 tgtcomp.target_type = 'oracle_database'
and
 tgtcomp.target_guid = ??emip_bind_target_guid??
and
 patch.installation_time>
mgmt_view_util.adjust_tz(??emip_bind_start_date??,
??emip_bind_timezone_region??,tgt.timezone_region)
and
 patch.installation_time<= mgmt_view_util.adjust_tz(??emip_bind_end_date??,
??emip_bind_timezone_region??,tgt.timezone_region)
order by
 installation_time desc
```

The database target is selected by this line in the SQL code:

```
and
 tgtcomp.target_guid = ??EMIP_BIND_TARGET_GUID??
```

On the execution of this report, you can select the database from a list of supplied database targets (Figure 6.13). This second customized report successfully displays the interim patches applied to the selected database during the specified period.

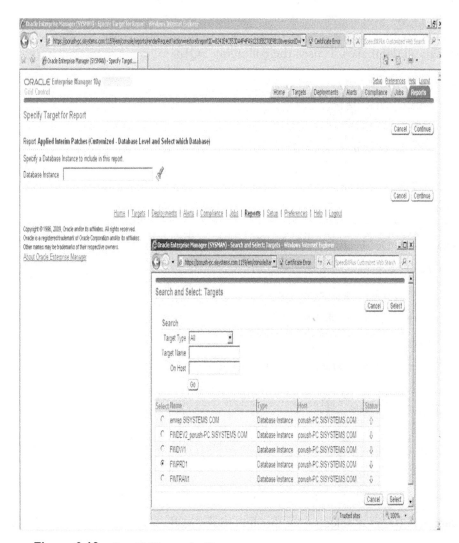

Figure 6.13: *Specify Target for Report*

It is obvious that a lot of customization is possible in Grid Control reports, making them even more powerful. This applies to database patching reports as well as other Grid Control reports.

The Repository Views

The OEM Grid Control repository, in itself, has a lot of information. As a reference, the *mgmt$* views of the repository are documented in detail in the OTN document "Enterprise Manager Extensibility Guide for 10g Release 5". The URL is: http://download.oracle.com /docs/cd/B16240_01/doc/em.102/b40007.pdf. This can be referred to if you need to find what information is in which repository view, which views are joined to other views, and so on.

Another way to find this information, and also learn something new, is by using Oracle SQL Developer Data Modeler. This is a brand-new utility able to be downloaded from OTN. The core product, Oracle SQL Developer, is a free and fully supported graphical tool used for database development. Using this tool, it is possible to easily browse database objects. The developer or DBA can also run SQL statements or scripts and edit or debug PL/SQL code using this free product.

Oracle SQL Developer has improved steadily over the past few releases, much like Grid Control has. The newest addition to SQL Developer is the Data Modeler, however this needs to be licensed separately for production. SQL Developer remains a free product. It should be noted here that licensing differs from company to company and the reader should check to make sure they are licensed to use any Oracle product.

The Data Modeler installs as a standalone utility rather than as a part of SQL Developer. This was intentionally done by Oracle so as to retain a smaller footprint for the core Oracle SQL Developer product.

Using the *data modeler* utility, it is possible to perform the reverse engineering of an existing Oracle Database instance. This is done by selecting File -> Import -> Data Dictionary. The data dictionary can be imported from any 9i, 10g, or 11g database. This can even be done from non-Oracle databases such as SQL Server, DB2 or a standard ODBC/JDBC driver, which makes it a very useful tool. The utility can be used to reverse-engineer the SYSMAN schema in the OEM Grid Control repository, such as the *mgmt$* views.

A data model of the Grid Control repository can then be created, which will aid in the understanding of what information is available in the views, how the

---

views have to be joined to one another, and so on. The information will be invaluable in the creation of customized Grid Control reports.

Analyze Before You Deploy

A new one-off patch on top of Enterprise Manager 10.2.0.5 was released by Oracle Corporation in July 2009. This is Patch Number 8653501, and it introduces a number of changes pertaining specifically to the patch automation feature.

Download this patch from My Oracle Support and apply it on all of your Grid Control OMS servers; also complete the additional steps in the *readme* file. The patch contains certain Patch Automation enhancements that are described below. After this patch has been applied, you will now be able to invoke the standard deployment procedures in analyze mode. This mode verifies that the patch is applicable on the database environment without actually applying it.

You can guess that DBAs from around the world had requested this feature, and so Oracle Development added this capability to the deployment procedures of Grid Control.

Two new mode buttons, analyze and deploy, are now visible on the review page during the deployment procedure execution. If you submit the deployment procedure in analyze mode, Grid Control will perform a total patchability check before the actual physical patching takes place. The Results tab will display the results of the check, along with recommendations.

The analyze mode checks the target properties, and it checks the target health. For example, in a RAC cluster the analyze mode will execute the *cluster verify* utility to make sure all components of the cluster are functioning properly. It then checks the patches selected and the patches already in the target to see if the patch can be applied or if there are any conflicts. You could possibly run this a few days before you run the actual deploy patching on your production database.

Patch Number 8653501 also adds two new patching-related reports to Grid Control under the Reports tab. The first new report is the EM Target Patchability report. This report describes the patchability, in a comprehensive manner, of the entire database environment that is visible to Grid Control.

The second new report is the Patching Deployment Procedure Execution Summary Report. This report provides a summary of the executions of the deployment procedures in any time period that is specified.

What Was Learned

In the financial institution, the DBA team was used to slogging through all database administration tasks manually for a large number of databases. When the Proof-of-Concept started, these DBAs were skeptical about the use of OEM Grid Control at their site for the purpose of the patching of databases. However, when the tests demonstrated how Grid Control could assist them in their recurrent database patching tasks, these same DBAs were very impressed.

OEM Grid Control supplies deployment procedures for database patching, and these procedures have reached a high level of maturity. DBAs can search for patches for any version of any Oracle software from My Oracle Support. They can then download the selected patch(es) to a staging area on the Oracle Management server. The patch(es) can then be applied on any target database(s) using the out-of-the-box or customized deployment procedure. They can be scheduled to be applied at any time with the Grid Control scheduler.

An Enterprise Manager blackout is automatically started for the database so that no alerts are generated. The procedure shuts down the database, applies the patch(es), and then starts the database again. The same set of steps is repeated for any other database that was selected for the patch application. It is also possible to customize the deployment procedure for any situations in which workarounds need to be added, new steps to be put in place for further automation, and modification of the error handling of each step.

After the completion of the POC, the general opinion among the DBAs was that deployment procedures, in the case of patches that have to be applied to many databases, would surely save them a lot of manual labour, time and repetition. These DBAs remembered how long it takes to perform a file transfer of a manually downloaded patch to their multitude of database servers and heaved a sigh of relief when they realized how Grid Control would help them. The patch, one or many, can be downloaded just once and stored in the software component library on the central Oracle Management server.

When the deployment procedure executes its initial steps, the patches are transferred to each database target host where they are placed in the patch staging location. This is under the Agent Home on the target host. The directory is *%oemd_root%/EMStage* if *%oemd_root%* is the target Agent Home location.

This transfer is done automatically in a lights-out manner with no human intervention – the time and labor savings for this step alone is evident. The patches are then applied from this staging area to the appropriate Oracle homes on that target host. This automatic transfer and application by the deployment procedure make the manual chore of file transfer and application of the patches to each home totally unnecessary and redundant.

Human error is also greatly reduced. A large telecommunications company found that using OEM to patch their databases reduced the DBA error rate in the entire process from about a hundred errors to an astounding total of just one.

Conclusion

At the end of the Proof-of-Concept exercise, the management and DBAs were convinced about the powerful capabilities in the Provisioning and Patch Automation Pack of Oracle Enterprise Manager Grid Control. The Pack is a boon to aid in the monotonous and mind-numbing task of database patching. Indeed, it would not be far wrong if this were to be called the next generation of patch management!

Another bonus: Do these deployment procedures only patch stand-alone Oracle database instances? Definitely not. The procedures also automate the application of patches to Oracle Real Application Cluster (RAC) database instances in zero-downtime rolling mode and non-rolling mode, Oracle Clusterware, Oracle Automatic Storage Management (ASM), and Oracle Application Server.

There are also deployment procedures for patching Solaris, Windows, and Linux hosts. The OTN document, *Enterprise Manager Administrator's Guide for Software and Server Provisioning and Patching*, has reference notes on this topic. The URL is: http://download.oracle.com/ndocs/cd/B16240_01/doc/doc.102/e14500.pdf.

OEM Grid Control and its world are growing very rapidly, all to the benefit of today's DBA. In this chapter, deployment procedures and patching were tested. Also created for the first time in Grid Control were a couple of customized patching reports.

The next chapter will examine another great use of Grid Control – to easily set up Data Guard configurations for disaster recovery purposes and to manage and monitor the standby databases in your company. Disaster recovery is also a very important aspect of DBA work, so find out how to reduce those sleepless nights.

Set Up Data Guard Standbys and Other Provisioning

Downtime of your databases and servers, as is well known, can either be meticulously planned or totally unplanned! Any type of downtime is expensive so far as business dollars are concerned, but the effects of planned downtime can more or less be mitigated by some means such as the new-fangled rolling upgrades concept from Oracle. In an Oracle RAC active-active cluster, that may mean upgrading one node at a time with the database always up and running.

It is actually unplanned, unpredictable downtime that is costlier to business since employees twiddle their thumbs idly and the corporate websites are unreachable, leading to business loss. A bit of a blow to the company prestige and worst of all, a dropping share price.

High Availability

High Availability (HA) is the main strategy that has been used by companies to protect themselves against server failures. This technology is often implemented in the form of active-passive clusters and such has been the case for many years. In an active-passive cluster, a storage unit known as a LUN (Logical Unit Number) is shared between two servers but only accessed by one primary server at a time. The database files are placed on this LUN, and the Oracle instance starts in memory on the primary server. When the primary server goes down, the LUN is switched over to the secondary server, and the instance is restarted in the memory of that server.

This active-passive technology was the HA norm in the corporate computer centers for many years. The only complaint was that the cluster could automatically and unexpectedly switch over to the passive server, even on very trivial grounds like slow network access to the active server or if the database were shut down for maintenance by a naive DBA. In the latter case, the cluster monitoring software has to be disabled first before any maintenance work is done on the database.

Oracle performed early experiments with active-active clusters. In this case, a single database had instances on multiple servers that all accessed the same database storage. The first versions were known as Oracle Parallel Server (OPS). However, at that time the clustering technology was primitive and used the shared storage itself as the method to transfer blocks from node to node. This had performance limitations and was very complex to set up; consequently, implementations of OPS were rare since DBAs who knew OPS fetched a premium when it came to employment benefits.

The picture was decidedly and vastly improved when Oracle developed the new version of active-active clusters and called it Oracle Real Application Clusters (RAC) in Oracle 9i onwards. This introduced the latest Oracle technology of cache fusion where, in a technical breakthrough, the database used the memory (cache) of the nodes for the first time to transfer requested blocks across the interconnect. The caches of the instances on the cluster nodes were fused together, in a manner of speaking. This technique improved cross-instance block-access performance dramatically, and made 9i RAC a very practical and scalable alternative to the active-passive technology.

RAC obviously afforded protection against server failures; if one of the nodes died, the database still stayed up since the other nodes kept on working. So this became a very valid HA solution. Additionally, the other great advantage was that an optimum use of all the servers in the cluster could be achieved via intelligent load balancing.

Because the load is shared across all nodes, the RAC can scale out horizontally – something which is impossible for an active-passive cluster to achieve unless the application and database is broken up into pieces. And how long can you continue to slice and dice an application and database? There is no need to do this in the RAC configuration so far as the majority of applications are concerned. Also, you can start with a small number of RAC nodes rather than initially deploy a large server to accommodate future growth.

In late 2009, a new HA technology was introduced by Oracle: Oracle RAC One Node in Oracle 11g Release 2. This is RAC running on one node in a cluster with failover protection, the same as the active-passive scenario. The difference is that RAC One Node can easily be upgraded online to a full active-active RAC cluster. This is not possible with the other third-party active-passive clusters.

Oracle VM, which is Oracle's virtualization solution, can be used with RAC One Node to allow migrating the database instance to another node in the cluster without application downtime. This is done by using the Oracle Omotion online migration utility, totally without failover. This is another advantage of using the latest Oracle technology.

Early Days of Oracle Disaster Recovery

Consider the situation of the entire computer site going down as in the case of an actual disaster, either natural or manmade. In such an event, HA technology just cannot cope. All the active-passive or active-active RAC servers in the one site hit by the disaster would be down! A genuine Disaster Recovery (DR) solution is needed with servers ready to take over at a totally different site, but distant enough not to be effected by the disaster at the primary site.

The concept of DR was first applied to Oracle databases by the Oracle consulting team in response to client requests. A manual standby database was the main instrument, this being in the days before Oracle 7.3. The technique was very primitive, but laid the groundwork for Oracle's ongoing concept of the standby database. The steps performed were basically as follows:

1. Install the Oracle database software on the standby server.

2. Shutdown the primary database, backup the database files, and FTP/SCP them across to the standby server.

3. Start recovery of the copied database.

4. Write UNIX shell scripts that keep transferring the archive logs from the primary database, as and when generated.

5. Write UNIX shell scripts that keep applying the archive logs on the standby database in a continuous recovery mode.

6. Write UNIX shell scripts that monitor the primary and standby databases, make sure logs are being applied and there are no gaps in log application.

7. Write UNIX shell scripts to failover to the standby database by stopping recovery, and opening it up as a read write database, in the case when the primary database was no longer workable due to a disaster.

Sometimes there arose gaps in log application in case the archive logs were not transported to the standby server due to network failure. Or, even if transported, they were not applied on the standby due to some reason such as unauthorized deletion or maybe hard disk corruption. The resulting gaps had to be resolved manually in all these cases.

Amazingly, there are some companies that even today deploy their standby databases using this manual scripted method. This is because they use the Oracle Standard Edition (SE) Database software and only the Enterprise Edition (EE) allows the use of the latter-day advanced standby technology from Oracle. This is one of the many advantages of using EE instead of SE.

Oracle official support for standby database mechanisms was first started in version 7.3 of the database software. As each version was announced, this support was developed rather considerably. In Oracle 8.1.7, the logs started to be transported between the primary and the standby via the mechanism of Oracle SQLNet 8, replacing the use of the FTP/SCP operating system utilities. The other new feature introduced at that time was Managed Database Recovery, which automatically applied the transferred archive logs on the standby.

As a result of these new features, some of the manual scripts used previously in the standby setup were now unnecessary. this is a good first step to automation, which is why this standby history is being covered, in case you are wondering.

But the big thing in Version 8.1.7 was the new Oracle Data Guard technology, a culmination and amalgamation of what went before. You had to download this separately from the Oracle Technical Network (OTN), and then unzip it in a subdirectory under your Oracle Home.

Oracle Data Guard, at that time, was a collection of UNIX shell scripts, such as *dgdeploy.sh*, which deployed the Data Guard configuration of the primary and standby databases. It also had a command line interface, Data Guard Control (*dgdctl*), which allowed you to perform a switchover or a failover to the standby database quite easily.

In Oracle 9i, Data Guard was promoted to become part of the Oracle kernel, resulting in better performance and memory management. A new Oracle background process DMON was now started specifically for the Data Guard broker along with all the other background processes.

Oracle, in Versions 10g and 11g, continued the enhancements to the Data Guard technology. But the setup, configuration and maintenance of Data Guard increased correspondingly in complexity, and human error became more likely in the entire process, especially if you had multiple primary databases and their corresponding standbys.

Enter Enterprise Manager

With the increasing complexity, a powerful tool was needed which would drive the setup and configuration of Data Guard. Oracle created just the right tool: Enterprise Manager 9i with a wizard that allowed the setup of Data Guard standbys directly from the Enterprise Manager console. You could also perform a database switchover or failover to the standby from Enterprise Manager 9i itself, instead of doing it manually using the Data Guard Command line interface.

The next version of OEM that handled standby databases was Grid Control 10g. This further enhanced the setup process of the Data Guard configuration and also included a monitoring interface for the entire configuration.

In general, Grid Control 10g, with its new architecture and interface, has already proven to be a great aid to the DBA. Grid Control excels at streamlining and automating many daily tasks of the DBA, tasks as varied as performance diagnosis, tuning, scheduling database and OS scripts, setting up and scheduling database RMAN backups as well as delivering and applying database patches, and configuration management and monitoring of the application, database, OS, and the server.

And of course, you can also easily set up Data Guard configurations, manage the configurations, switchover or failover the database, and monitor the primary and standby databases using Grid Control, which is an ideal way to set up disaster recovery capabilities in your company.

One marvelous thing is that Oracle 9i, 10g and 11g databases are all included in the Data Guard capabilities of Grid Control. Typically, a large company would have existing versions of these databases although it is always advisable to upgrade, considering that extended support for 9i ended on 31st July 2010, and 10g needs extended support after this date.

Before starting with the demonstration of our standby setup, it is assumed as before that the central Grid Control site has been deployed using scalable architecture and best practices. For a refresh, refer to Chapter 2 of this book titled "Scalable Architecture for Large Sites". This chapter explains the scenario of a very large Grid Control site monitoring and managing many hundreds of database, server and listener targets.

The wizard for creating the standby database is a step-by-step, guided, error-free procedure to set up Oracle Data Guard. Using this procedure, you can set up the standby database on any server in your corporate space, provided the Grid Control agent is already installed and running on that server prior to the actual setup. If a large company standardizes the use of Grid Control, it would be possible to set up disaster recovery very painlessly and seamlessly for Oracle databases in the entire corporate.

A lot of time can be saved, customized scripts can be eliminated, and human error greatly reduced. Not least importantly, you would definitely be extending the life of your DBA.

Standby Oracle Home Creation

Oracle Enterprise Manager Grid Control 10g Release 5 (10.2.0.5.0) has been installed on a test server, and this will be used as the basis for your demonstration in this chapter. Figure 7.1 will look familiar. This is the Enterprise Manager console's home page.

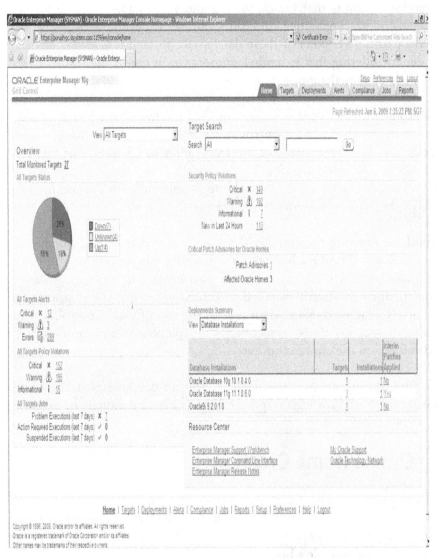

Figure 7.1: *Console Home Page*

On every host that you wish to monitor and manage via OEM 10g Grid Control, the OEM 10g Agent must be installed and running. This is a prerequisite since the Agent is used to communicate between the targets on the host and the Oracle Management Service (OMS).

Presuming that the primary database is already managed by Grid Control, you now turn to the server that is to be used as the standby. As per Oracle Data Guard requirements, the primary and standby should have the same Operating System, but the OS patchset release may be different. The requirement for the Oracle software is stricter. The Oracle software should be the same version including the Oracle patchset release.

The first thing to do on this standby server is to install the OEM 10g Agent using a separate Agent Home located on the target server. Once the OEM Agent starts communicating with the central OMS, all information about the standby server is available on the central Grid Control site. After this Agent installation is complete, the standby server now has the Agent Home, but there is no Oracle Home since the Oracle database software has not been installed on this server.

You can manually install the Oracle Enterprise Edition (EE) software from a CD or use the downloaded installation files from the Oracle Technology Network (OTN). Make sure you do not install the Standard Edition (SE) since the use of Data Guard is not allowed with the Standard Edition.

Another faster, better way to do this is to select the *Clone Oracle Home* utility, which is visible in the Cloning section of the Deployments tab in Grid Control. Figure 7.2 demonstrates this feature. This is also known as the Clone Wizard.

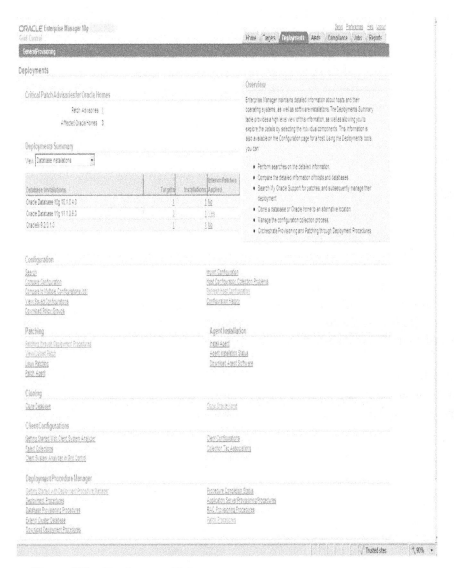

Figure 7.2: *Deployments Tab*

Please note that you must make sure you are licensed to use the OEM Provisioning and Patch Automation Pack. Sometimes the license may only be required if the *Clone Oracle Home* utility is to be used on production and test servers, but you must make certain this is true.

Cloning Oracle Homes in this manner is not the only use of this powerful pack. It also allows you to clone Oracle databases fast and seamlessly either to the same server or to totally different servers. You can easily create test or development instances from production, for example. Remember to combine this feature with the OEM Data Masking Pack, which helps you to change confidential data in production at the end of the cloning process. The Provisioning and Patch Automation Pack also assists in the automated patching of Oracle databases via the new and powerful deployment procedures.

Select *Clone Oracle Home* on this page. The Source Home page now appears (Figure 7.3). This is the starting page of the Clone wizard. On the Source Home page, you can now select the source Oracle Home that is to be cloned.

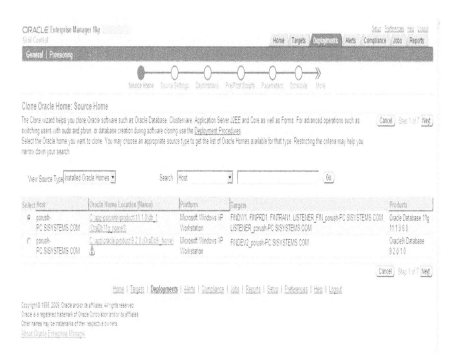

Figure 7.3: *Clone Oracle Home - Source Home*

Take note of the View Source Type dropdown box that is displayed on the Source Home page. By selecting a different source type, you can select the source home from any existing Oracle Home, or you can select it from the Software Library that has been set up on the central OEM site.

Gold Copies

When is a Software library used as the Source Type? This is when you have created a Gold copy in the library, e.g. an image of an Oracle Home, fully patched and with all the company standards and licensed options installed.

Your database Gold copy of 10g or 11g may be patched up to a particular patchset such as 10.2.0.5 or 11.2.0.2. It can have appropriate security patches, interim patches, and/or Critical Patch Updates (CPUs) applied. The Gold copy can also have particular database options like Label Security and Oracle Database Vault options installed, as seen in Advanced Installation – Custom when you install Oracle software from the CD, since the corresponding licenses have been purchased by the company and are deemed mandatory for all new databases to be deployed in the company.

On the other hand, if licenses for some of the options have not been purchased, you would not want your DBA to automatically install options like Oracle Partitioning and Oracle Advanced Security in your Oracle Home. These options are preselected when Advanced Installation – Enterprise Edition is used to install 11g via the GUI Oracle Installer. Another benefit of the Gold copy is patently obvious: you can prevent unlicensed Oracle options from being used.

When the Gold copy is ready, you can use the *Clone Oracle Home* utility to create production Oracle Homes on new servers as clones of the Gold copy. The cloned Oracle Home is a perfect copy of this one master copy with all the patches, standards and licensed options in place in the clone. Thus, you have effectively provisioned a new database server in a fraction of the time it would take you to install the Oracle software, patch it, and make sure all the standards are followed and only the licensed options are used.

The same applies to Gold copies of Oracle databases; you can create databases that conform to your company standards including database sizing, structure, tablespace and datafile naming, appropriate database parameters, and enabling the licensed options. This then becomes your master database copy, and it can likewise be cloned to any server in your company that can be accessed by Grid

Control. DBAs may remember at this point the long checklists for new database installations that are followed to the letter in certain financial institutions and which take an eon to complete.

If you use the Gold copy and the cloning mechanism, you no longer need to tick all the points in the checklist since all the requirements are in the Gold copy itself. This has a dramatic effect on the implementation time of new projects which can now be provisioned much faster than before and with less chance of human error in the provisioning process.

There is also no need to have another DBA check and review what you have done as happens in some companies that like to base everything on long drawn out processes and a ridiculous waste of DBA time. From the Source Home page in the Clone Oracle Home wizard, select the Oracle Home that is already installed on the primary server, and then Next to move to the following page (Figure 7.4).

Here you can enter the working directory to be used in the copy process. You can also specify the files you want to exclude in the copy.

Figure 7.4: *Clone Oracle Home - Source Settings*

Under the section Files to Exclude on this page, there is a default list of files that will not be copied to the new Home:

```
*.log,*.dbf,*.aud,*.trc,EMStagedPatches,sqlnet.ora,tnsnames.ora,listener.ora
,oratab
```

The reason behind this is, obviously, log files and trace files need not be copied. Oracle SQLNET files such as *tnsnames.ora*, *listener.ora*, and such are highly specific to the source server since they contain the hostname or IP address, so these too should not be copied since the destination server for the cloned home has a different hostname and IP address.

Dbf (database) files and *Aud* (audit) files are also not required because they relate more to the database on the source server. Sometimes database files may be placed in the Oracle Home, so they should be excluded. You can also add to this exclude list if required.

Move to the next page (Figure 7.5). You can select the destination host from a list of hosts. Note that only hosts that have the same OS as the source host are displayed.

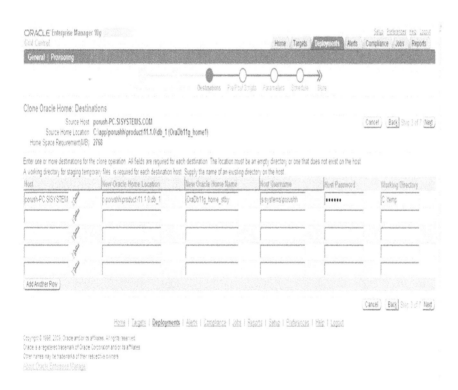

Figure 7.5: *Clone Oracle Home - Destinations*

Choose the particular host on which the standby database is to be installed. You can specify the Home location on this page as the following:

```
D:\app\porushh\product\11.1.0\db_1
```

The source Home will be copied to this location.

Name the new Oracle Home as *OraDb11g_home_stby* and enter the credentials to be used to logon to the standby host. This page allows you to add multiple destinations. So, you can easily create multiple cloned Oracle Homes on different hosts from one master Gold copy or an existing Oracle Home.

This is yet another advantage of the *Clone Oracle Home* utility in Grid Control: mass cloning. If there are pre-cloning and post-cloning scripts you want to use to customize the cloning operation, you can specify them in the next step. Either a host command or a script can be used.

After this, the hostname and the Oracle base for the destination Home can be specified; this is entered as *D:\app\porushh*. The original Oracle base is *C:\app\porushh*. The cloning operation can be scheduled on the next screen (Figure 7.6) to run either immediately or at a later time and to be started by the Grid Control Job Scheduler. Set the job to run immediately.

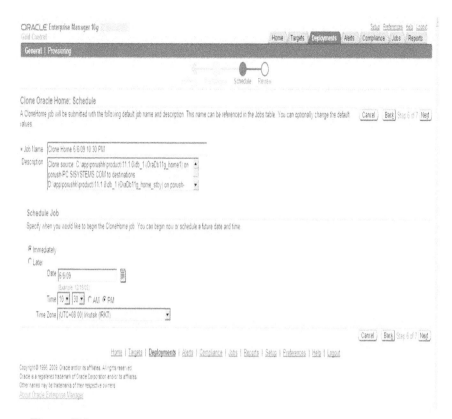

Figure 7.6: *Clone Oracle Home - Schedule*

Finally, on the Summary page, you can confirm that all details are correct and let the cloning operation proceed. The progress of the cloning operation can be observed by selecting View Job (Figure 7.7). The cloning proceeds at once as the schedule was set to immediate.

Figure 7.7: *Clone Oracle Home Job Execution*

The job execution displays an initial first step: Prepare Source Home. Selecting this step shows that the mechanism of cloning is actually performed through the creation of a zip archive located in a temporary directory. The creation excludes certain files that are not required to be copied.

```
C:\OracleHomes\agent10g\bin\zip -r -S -9
"C:\temp\oemchsED724047ACDB4DBCB7C2EE14AC386371\homeArchive" * -x "" "*.log"
"*.log/*" "*.dbf" "*.dbf/*" "*.aud" "*.aud/*" "*.trc" "*.trc/*"
"EMStagedPatches" "*/EMStagedPatches" "EMStagedPatches/*"
"*/EMStagedPatches/*" "sqlnet.ora" "*/sqlnet.ora" "sqlnet.ora/*"
"*/sqlnet.ora/*" "tnsnames.ora" "*/tnsnames.ora" "tnsnames.ora/*"
"*/tnsnames.ora/*" "listener.ora" "*/listener.ora" "listener.ora/*"
"*/listener.ora/*" "oratab" "*/oratab" "oratab/*" "*/oratab/*" 1> NUL
```

After creation, the zip file is transferred to the destination host and extracted in the destination directory. This is followed by other job steps such as updating the Oracle inventory and discovering the new Oracle Home by the Grid Control Agent.

You may well ask, "Can you simply copy the Oracle Home manually using operating system utilities such as *zip*, *tar* and more?" The answer is a resounding no because manual copying of Oracle Homes is not supported by Oracle Worldwide Support. The manual process you may use does not maintain the Oracle Inventory, and the databases using this manually copied Oracle Home are not discovered by the Grid Control Agent.

As Oracle RAC 10g onwards has many more integrated components than 9i, it is not advisable to clone homes using the manual method. It is better to use the Grid Control Clone Oracle Home feature instead, which is licensed with the Provisioning and Patch Automation Pack.

Finally, the cloning job has completed and you have a new Oracle Home. It is now possible to proceed with the creation of the standby database.

Creating the Standby Database

Go to Targets..Databases on the Grid Control console, and select the FINPRD1 production database. This will be the primary database in the Data Guard configuration. When the FINPRD1 database home page appears, move to the Availability tab (Figure 7.8). Click on Add Standby Database which can be seen in the Data Guard section on this page.

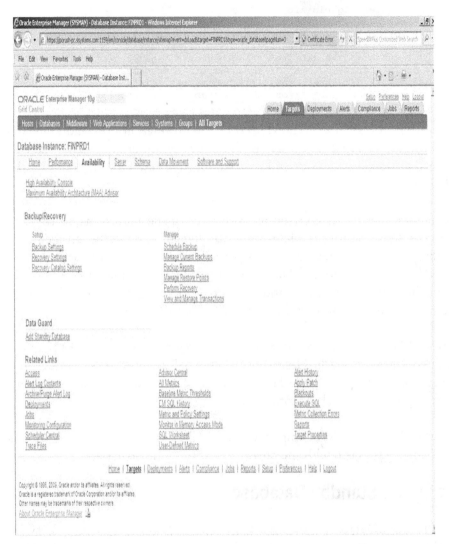

Figure 7.8: *Database Instance - Availability*

If you have not logged in to the FINPRD1 database previously, you will have to do so at this point; the login screen appears. Connect with SYSDBA privileges.

On the next screen (Figure 7.9), you can see that there are no existing standby databases in this configuration. Select Add Standby Database on this page to proceed.

Note that if you are setting up the Data Guard configuration in this way in production, apparently you may not need the Provisioning and Patch Automation Pack license as per what Oracle Product management has told us. The license for this pack may be only required if you are cloning Oracle Homes, Oracle databases, or patching the databases, but not if you are just creating a standby database. However, please check with your Oracle licensing representative to clarify the license agreement in place for your company.

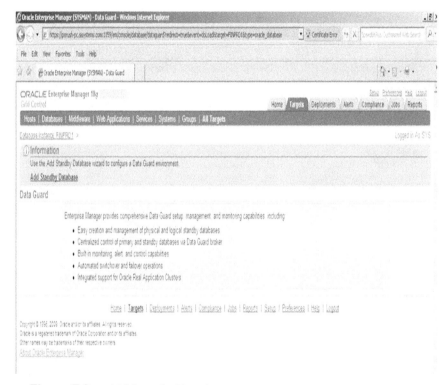

Figure 7.9: *Add Standby Database*

Choosing the Standby Type: Physical or Logical

The wizard now displays the next page (Figure 7.10) where you can select the type of standby database that is to be created. The main options are a new physical standby or a new logical standby. However, if you have already set up a standby database manually, it is also possible to add it at this stage to the Data Guard configuration. You can do this by choosing "Manage an existing standby database with Data Guard broker".

Figure 7.10: *Standby Database Types*

In most cases, a physical standby database is suitable for it has the better performance as compared to a logical standby.

The logical standby also has a number of restrictions as to the data types allowed. Hence, click on "Create a new physical standby database" to use a physical standby.

Backup Type

Now choose the backup method that will be used to create the physical standby (Figure 7.11). The easiest option is to perform an online backup of the primary database via Oracle Recovery Manager (RMAN). The backup files will be copied by RMAN to the standby server. This will provide the most recent copy of the primary database which is the physical standby being an exact copy of the primary.

It is also possible to use an RMAN database backup that has been created previously, perhaps your nightly backup. You can do this if the database is large and you do not want to take an online backup again at this time.

Figure 7.11: *Add Standby Database - Backup Type*

Select "Perform an online backup of the primary database" and "Use Recovery Manager (RMAN) to copy database files". In this case, the files will be copied by RMAN to the standby server, so a staging area is not required. However, if you wish, you can select a staging area to be used. This must be on both the primary and standby servers.

The next page appears. This is the Add Standby Database: Backup Options page (Figure 7.12).

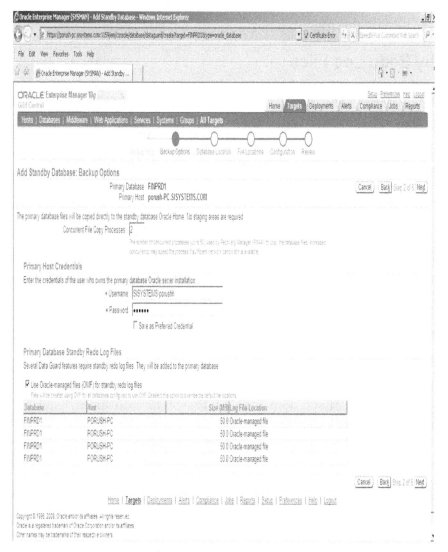

Figure 7.12: *Add Standby Database - Backup Options*

On this page, you can enter the number of concurrent File Copy processes. This will be used by RMAN to copy the database files to the standby.

Increase the number of processes (two by default), but only if sufficient bandwidth is available. Using a higher number of processes can potentially speed up the creation of the standby. The Primary Host Login credentials can also be specified on this page.

Standby Redo Log Files

The section Primary Database Standby Redo Log Files indicates that standby redo log files will be added to the primary database automatically by the wizard. Standby redo logs are very important for the functioning of Data Guard. Their main purpose is to enable real time application of redo data onto the standby by populating the standby logs with redo data almost at the same time as the redo logs in the primary database. So you do not have to wait for the archive log to be shipped to the standby.

This means that if there is a failover, the loss of data will be minimal in the case of real time apply since no redo data would have been lost. Consequently, when either the synchronous or asynchronous redo transport modes are used, standby redo logs are mandatory at the redo transport destination. But why are they created at the primary? Quite simply, because they enable the primary to receive redo log data after it assumes the standby role.

In order to simplify the setup, you can use Oracle-managed Files (OMF) for the standby redo files. Oracle will automatically name and place these files in the directory structure. If you do not use OMF, you have to specify your own file names and directory locations.

Specify the standby database attributes on the following page (Figure 7.13). The instance name must be unique on the standby host. In this case, you can name the standby database FINSTBY1. Choose File System as the database storage type for the standby database.

The other alternative is Oracle Automatic Storage Management (ASM). You can specify this as the standby database storage only if an ASM instance is operating on the standby server.

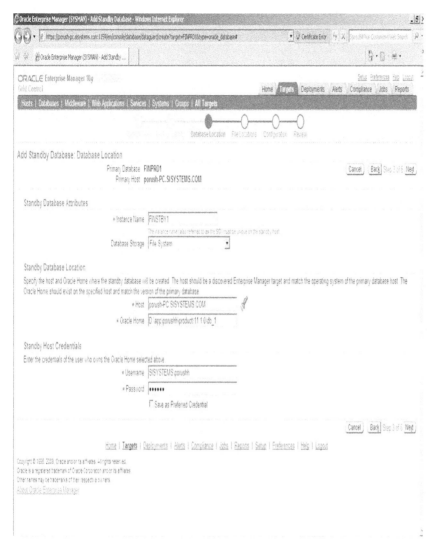

Figure 7.13: *Add Standby Database - Location and Attributes*

Under Standby Database Location, enter the hostname and the Oracle Home location for the standby database you are creating. You can select this from a list of host targets in the Grid Control system. The list displays only hosts with the same operating system as that of the primary because this is a requirement of Oracle Data Guard and Grid Control understands this. The Oracle Home for the standby also needs to be of the same version as the Oracle Home on the primary. You can refer to Metalink Note 413484.1 for a list of Data Guard configurations that are supported.

Differences in Oracle Home binaries may exist due to word sizes at the database or OS level or due to different hardware, different operating systems or even different Linux distributions. In such cases, you cannot create standby databases using the Data Guard standby creation wizard on such different primary and standby platforms, but you can create them manually and then start to manage them with the Data Guard broker. This option to manage existing standby databases is seen in Figure 7.10 in the previous pages.

Remember that the new Oracle Home has already been created on the standby host. This was done via the Clone Oracle Home wizard. You can now go to the next step.

Standby Database File Locations

You can now specify the Standby Database File locations (Figure 7.14). One option is to accept the suggested Optimal Flexible Architecture (OFA) locations, or you can change the file locations manually.

Figure 7.14: *Add Standby Database - File Locations*

The section Backup File Access is only visible on this page if you are creating the standby on a separate host (not the primary host), and you are not using RMAN to copy the database files in the case of an 11g database. In this case RMAN is being used, so Figure 7.14 does not display this section, indicating the dynamic nature of the screens. The wizards also display different options in different database versions as per the technological advances in that version.

In the event that the Backup File Access section is displayed, you must specify the method to make the primary database's backup files available to the standby host. You can choose to transfer files from the primary's working directory to a directory on the standby. In this case, you need to specify a temporary location on the standby where the primary backup files can be stored.

FTP is the fastest method to use for the file transfer. But in the case that FTP has been disabled on the servers due to security policies in force in the company, you can use the Enterprise Manager HTTP Server option. It is also possible to use HTTPS so that the transfer is secure.

If you have a very large primary database, the file transfer would need quite some time to complete. You can avoid the file transfer altogether by using the NFS method to access the backup files. Besides the time factor, this will also save the disk space that would be used if the backup files had to be transferred instead to the standby host server.

What you have to do is to access the primary's working directory via NFS, a share, or another network method from the standby. You can then select the option "Directly Access the Primary host working directory location from the Standby host using a network pathname".

Next, answer the other questions as seen in Figure 7.14, such as the "Network Configuration File Location". This identifies the directory where the *listener.ora* and *tnsnames.ora* files are located; by default, the standby Oracle Home's network/admin subdirectory. Configuration information for the new standby database will be added to these files.

Select Customize, and this will allow you to see the suggested file locations for the standby database. Based on OFA, the locations are seen as follows:

```
D:\app\porushh\product\11.1.0\db_1\oradata\FINSTBY1
```

It would be more appropriate to change these locations. This can be done for a group of files at a time, such as for all datafiles together or for tempfiles, logfiles, control files, directory objects and external files that are seen in various sections on the page. You can set the location for all the different groups of files, a group at a time, to the following directory:

```
C:\ORADATA\FINSTBY1
```

The changed locations can be seen in Figure 7.15. In the Log Files section, the standby redo logs recently added to the primary database are seen to be Oracle-managed Files.

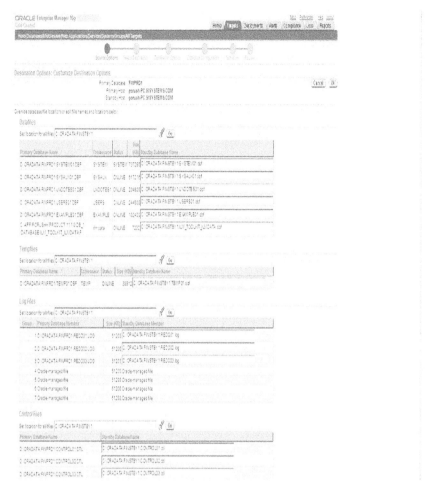

Figure 7.15: *Customize Destination Options*

When you accept the changes by selecting OK, a warning appears.

This indicates that the directories you specified will be created automatically since they do not currently exist on the server. This is fine, so you can proceed.

Standby Database Configuration Page

The Standby Database Configuration page is now displayed (Figure 7.16). The parameters controlling the standby can be set here. First of all, you can set the unique name of the standby database via the *db_unique_name* parameter.

This is set to FINSTBY1. There should be no database with this name elsewhere in the company; it should be a unique name.

Figure 7.16: *Standby Database Configuration Page*

Next, set the target name of the standby database. This is used as the display name of the target on the Grid Control screens. Keep this the same as the unique name, so this would be FINSTBY1 again.

Change the standby archive location and configure it as the Flash Recovery area as follows. This is where Data Guard will place the archived redo logs that are received from the primary database.

```
D:\flash_recovery_area\FINSTBY1
```

Normally as a rule of thumb, the size of the Flash Recovery area should be twice the database size. However this estimate is treated differently in different companies. In this case, decide on 4000 MB.

The OEM monitoring credentials for Data Guard are also specified on these pages. A SYSDBA login should be used if you intend to monitor a mounted physical standby database because only a SYSDBA can connect to a mounted database. Otherwise, use ordinary credentials; for example, the dbsnmp user to satisfy the security requirements of your company.

Under the Data Broker section, it is recommended that you use the Data Guard broker to manage the Data Guard configuration. You can either use the OEM connect descriptors as the Data Guard Connect Identifiers for both databases, or you can use the service names that already exist.

Figure 7.17 shows the Review page. On this page, the Standby Database Storage section can be expanded if you wish to verify that all the locations are correctly specified. Then select Finish.

Figure 7.17: *Add Standby Database - Review*

A few preliminary steps now begin which create the Data Guard configuration and the job preparation. Figure 7.18 shows the initial steps, which can be cancelled if required. OEM now submits a job for creation of the standby database.

Figure 7.18: *Processing - Add Standby Database*

Figure 7.19 shows the final stages of the preliminary steps. The process can no longer be cancelled when it has reached this stage.

Figure 7.19: *Completing Processing - Add Standby Database*

The OEM job system now submits the standby database creation job. This starts to create the standby database using the techniques selected in the Wizard pages, whether using an RMAN backup and copy or a NFS mount.

The standby creation job finally completes after a period of time which depends on the size of the primary database and the method chosen to create the standby. The NFS method, for example, is faster than other methods since it does not need to copy the backup files. At this point in time, the Targets..Databases list of OEM Grid Control will display the primary and standby databases in the form of a Database Instance: Primary and a Database Instance: Physical Standby.

This is seen in Figure 7.20 where the status of both the databases is displayed as Up.

Figure 7.20: *Database Targets Showing Primary and Standby*

Management Options for Data Guard

Move to the primary database's Home page in Grid Control. Select the Availability tab. You can now see some new options under the Data Guard section (Figure 7.21). The options have appeared since OEM is aware there is a Data Guard configuration that is active for this primary database. The section displays the options as Performance, Verify Configuration, and Add Standby Database. These options are in addition to Setup and Manage that were noticed previously.

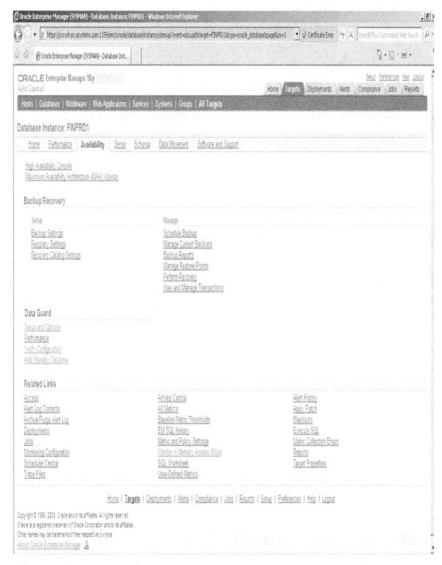

Figure 7.21: *New Visible Options for Data Guard*

Data Guard Management Page

Click on Setup and Manage. This brings up the Data Guard Management page, seen in Figure 7.22.

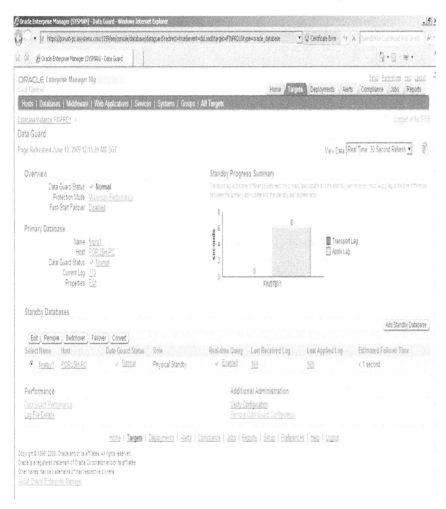

Figure 7.22: *Data Guard Management Page*

This page is used for the management of the entire Data Guard configuration for this primary database and the standby databases associated with it. Regarding the licensing aspects: the monitoring of the Data Guard configuration from this page is normally free and does not require the Provisioning and Patch Management Pack, but check with your Oracle licensing representative for your company's license agreement with Oracle.

The Data Guard Management page shows the Data Guard Status, which is displayed as normal. It also shows the Protection Mode used. By default, this is Maximum Performance. You can also see if Fast-Start Failover is enabled or not. By default, the latter is disabled.

Fast-Start Failover was introduced as a new feature in Data Guard 10g. If this feature is enabled, the standby database is able to assume primary status, i.e. a failover is performed without human intervention in case the primary database has failed for any reason.

Look at the Standby Progress Summary section. This displays the Transport lag and the Apply lag in a bar chart format. The Transport lag is the time difference between the last update on the primary database, and the last received redo on the standby. Whereas, the Apply lag is the same difference but pertaining to the last applied redo on the standby.

From these two lag calculations, the DBA can understand at a glance how far the standby is behind the primary, regarding both the transport of the logs and the application of the logs. You can also see the status of both these databases: they are at status Normal. The management page also displays the current log of the primary and the last received and last applied log on the standby. The estimated failover time is calculated as less than one second.

The Data Guard Management page also allows you to edit the Data Guard properties of the primary or the standby. You can even add additional standby databases to this Data Guard configuration, up to nine standby databases can be added in total. The DBA can also elect to perform a switchover or a failover directly from the management page to the selected standby database. A disaster scenario resulting in unplanned downtime would necessitate a failover, whereas a switchover can be used for planned downtime such as the installation of operating system patches or a machine upgrade.

Verify Configuration

In the section Additional Administration on this page, you can select Verify Configuration to go through scripted and automatic checks on the Data Guard configuration to make sure the machinery of log transport and application works as expected without actually performing a failover or switchover. This is recommended to be performed on initial setup as well as periodically. Various primary and standby database settings are verified by this step, as can be seen in Figure 7.23.

As a part of this process, the current log on the primary database is switched, followed by a verification of the protection mode. The standby redo log files are then checked. The log switch is verified as successful. The Verify Configuration process then produces a detailed report on the health of the Data Guard configuration, which helps in bringing any urgent issues to the attention of the DBA.

Figure 7.23: *Processing - Verify*

Editing Data Guard Properties

From the Data Guard Management page, displayed in Figure 7.22, you can edit the Data Guard properties of the primary or standby databases. Selecting this displays a series of property tabs (Figure 7.24).

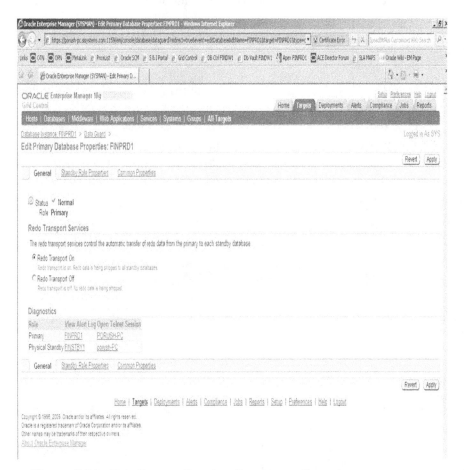

Figure 7.24: *Edit Primary Database Properties - General*

In the General properties tab for the primary database, it is possible to turn the redo transport on or off so that all transport of redo logs to any of the standby databases is either restarted or suspended. You would do this in the case of a network outage or any similar event when you know the logs cannot be sent to the standby and it is pointless for the primary to keep trying to send the logs across. Or if the primary database was being brought down for maintenance work, turning the redo transport off would be a good practice. The Standby Role Properties are seen on the next tab (Figure 7.25).

Here you can modify the redo transport mode to SYNC, which is the opposite of the default ASYNC. You can also change the net timeout property in case it is a slower network and the apply delay to specifically leave a time gap of applying logs between the standby and the primary.

If any manual errors are committed by users on the primary database, and if the DBA becomes aware of this in time due to the time gap, it may be possible to recover the data from the standby or simply failover to the standby. These are important Data Guard properties, most definitely, and must be carefully understood and implemented. Grid Control shows you all the properties at a glance which aids in understanding the possibilities.

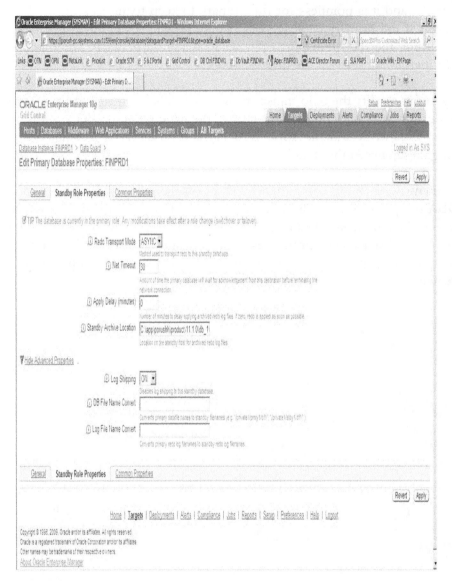

Figure 7.25: *Standby Role Properties*

Suppose 20 minutes has been specified as the apply delay.

This means that logs transported to the standby server will not be applied on the standby database until 20 minutes has passed. If a user now drops a table

Oracle Enterprise Manager Grid Control

and they make the DBA aware of this immediately, the DBA can stop the application of logs on the standby and then make an effort to recover the dropped table from the standby or failover to the standby, if need be.

Common Properties are displayed on the third tab (Figure 7.26). This tab shows the Data Guard Connect Identifier in use and the number of log archive processes. It also displays the log archive trace level. The latter can be set to a higher value when debugging the Data Guard configuration.

Figure 7.26: *Common Properties*

Procedures for Database Provisioning

Previously in this chapter, the Clone wizard has been used for a simple cloning of an Oracle Home as the first step in creating a standby database. However, you can see the limitations in this approach. The Clone wizard procedure cannot be customized and has to be executed as supplied by Oracle.

Instead, there is a much better facility available: the deployment procedures. These have been seen before in the previous chapter which demonstrated the automated patching of databases. Using similar procedures supplied out-of-the-box for database provisioning, you can also include the cloning of databases along with the cloning of Database Homes. To take a look at these procedures, open the Grid Control console and click on the Deployments tab. Select the database provisioning procedures link on this tab.

You will now see a list of all the available deployment procedures for deploying databases and replay clients, an executable part of the Oracle Client used for database replay purposes. These include out-of-the-box procedures as well as customized procedures as seen in Figure 7.27.

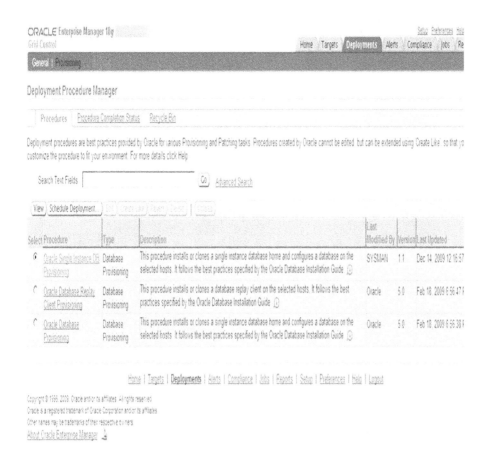

Figure 7.27: *Deployment Procedure Manager - Procedures*

Customize Any Procedure

In order to customize a procedure on this page, you can select any of the out-of-the-box procedures and then click on Create Like. This will let you create a brand new deployment procedure that you can give a new name to.

As shown in Chapter 6 about using customized deployment procedures for patching databases, the steps of the customized procedure can be changed to either stop on error or continue on error, and you can add additional steps or disable existing steps.

Oracle Single Instance DB Provisioning is one such customized procedure that has been created by SYSMAN after the Grid Control install, as can be seen by the more recent update date. This has been copied from the out-of-the-box Oracle database provisioning procedure and customized with some minor steps disabled. This procedure will be used in the following sections.

You can select this procedure, and then view the contents by clicking on the View button. The steps in this procedure are displayed. Figure 7.28 shows the first few steps.

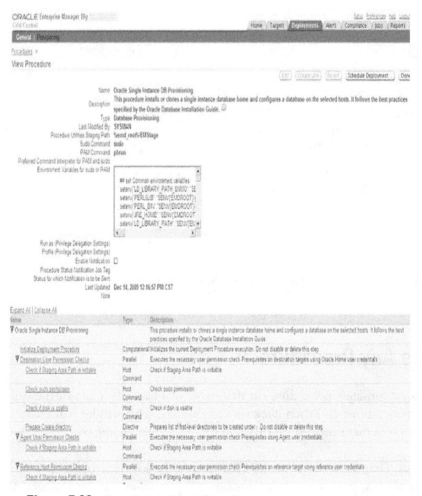

Figure 7.28: *Procedures - View Procedure*

Deploy the Procedure

To deploy the procedure, you can select it in the main list and then click on Schedule Deployment. The Select Source and Destination screen appears as seen in Figure 7.29.

Figure 7.29: *Select Source and Destination*

You want to use a Gold image from the software library as the source for this provisioning, so select the Software Library radio button. The other alternative is to choose an existing database installation, a reference installation, as the source or to use a staging location. If you choose the latter, you can use installation media to create the components in the software library and then use those components for the provisioning.

Your preference right now is the Gold image, so use the Software Library radio button and perform a search. A screen appears (Figure 7.30) displaying the available components and you can select the only Gold image you find on this page. Notice the Upload link on this page by which you can upload a new component to the Software Library at this point if no suitable image is available.

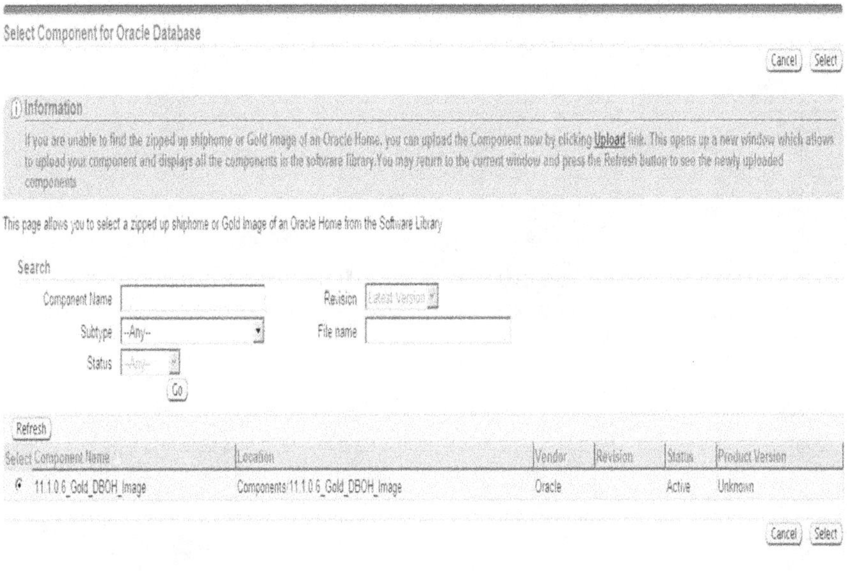

Figure 7.30: *Select Gold Image*

When the Gold image has been selected, the screen returns to the Select Source and Destination page on Figure 7.29. You can now add the destination host by clicking on the Add button under the section Specify Destination Host Settings. The screen on Figure 7.31 is displayed.

To display all the hosts, click on Show All Hosts; otherwise, by default only hosts suitable for the provisioning will appear in the list when you click on the Go button. Select tdsmaa03-d2.oracleads.com as the host you want.

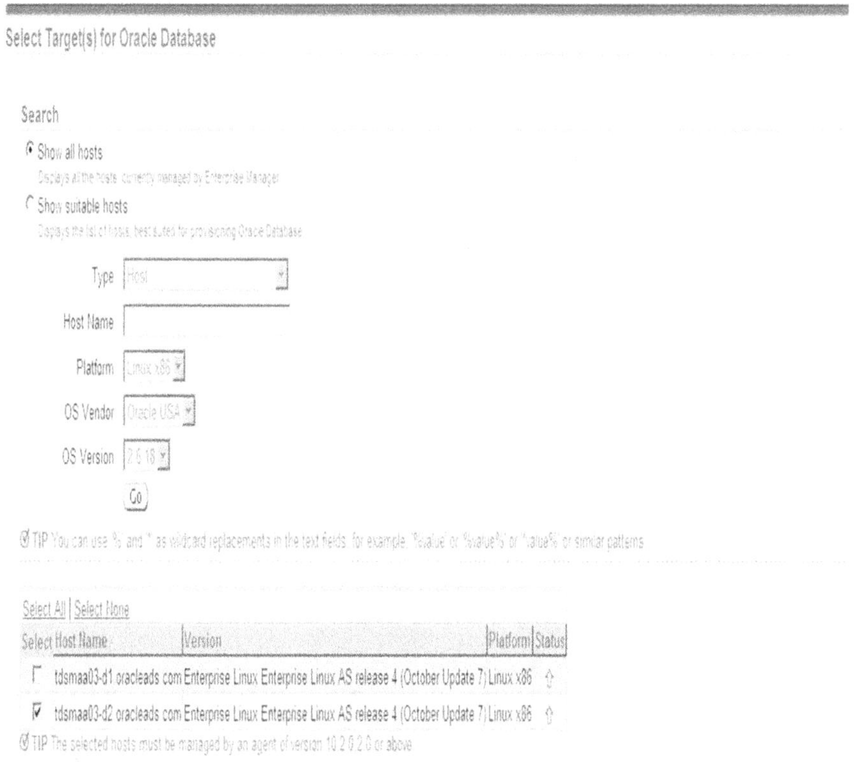

Select Target(s) for Oracle Database

Search

⊙ Show all hosts
Displays all the hosts currently managed by Enterprise Manager

○ Show suitable hosts
Displays the list of hosts best suited for provisioning Oracle Database

Type [Host ▾]

Host Name [ ]

Platform [Linux x86 ▾]

OS Vendor [Oracle USA ▾]

OS Version [2.6.18 ▾]

[Go]

TIP You can use % and * as wildcard replacements in the text fields, for example, %value or %value% or %value% or similar patterns

Select All | Select None

Select	Host Name	Version	Platform	Status
☐	tdsmaa03-d1 oracleads com Enterprise Linux Enterprise Linux AS release 4 (October Update 7)	Linux x86	↑
☑	tdsmaa03-d2 oracleads com Enterprise Linux Enterprise Linux AS release 4 (October Update 7)	Linux x86	↑

TIP The selected hosts must be managed by an agent of version 10.2.0.2.0 or above

Figure 7.31: *Select Targets*

The screen again returns to the Select Source and Destination page (Figure 7.29).

At this stage, if you wish to provide more information such as different credentials for your OEM Agent, a Custom Oracle Home name or a Custom Host name, then select Customize Host Settings. The Customize Host Settings screen appears as seen in Figure 7.32.

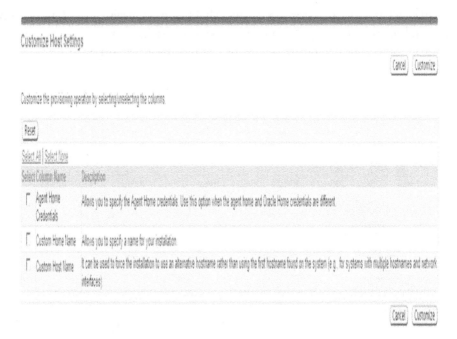

Customize Host Settings

Cancel Customize

Customize the provisioning operation by selecting/unselecting the columns.

Reset

Select All | Select None

Select	Column Name	Description
☐	Agent Home Credentials	Allows you to specify the Agent Home credentials. Use this option when the agent home and Oracle Home credentials are different.
☐	Custom Home Name	Allows you to specify a name for your installation.
☐	Custom Host Name	It can be used to force the installation to use an alternative hostname rather than using the first hostname found on the system (e.g. for systems with multiple hostnames and network interfaces)

Cancel Customize

Figure 7.32: *Customize Host Settings*

Click on the Customize button after selecting Agent Home Credentials. The screen now returns to the Select Source and Destination page and you can see that the Agent Home credentials also have appeared on this page, allowing you to type in different credentials. See Figure 7.33.

Enter more details for the target server on this page such as the location of the Oracle Base and Oracle Home and the different credentials. You can also specify the working directory.

Provision Multiple Targets

Multiple destination targets can easily be entered on this screen and these will be provisioned in the same session. From one corporate Gold image, a reference installation or the staging location, you are actually able to provision a number of targets and you can schedule this job to execute automatically at any time.

If you add multiple targets to this page (Figure 7.33), the paths can be changed to Different for each host. Also, the Credentials can be changed to Override – Different for each host.

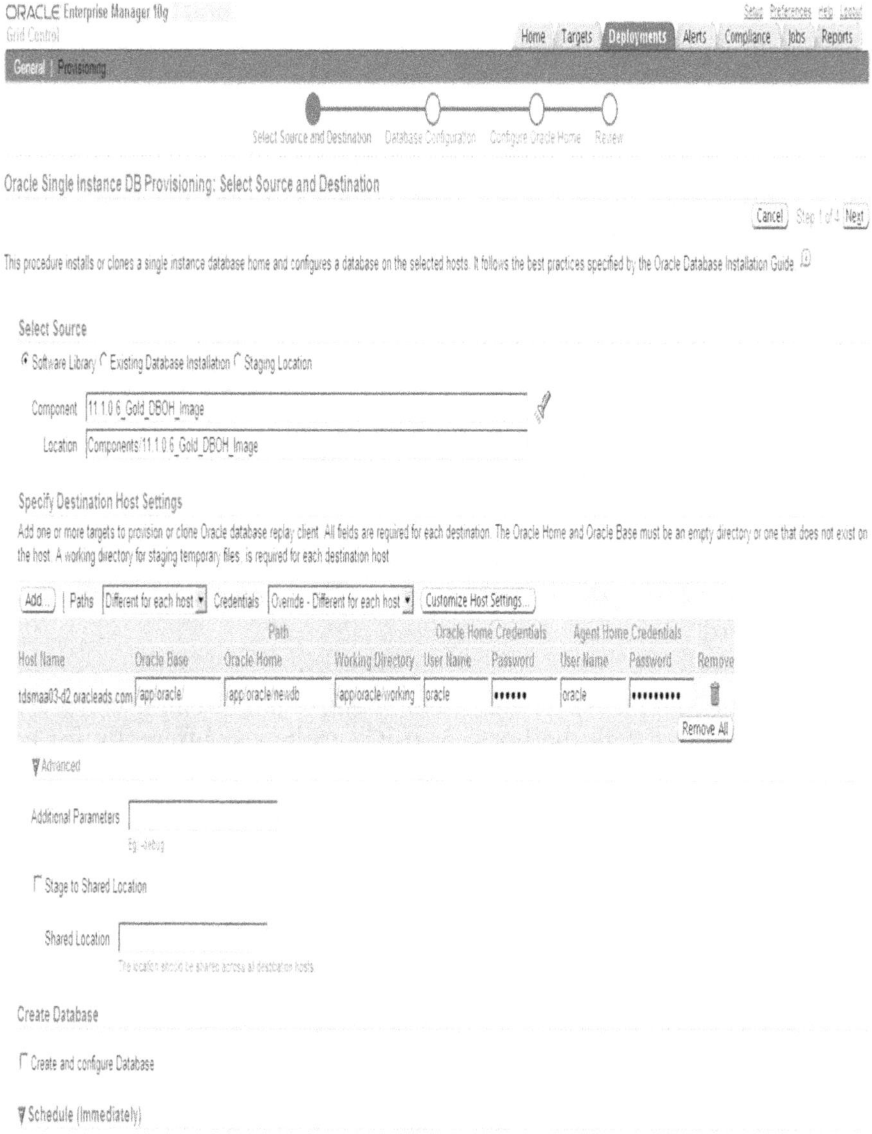

Figure 7.33: *Select Source and Destination*

Oracle Installer parameters can be specified in the Additional Parameters space on this screen and a shared location used to stage the binaries. This location, which must be shared across all the destination hosts, can be used to reduce the overall provisioning time in the case of multiple target provisioning since the binaries would only be copied once to this shared location and not to each target before the start of the installation.

You can include the creation of a database in the provisioning procedure by simply selecting the Create and configure Database option on this screen. By doing this, you can avoid using the Oracle Database Configuration Assistant (DBCA) to manually create and configure the database after the software is provisioned. Another glimpse of how DBA productivity is increased.

The provisioning procedure can now be scheduled to run at any time in the future if not immediately. Move to the Next screen.

Database Configuration

On the screen that appears, you must now enter the Database Configuration details (Figure 7.34). Enter the Data File location, SID and Domain that pertains to each of the destination targets. Also enter and confirm the Database Password.

You can decide on this screen if the Data File location path and the database password is the same for all the hosts or if it is to be set differently for each host.

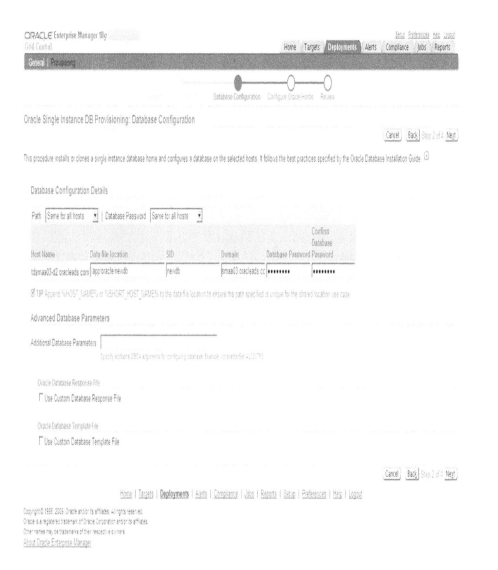

Figure 7.34: *Database Configuration Page*

Also on this screen, special DBCA arguments can be specified as Additional Database Parameters. One example is a non-default characterset for the database to be created.

You can also decide if DBCA should use custom database response files or template files; this is important. Why?

Because, in this way, you can force company database and security standards to be used during the database provisioning such as installing licensed database options and no other options, or setting any database initialization parameters to non-default values as per database standards and best practices, or creating a database with Oracle Automatic Storage Management (ASM) configured to store the data as well as the redo and archive logs. Of course, if no templates are specified, DBCA will use default out-of-the-box templates.

The next screen (Figure 7.35) shows the Oracle Support Details you can enter, such as your Email address and Oracle Support Password. This will enable you to receive security updates directly from the Oracle Support site and initiates Configuration Manager, which will also assist in future Oracle Service Request (SR) issues. After entering these details, move to the next page.

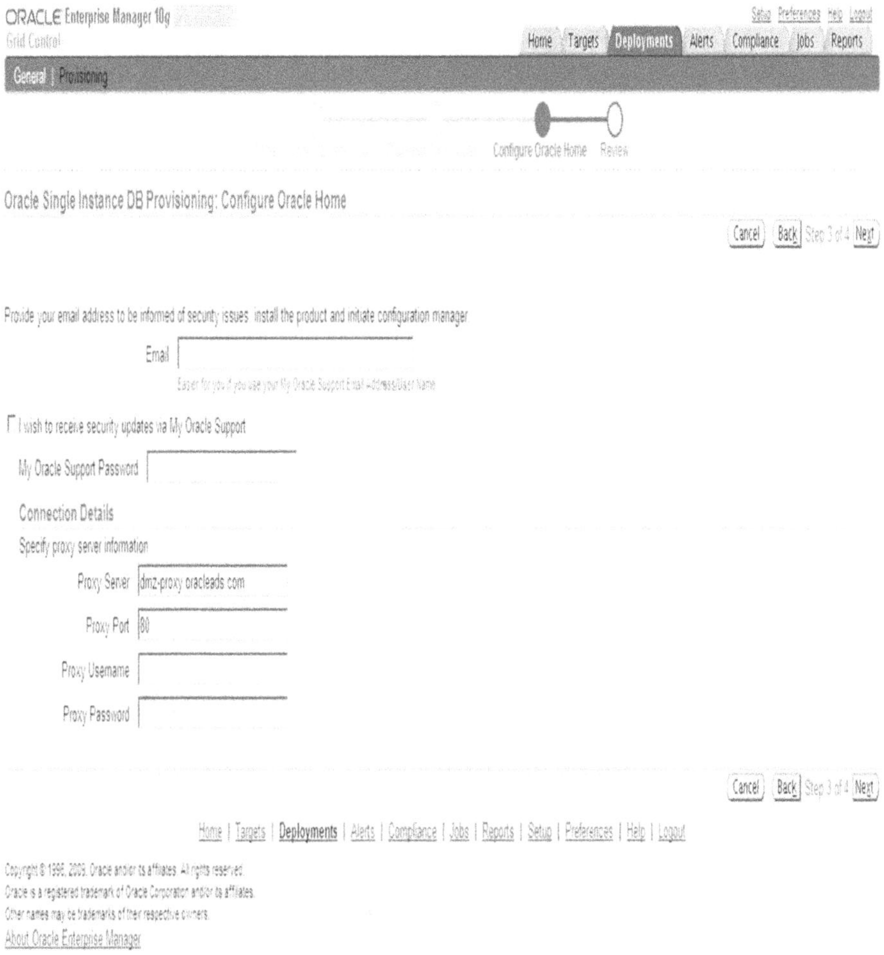

ORACLE Enterprise Manager 10g
Grid Control

Setup Preferences Help Logout

Home Targets **Deployments** Alerts Compliance Jobs Reports

General | Provisioning

Configure Oracle Home   Review

Oracle Single Instance DB Provisioning: Configure Oracle Home

Cancel   Back   Step 3 of 4   Next

Provide your email address to be informed of security issues, install the product and initiate configuration manager

Email [   ]

Easier for you if you use your My Oracle Support Email Address/User Name

☐ I wish to receive security updates via My Oracle Support

My Oracle Support Password [   ]

Connection Details

Specify proxy server information

Proxy Server [dmz-proxy.oracleads.com]

Proxy Port [80]

Proxy Username [   ]

Proxy Password [   ]

Cancel   Back   Step 3 of 4   Next

Figure 7.35: *Oracle Support Details*

Finally, the screen shows the Review information (Figure 7.36). When satisfied with the details, click on the Finish button.

Figure 7.36: *Review*

Provisioning Launch

Now, the entire provisioning operation is launched. You can see the procedure appearing in the Procedure Completion Status screen (Figure 7.37) and starting its run.

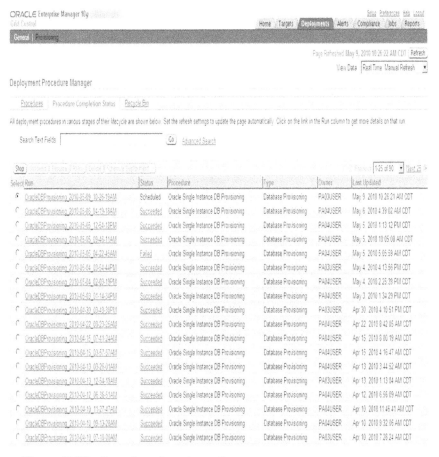

Figure 7.37: *Procedure Completion Status*

Click on the Procedure link, and this displays the progress of the deployment procedure as it proceeds with the execution of each of the steps (Figure 7.38).

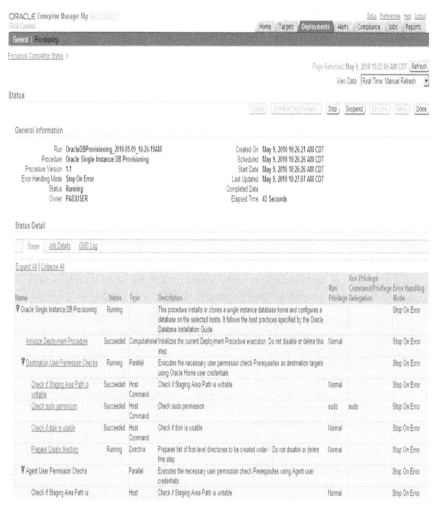

Figure 7.38: *Progress of Deployment Procedure*

Now, simply wait for the procedure to complete. Software and hardware prerequisites are checked by the procedure and Oracle recommended best practices are used to provision the database. If some requirments fail, they are fixed automatically; for example, improperly set kernel settings.

After some minutes, the deployment procedure completes successfully (Figure 7.39).

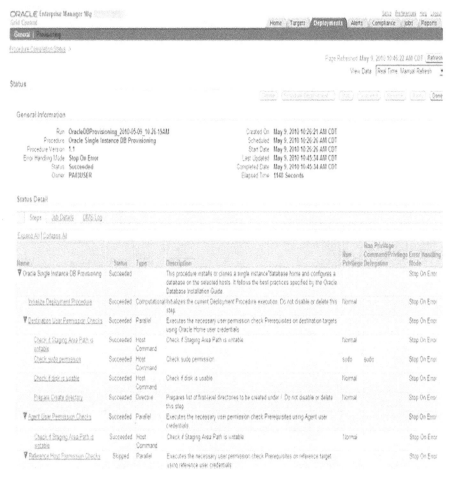

Figure 7.39: *Status Succeeded*

As part of the procedure, the new targets that are provisioned are also registered in OEM. As a result, you will be able to see the new database and its new Oracle Home in the list of targets. But there may be a slight delay of a few minutes before the targets appear. A screen refresh may be required after a few minutes.

Have a look at the Host Targets screen (Figure 7.40).

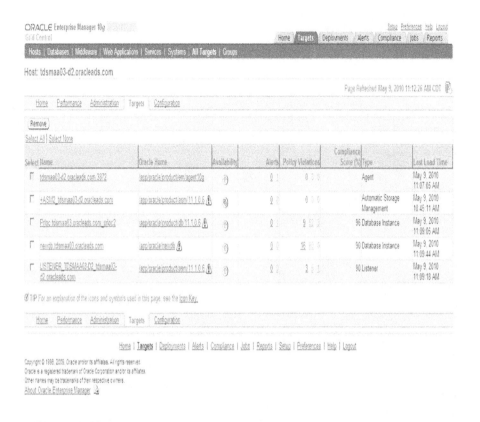

Figure 7.40: *Provisioned Database Appears in Target List*

From this demonstration, the power and benefits of the database provisioning deployment procedures are obvious. You have been able to set up and configure a new Oracle Home as well as an Oracle database in a fully automated and scheduled manner in a time frame that would surely be a fraction of the time taken by the normal DBA manual process. Great going! At the same time, you have been successful in eliminating a major part of human error due to the automated nature of this procedure.

The cost, of course, is that the OEM Provisioning and Patch Automation Pack license must be purchased to use the Deployment procedures. But it is well worth it in the long run, with the Return on Investment (ROI) being very quick as per various independent studies and the DBA productivity increasing dramatically.

Manual Copy Not Supported

It is worth noting here that Oracle Support does not certify the use of tar or zip in UNIX or Windows to manually wrap up Oracle Homes and copy them to different servers. As a result, no one would recommend such a manual method to be used in any company. However, there are still some sites that use scripts to create the copies. These scripts need to be manually maintained by a number of DBAs over the years and may not properly update the Oracle Inventory or the /etc/oratab file on the target server, leading to all sorts of issues in the future.

The rock-solid database provisioning deployment procedures offered by Oracle are a far better alternative because they are fully certified by Oracle Support. These procedures are customizable and can be used to provision Oracle single-instance as well as RAC databases and also Oracle Clusterware. They are comprehensive enough to cater to all aspects of the Oracle software which is ever increasing in complexity with newer and newer versions.

Database Gold Copy

As you have seen, you can have an Oracle database as a Gold copy, which is a database set up as per the company database and security standards. ASM can be mandated for use, or file system directories can be enforced as per Oracle Flexible Architecture (OFA) standards, initialization parameters can be changed from the default, and only licensed options can be included in the installation.

Such a database can be set up and certified by the central Database Engineering department, and it can then be uploaded to the Enterprise Manager Software library, creating a database Gold image. The image can then be used by DBA teams in the company to provision to any new server requiring the installation of a new database.

The Provisioning and Patch Automation Pack, besides allowing you to clone Oracle Homes, also lets you clone Oracle databases in this manner. It is possible to quickly create development or test databases from production by this provisioning process. You can easily combine this cloning with the OEM Data Masking Pack so that confidential data in production can be masked in the cloned database as one of the steps that execute before the completion of the cloning process.

To create a Gold image of an Oracle database (single-instance or RAC), use the Create Component page which can be accessed from the Provisioning tab on the Deployments page. The procedure to create a Gold image is fully explained in OEM documentation. Download the documentation library from the OTN and look for the OEM Administrator's Guide for Software and Server Provisioning and Patching, 10g Release 5 (10.2.0.5.0).

Bare Metal Provisioning

Bare Metal Provisioning enables you to provision the operating system on an empty server. This is done using a standardized PXE (Preboot Execution Environment) booting process and kickstart mechanism. The new hardware is booted and the Linux operating system is automatically installed on the hardware. Alternatively, Oracle VM server software can be installed. In this way, you can provision 32-bit/64-bit Oracle Enterprise Linux, Oracle VM for x86, RedHat Enterprise Linux (RHEL) and Suse Linux (SLES) out of the box.

The network boot for the startup of the hardware is performed by a required boot server, and the OS image that will be deployed is staged on a required stage server. An RPM repository is also required. This must be configured as a YUM repository. Software components and directives from the OEM software library will be installed on top of everything else.

In the case of provisioning a Linux system, the OEM Agent is automatically installed on completion of the Linux install. However, in the case of provisioning an Oracle VM server, Oracle VM server software gets installed. The new Oracle VM servers then need to be registered manually in Oracle Enterprise Manager in order to start managing them.

The Oracle Enterprise Manager Agent RPM Kit for Bare Metal Provisioning is the best practices kit for bare metal and can be referred to at the following link on the Oracle Technology Network (OTN).

```
http://www.oracle.com/technology/software/products/oem/htdocs/provisioning_a
gent.html
```

Conclusion

This chapter showed it was possible to easily set up, manage and monitor standby databases for any primary database using Oracle Enterprise Manager Grid Control. The web interface provided by Oracle for creating and managing Data Guard configurations seems to be reasonably advanced in all aspects and easy to use.

The DBA can easily use OEM for the day-to-day monitoring and management of Data Guard configurations. Also, they can perform switchovers or failovers to the standby, in the case of planned or unplanned downtime, and they can do all this from the OEM Grid Control console.

Grid Control supplies a common standard interface to set up and manage Data Guard for Oracle 9i, 10g and 11g databases. Advanced features of Data Guard in different database releases are visible corresponding to the release, and automatically offered to the DBA, thus reducing the learning curve. OEM Grid Control can, therefore, be very useful in implementing Data Guard for the varied Oracle database releases in a real world company.

This chapter has also shown the power of the database provisioning deployment procedures that can be customized to easily deploy multiple Oracle Homes and databases in the corporate space using Software Gold copies or Database Gold copies, or by using reference installations or a staging location. Such provisioning can be done to multiple new destinations in an automated, seamless and error-free manner.

Also shown were the uses of Bare Metal Provisioning for provisioning hardware from scratch with the entire software stack including the operating system, thus cutting down on incredible amounts of administrator time and increasing DBA productivity.

The next chapter will look at how Grid Control is a great benefit to System Administrators, DBA troubleshooters, company regulators and IT managers. Also, the various OEM Management Packs will be examined.

Grid Control for Everyone

Throughout this book, examples have been given of the practical uses of Oracle Enterprise Manager Grid Control in real life situations such as backing up databases or setting up standby sites. Most of these scenarios are mainly useful for the DBA community. But what about the other people in the IT world, such as System Administrators and IT managers? Would they be interested?

Grid Control for System Administrators

As was mentioned in the beginning, Grid Control can also be used by System Administrators since most of them would appreciate what it can do. Now take a brief look.

From the Grid Control console, move to Targets..Hosts. What appears is a list of hosts in the corporation that have been added to the OEM Repository (Figure 8.1). The host target list displays the status of each host server whether it is running or down, the alerts and policy violation for the host, CPU utilization, memory utilization, compliance score, Total IO per second, and so on, all at a glance on the screen.

Also observe the exclamation marks. These indicate that there may be an issue with either the state of the node or one of its components or services and more.

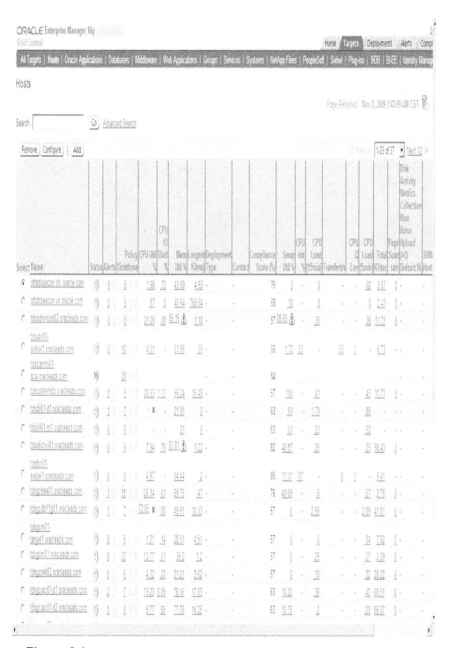

Figure 8.1: *Targets..Hosts*

Now select any of the hosts from this page. The Host Home page appears (Figure 8.2) with more information on the operating system, hardware platform, IP address, memory, CPUs, alerts, policy violations, security evaluations, and job activity.

Figure 8.2: *Host Home Page*

From the Home page, move to the Host Performance tab, as seen in Figure 8.3. This is the interesting part.

Figure 8.3: *Host Performance Tab*

The Host Performance tab (Figure 8.3) displays the host's CPU, memory and disk I/O utilization, and you can also drill down to the swap utilization, paging activity and disk activity. The top 10 operating system level process can also be seen, ordered by CPU utilization or memory utilization. It is like remotely running the UNIX *top* command without having to log in to every UNIX server. You can also select to see these details for the last 24 hours, the last seven days or the previous 31 days!

For the first time, host performance details are stored in the OEM repository and their history can be seen from the Grid Control console. This is of great interest to your System Administrator friends who traditionally have used UNIX scripts to capture these details, then upload into an Excel spreadsheet to show the CPU and memory utilization trends to management and finally, ask for a hardware upgrade. This kind of manual collation of information is required no longer. OEM Grid Control has the perfect answer.

Using the history feature, the System Administrator can also relate spikes in the host performance to issues the DBA and the database users have reported at the database level. The following Figure 8.4 displays host performance history for the previous 31 days. As can be seen, the information is detailed and a number of other graphs are also displayed.

Figure 8.4: *Host Performance History – Previous 31 Days*

If you were to drill down on the CPU utilization link on the Host Performance tab, the next page (Figure 8.5) can be seen. This page provides the details about the host's utilization and also shows the warning and critical thresholds, that if exceeded, would cause OEM to issue an alert. You can view historical data as well for this metric on this page.

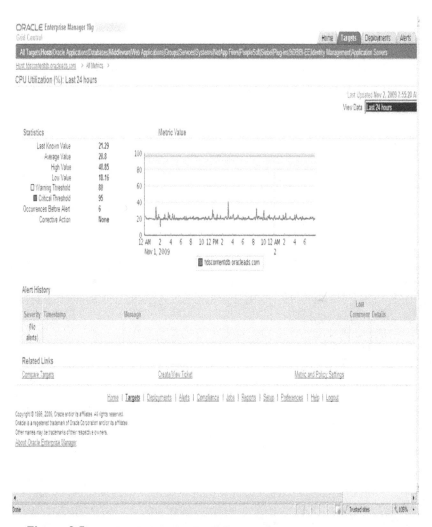

Figure 8.5: *CPU Utilization Drill Down*

Now move to the Host Configuration tab (Figure 8.6). This displays detailed information about the hardware, the operating system details and packages, the

Oracle software installed on the host with the location and time of install and all the OS registered software as well. In short, your host inside out.

Figure 8.6: *Host Configuration Tab*

The Host Configuration tab requires you to be licensed to use the OEM Configuration Management Pack. All the information you see is collected by the Agent and stored in the central Grid Control repository database.

Select the Operating System Details link. This displays the Host Operating System Details..General tab (Figure 8.7) where all the operating system properties are displayed.

Figure 8.7: *Host Operating System Details – General*

Moving to the File Systems tab (Figure 8.8) shows the file systems, types, mount locations and even the mount options used on the host!

Figure 8.8: *Host Operating System Details – File Systems*

Next, the Packages tab displays the operating system packages installed on the host (Figure 8.9). In this case, it shows all the SUSE Linux packages that have been installed.

Figure 8.9: *Host Operating System Details – Packages*

Now comes a very important aspect of configuration management: the history of all configuration changes. This is accessed from the Host Configuration tab (Figure 8.6). Click on the History button. This displays the Configuration History page (Figure 8.10) where you can search for specific changes.

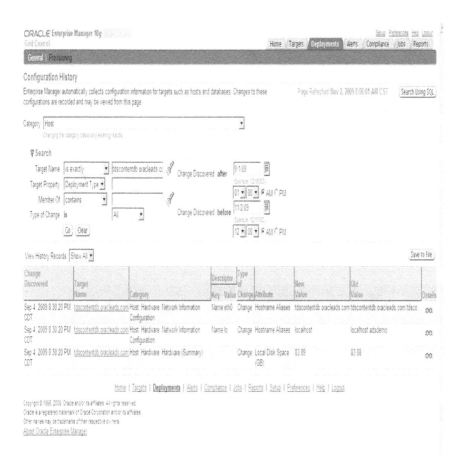

Figure 8.10: *Configuration History*

Grid Control for DBA Troubleshooters

This is where DBA troubleshooters find things getting very interesting. If things stop working all of a sudden, this may lead you quickly to the root cause and a speedy resolution by identifying who has changed what.

As is shown on the Configuration History page, a search has been done for host level changes discovered by the Agent in a certain period and on a specific host target. Three configuration changes were found that occurred on a certain date in September: the *host name alias* attribute of two network cards was changed and the local disk space also changed. The previous as well as the current values are shown.

Such a configuration history, collected seamlessly and stored in the Oracle repository, is of incredible value during the troubleshooting of production issues since it is possible to see at a glance what has changed at the hardware or operating system level and pinpoint the cause of the production issue. This is very important for root cause analysis.

Back on the Host Configuration Tab (Figure 8.6), click on the Compare Configuration button. This displays the Compare Configurations page (Figure 8.11). In this page, you can select the first configuration you wish to compare.

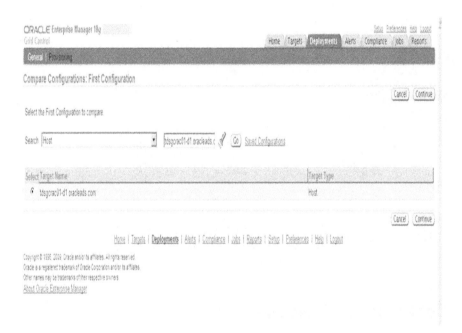

Figure 8.11: *Compare Configurations - First Configuration*

When you select Continue in the next page (Figure 8.12), you can decide on the second configuration to use in the comparison.

Oracle Enterprise Manager Grid Control

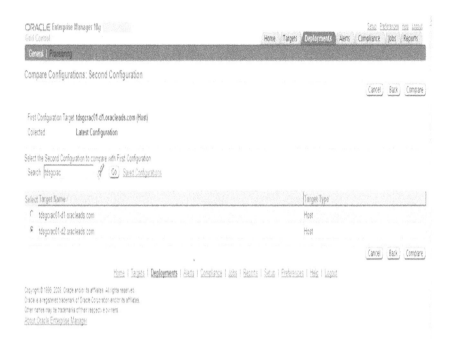

Figure 8.12: *Compare Configurations - Second Configuration*

The process of comparison of the configurations starts, as can be seen in Figure 8.13.

Figure 8.13: *Comparing Selected Configurations*

The Comparison Results Summary now appears (Figure 8.14). This shows the differences between the two servers in terms of the Hardware and Operating System, the Oracle Software differences, and also the OS-Registered software differences.

Figure 8.14: *Comparison Results Summary*

Drilling down on the very first Different link shows the actual differences in Figure 8.15. In particular, you can see that the main difference in the System Details is that the local disk capacity is slightly different between the two servers: one is 14.04 Gb, the other is 14.17 Gb, and such differences are clearly highlighted in red on your screen.

Figure 8.15: *Comparison Results - Hardware*

Going back to the Comparison Results Summary page in Figure 8.14, click on the second Different link. This will show the Operating System software differences (Figure 8.16). The main difference is that the kernel hostname is different, which is expected. This is on the General tab.

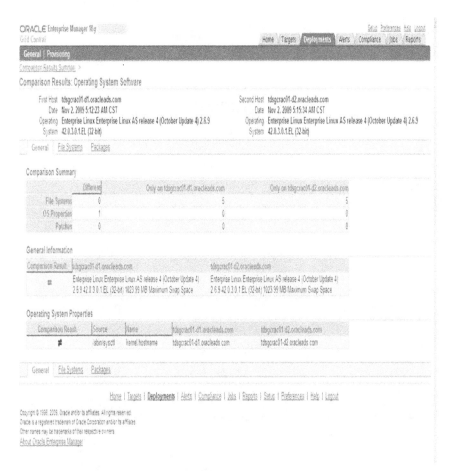

Figure 8.16: *Comparison Results - OS Software..General*

Move to the File Systems tab (Figure 8.17). This shows the differences between the file systems that are mounted on the two servers, and the mount options for each file system are also displayed.

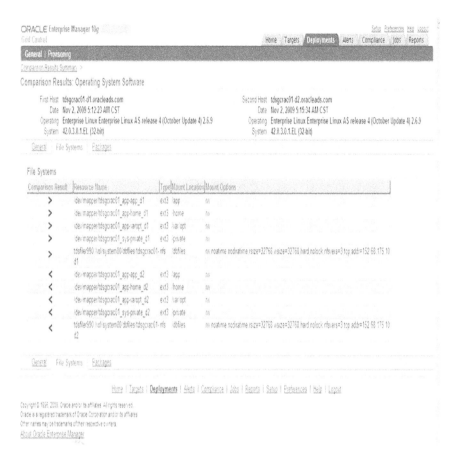

Figure 8.17: *Comparison Results - OS Software..File Systems*

The final tab is the Packages tab, showing the differences in operating system packages between the two servers (Figure 8.18). There are no differences in this case.

Figure 8.18: *Comparison Results - OS Software..Packages*

Going back to the Comparison Results Summary page in Figure 8.16, click on Compare Products. The resulting page (Figure 8.19) displays the Oracle products installed on each server, and you have to select a product from each table to compare.

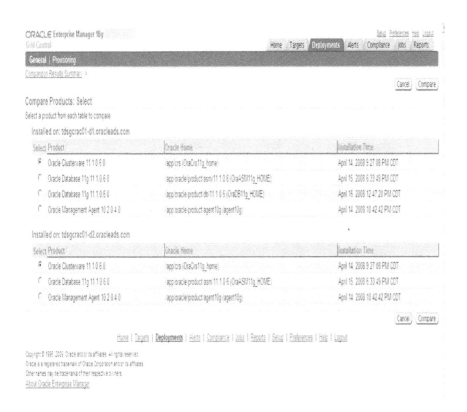

Figure 8.19: *Compare Products - Select*

Comparing two products from the two servers will display the Oracle component differences, the Oracle patch set differences, and the differences in the interim patches on the two servers. This can be demonstrated when trying to compare the Oracle Clusterware product with the Oracle Database product, which shows the numerous different components belonging to the two products (Figure 8.20). As for the patch sets and the interim patches, there are no differences.

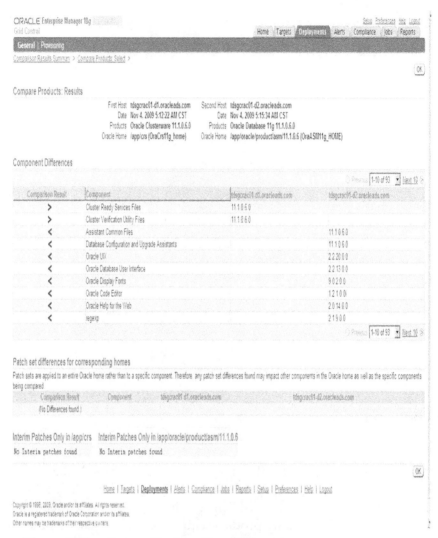

Figure 8.20: *Compare Products..Results*

Obviously, a lot of configuration information is being collected by Grid Control about the hardware and software components in the entire company. This includes the hardware configuration, such as CPU, memory, storage, and network, the OS-level patches and packages, the kernel parameter settings, and the installed Oracle software, i.e. databases and Middleware.

Information about the Oracle patch sets, interim patches, initialization parameters, and configuration settings for both the Oracle database and application server is also collected as well as the Oracle WebLogic Server configuration settings, i.e. the deployed applications, JDBC resources, ports in use, and the resource usage settings. Configuration management solution features are actually covered within three products, and these are all included in the Oracle Enterprise Manager Configuration Pack license as follows:

1. Baseline Configuration management, as provided in Grid Control. This provides integrated configuration management for all the targets monitored, as has been seen in the previous screens.

2. Configuration Change console for real-time change detection. This interacts with change management systems like Remedy to find out if a change was authorized or not authorized.

3. Application Configuration console from the mValent acquisition. This is for application level configuration management.

In fact, more than 30 non-Oracle systems are covered by the Change Management Pack. Next will be a brief review of the Configuration Change console, which provides you with extreme control of all changes.

Extreme Control – Grid Control for Regulators

The Oracle Configuration Management Pack now includes real-time configuration monitoring. There is a separate download available on the OTN Enterprise Manager downloads page: Oracle Configuration Change Console Release 5 (10.2.0.5). You need to download this and install it separately from the main Grid Control install.

The Configuration Change console server is installed on either a Windows or Linux platform, and then the Change Console Agent can be installed on different operating systems like AIX, HP-UX, Solaris, Linux, Windows and OS/400.

What does the Change console do? It provides continuous detection, validation and reporting associated with any authorized and unauthorized configuration change. This kind of change control is in accordance with regulatory and industry standards like Sarbanes-Oxley, PCI and ITIL, which is being implemented today by many organizations.

Real-time configuration change detection and reporting is crucial to these compliance frameworks and is achieved by the Oracle Configuration Change console. This console integrates with change management systems such as Remedy and examines the open Requests For Change in such systems. This enables the Configuration Change console to determine if a detected change was unauthorized or authorized.

Have a look at the Console Dashboard (Figure 8.21). This shows you at a glance the compliance status of the entire company as per out-of-the-box frameworks such as the PCI framework or as per your own defined compliance framework. The PCI DSS standard is the worldwide Payment Card Industry Data Security Standard from the PCI Security Standards Council. The five key policies that make up PCI are displayed on the Dashboard.

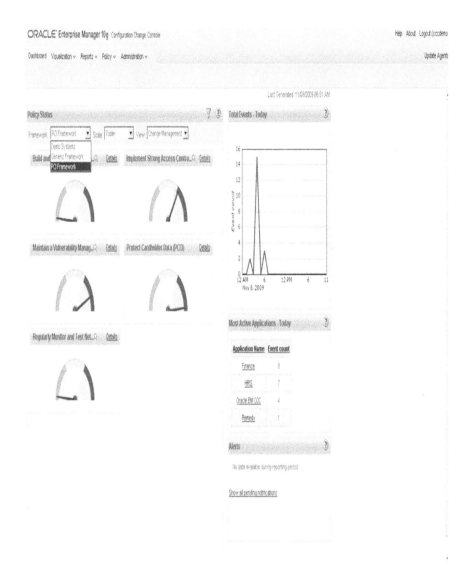

Figure 8.21: *Configuration Change Console Dashboard*

The dials on the page are based on the number of unauthorized changes versus authorized changes. As can be seen, a number of dials appear in red, which means unauthorized changes have occurred. Drill down to the Vulnerability Management Dial to examine the changes. Figure 8.22 is displayed.

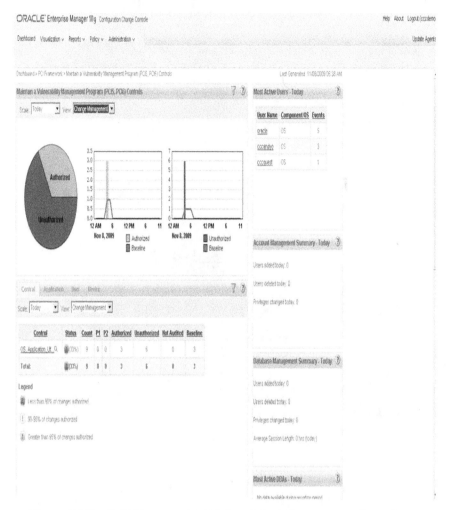

Figure 8.22: *PCI Framework - Vulnerability Management..Control*

The authorized and unauthorized changes under this PCI policy are clearly displayed. The Control tab that is visible shows the OS, Application Utility changes, which are file level changes like the change of file content.

Move to the Application tab (Figure 8.23).

Figure 8.23: *PCI: Vulnerability Management..Application*

In the Application tab in Figure 8.23, you can clearly see the applications such as Finance, HRIS and such, that have had authorized and unauthorized events or changes.

These events have been detected under the PCI Framework's Vulnerability Management program controls.

For further exploration, drill down to the Finance Events. A list of Events is visible (Figure 8.24) that shows changes to the Finance application's configuration, executables, libraries and logs and an event on the sensitive data. The dashboard offers further drill-down capabilities to the actual Event itself. If the Sensitive Data Event is selected, you can now see the details about what happened. This is shown in the smaller-sized Event Details window in Figure 8.24, which is the drill-down window.

The Event Details window shows that the change was actually on the Entity Name FINANCE.CREDITCARDS and the actual Event was selected. This seems serious and a security breach, so the user dba1 can be tracked down. The exact time the event took place is also known.

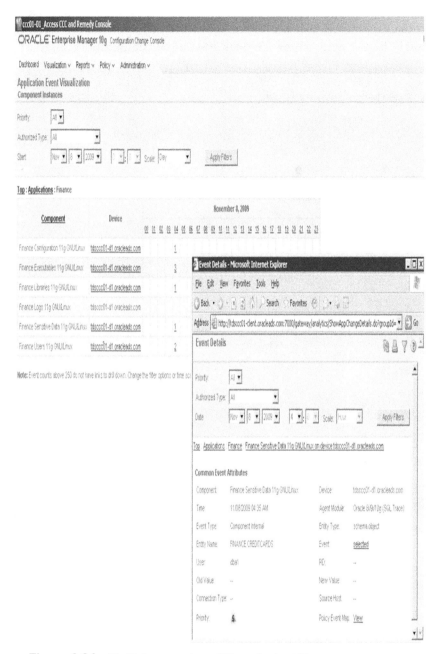

Figure 8.24: *Drill-down to Actual Unauthorized Events*

The Configuration Change console allows you to create custom policies in addition to the predefined policies pertaining to the different frameworks that are displayed in Figure 8.25. There are over 200 out-of-the-box policies.

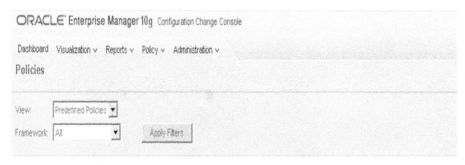

ORACLE Enterprise Manager 10g Configuration Change Console

Dashboard   Visualization ˅   Reports ˅   Policy ˅   Administration ˅

Policies

View: Predefined Policies ▼
Framework: All   ▼   Apply Filters

Framework	Policy	Description	Controls
Generic Framework	Access	View information about login/logout events through...Q	8
PCI Framework	Build and Maintain a Secure Network (PCI...Q	Maintain a secure network by tracking firewall con...Q	2
Generic Framework	Change and Configuration Management	Monitor change management activity associated with...Q	7
Generic Framework	Database	Monitor the activity, events, and users associated...Q	4
Generic Framework	Emergency Change	Identify issues related to emergency tickets. Moni...Q	4
Generic Framework	IT Operations	View data related to backup/restore processes, ava...Q	4
PCI Framework	Implement Strong Access Control Measures...Q	Restrict access to data to authorized individuals	3
PCI Framework	Maintain a Vulnerability Management Prog...Q	Develop and maintain secure systems and applicatio...Q	6
Generic Framework	Network Security	Track activity and configuration changes to firewa...Q	3
PCI Framework	Protect Cardholder Data (PCI3)	Protect cardholder data by tracking encryption and...Q	4
PCI Framework	Regularly Monitor and Test Networks (PCI...Q	Monitor access to network resources	4
Generic Framework	Segregation of Duties	Track individual responsibilities for the change m...Q	1

Create Custom Policy

Figure 8.25: *Predefined Policies for All Frameworks*

Custom policies also have been created for various frameworks, and these are displayed in Figure 8.26.

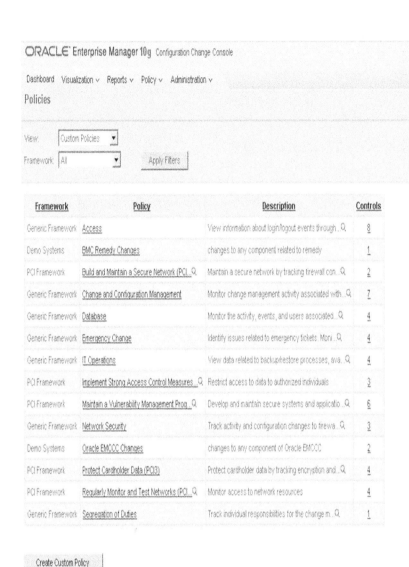

ORACLE Enterprise Manager 10g Configuration Change Console

Dashboard   Visualization ∨   Reports ∨   Policy ∨   Administration ∨

Policies

View: Custom Policies ▼
Framework: All   ▼   Apply Filters

Framework	Policy	Description	Controls
Generic Framework	Access	View information about login/logout events through...	8
Demo Systems	BMC Remedy Changes	changes to any component related to remedy	1
PCI Framework	Build and Maintain a Secure Network (PCI...	Maintain a secure network by tracking firewall con...	2
Generic Framework	Change and Configuration Management	Monitor change management activity associated with...	7
Generic Framework	Database	Monitor the activity, events, and users associated...	4
Generic Framework	Emergency Change	Identify issues related to emergency tickets. Moni...	4
Generic Framework	IT Operations	View data related to backup/restore processes, ava...	4
PCI Framework	Implement Strong Access Control Measures...	Restrict access to data to authorized individuals	3
PCI Framework	Maintain a Vulnerability Management Prog...	Develop and maintain secure systems and applicatio...	6
Generic Framework	Network Security	Track activity and configuration changes to firewa...	3
Demo Systems	Oracle EMCCC Changes	changes to any component of Oracle EMCCC	2
PCI Framework	Protect Cardholder Data (PCI3)	Protect cardholder data by tracking encryption and...	4
PCI Framework	Regularly Monitor and Test Networks (PCI...	Monitor access to network resources	4
Generic Framework	Segregation of Duties	Track individual responsibilities for the change m...	1

Create Custom Policy

Figure 8.26: *Custom Policies for All Frameworks*

The Compliance Dashboard, therefore, offers a view at a glance of how the company systems are complying with best practices, security policies, storage policies, and other user-defined policies.

Data collection is automated; the Configuration Change console detects and captures all actions by users or applications resulting in infrastructure changes. As examples, all these components are monitored continuously for changes: files, directories, processes, databases, networks, user accounts, server resources and so on.

Grid Control for IT Managers

You have seen how Grid Control can benefit database-administering DBAs, UNIX-monitoring system administrators, and troubleshooting DBAs. You also saw how eagle-eyed company regulators concerned with PCI and other compliance frameworks would be keenly interested in the Configuration Management Pack capabilities. Now how about IT managers?

IT managers would be interested in how Grid Control can help them achieve an overall end-to-end corporate view of its infrastructure system, such as the availability of the systems, the database versions in use, Oracle licensing aspects, and the different hardware systems out there in the company. They would like to see the dashboards that display the performance of the application system components as a whole including the databases, listeners, application server instances, hosts, and other components that make up the application in total. If any of these components were to stagger and fall, the entire application system would be affected adversely.

IT managers would also be keenly interested in the proper use or wastage of expensive storage space, and they would appreciate the automation of jobs without scripts, removing much of the dependence on UNIX shell scripts and cron jobs. They would like to see if the security compliance requirements and the SLAs (service level agreements) for the various systems in the company are being achieved, just as the managers of the Oracle Data Centre in Texas do. Oracle itself uses OEM Grid Control to manage its entire data centre, meeting the service level agreements to the various departments throughout Oracle that are using the Centre.

Figure 8.27 displays the OEM Grid Control console. This main screen alone holds a wealth of information for the IT manager. Under the Deployment Summary section on this page, it is possible to select the Hardware, Operating Systems, Database Installations and Application Server Installations in use in the company.

In this figure, the Database Installations have been selected. This shows that Releases 10g through 11g have been installed in the company and patched up to versions like 10.1.0.5, 10.2.0.2 and such. One of the columns in this table even tells whether or not interim patches have been applied. The total number of targets monitored and their availability status is visible at a glance as is the security policy violations count and the Critical Patch Advisories that have been provided by Oracle for the Oracle Homes.

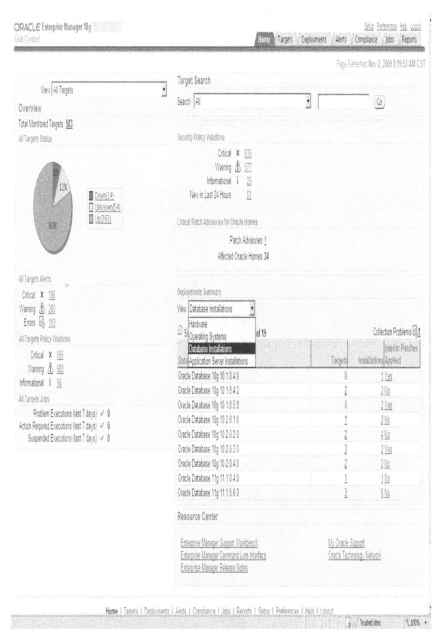

Figure 8.27: *Deployments Summary..Database Installations*

If now you select the Operating Systems from the list, Figure 8.28 is seen displaying all the operating systems in use throughout the company. You can see Oracle Enterprise Linux in use as well as Red Hat's version, SUSE Linux, and Microsoft Windows installations.

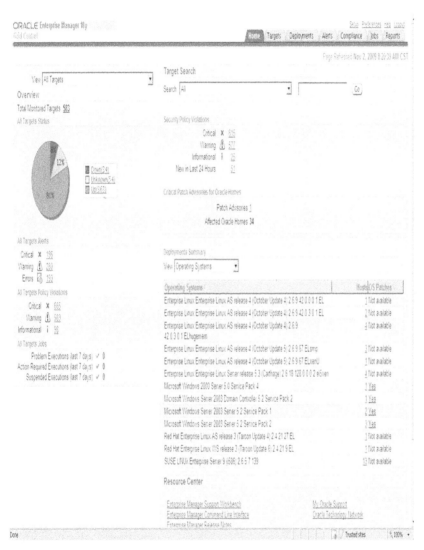

Figure 8.28: *Deployments Summary..Operating Systems*

Now move to the Targets tab in Grid Control, and then select Groups. The screen (Figure 8.29) shows the various target groups that have been defined in Grid Control.

Figure 8.29: *Targets..Groups*

Select one of the groups, such as the DB Mixed Group. The Group Home Page appears (Figure 8.30). This shows the information about all the group targets as a whole including the uptime and the policy violations.

Figure 8.30: *Group Home Page*

Click on the interesting-looking Launch Dashboard button. This launches the Group Dashboard (Figure 8.31).

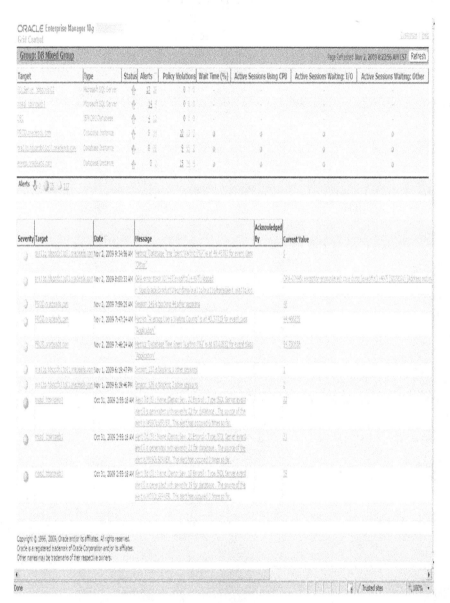

Figure 8.31: *Group Dashboard Launched*

This shows that the Group Dashboard gives a clear view of the targets in the group, showing their status, alerts, policy violations, wait time (%), and other performance indicators. The alerts that have been raised for any of the targets in the group are shown below the screen.

This would be very useful to understand the status and performance of an entire application system: simply place all the application components together in a target group, and you can monitor the full system on one Dashboard page as can be seen on Figure 8.31. Very informative for the IT manager.

Real User Experience Insight (RUEI)

Oracle also has other performance dashboard products such as Real User Experience Insight (RUEI), an acquired product; Oracle's strategy being to buy the best of breed. This can perform a powerful analysis of your network and business application infrastructure and allows you to monitor the real user experience.

The product is built using state-of-the-art Network Protocol Analysis (NPA) technology. This is 100% accurate and data collection is 100% non-intrusive with no impact on the web application performance. The RUEI data collector is simply plugged into a network switch.

Using RUEI does not require any modification or changes to the web applications since it has a passive monitoring approach. There are various accelerators available, which are out-of-the-box real user monitoring solutions for applications such as Oracle E-Business, PeopleSoft, and Siebel. RUEI allows you to define the Key Performance Indicators (KPIs) and Service Level Agreements (SLAs) of the business. The Executive Dashboard (Figure 8.32) displays at a glance the KPIs of the organization and whether they have been met.

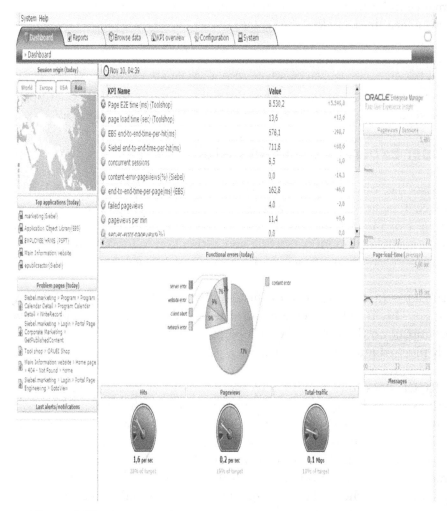

Figure 8.32: *Real User Experience Insight (RUEI) Dashboard*

Problem Pages and alerts/notifications, if any, can also be seen on this main page of the Dashboard. Moving now to the KPI Overview page (Figure 8.33), the management gets a further detailed overview of which KPIs have been met and which ones have not been met.

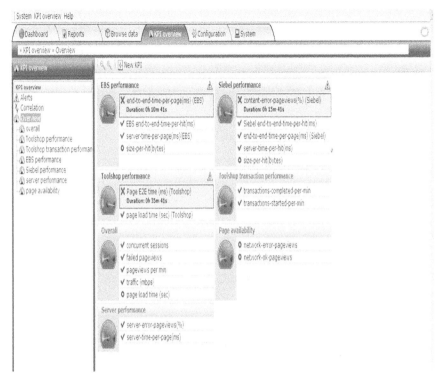

Figure 8.33: *RUEI KPI Overview*

This information can also be seen under the Reports tab where you can select the KPI Overview report after selecting the range of dates in a graphical calendar (Figure 8.34). The report vividly shows the percentage of KPI success.

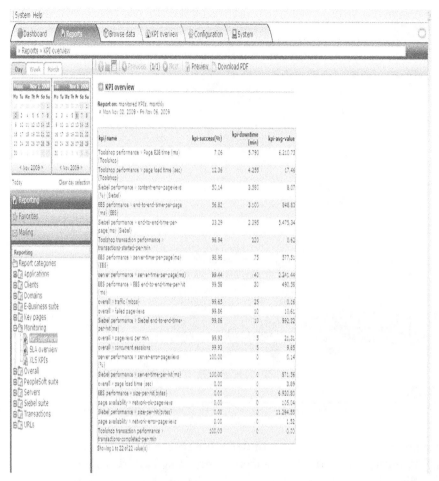

Figure 8.34: *RUEI Reports..KPI Overview*

Now move from RUEI back to the Grid Control console. Go to the Compliance tab on the console, where it is possible to search for all the policy violations on any kind of target. In this case, a search has been done for all such violations on Cluster Database targets, and a list of violations immediately appears (Figure 8.35).

Figure 8.35: *Compliance..Policies - Violations for Cluster DB*

As can be seen in the list, the violations are mainly security based, such as the presence of restricted privileges, the grant of unlimited tablespace quota, and so on. These policies are based on an out-of-the-box Policy Library (Figure 8.36) that contains supplied policies on security, configuration and storage.

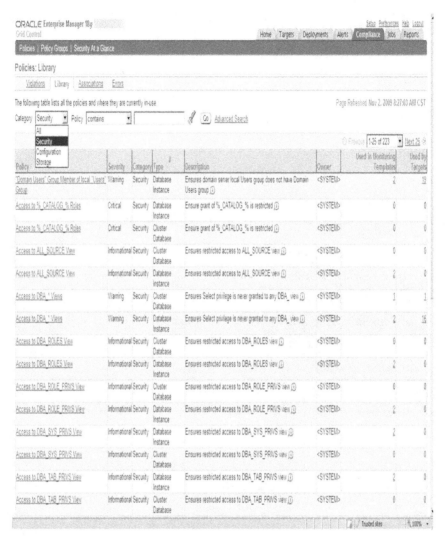

Figure 8.36: *Compliance..Policies - Library*

Any one of these policies is only deemed to be compliant if none of the managed targets violate it. If a policy has one or more policy violations, it is considered to be non-compliant. On detection of a policy violation in any target, OEM Grid Control allows you to optionally specify an action to bring the target back into compliance via a corrective action. This can be defined as a special job to automatically make the correction whenever there is a violation of the specific policy.

In addition to the out-of-the-box policies seen in the Policy Library (Figure 8.36), you can define your own company-specific policies which can enforce the standards in the company. There is a Create Policy wizard, accessed via the Create button on the Policies..Library page, that enables you to do this very easily.

This again is a tremendous help to IT management for the adoption and enforcement of standards across the company. It is possible now for any company to create policies to fulfill the demands of security compliance and audit compliance. The user-defined policies can be mapped by the company to governance controls and standards such as Sarbanes-Oxley, COBIT and ISO. Thus, it follows that the company's ability to meet regulatory requirements, adopt best practices, and follow industry standards is considerably enhanced. All this due to the Oracle Enterprise Manager Configuration Management Pack.

Monitoring Entire Systems and Services

On the Targets tab, OEM Grid Control allows you to define new systems as well as services. A system is a grouping of infrastructure targets such as hosts, databases, listeners, application servers and so on. The application that runs on this system, like a finance application, is defined as a service.

Move to Targets..Service and select one of the services. The Service Home Page appears (Figure 8.37), which shows the overall status of the service, the performance and usage, and the status of its individual components. You can also add Key Tests that define the availability of your service.

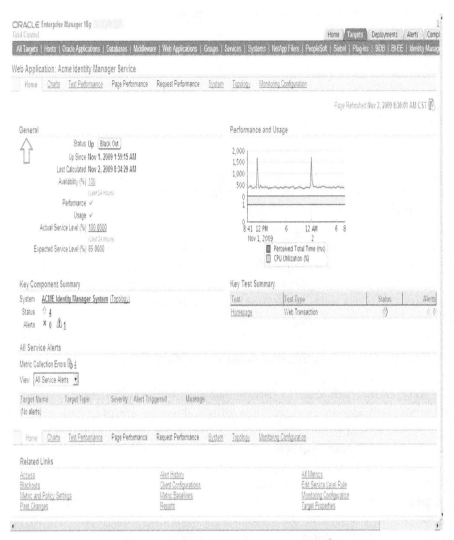

Figure 8.37: *Targets..Service Home Page*

In any system, it is possible to define associations between its components that show a relationship between them; for example, between a database and listener. These associations are displayed in the topology viewer, which can be seen on the Topology tab (Figure 8.38) of the service or system.

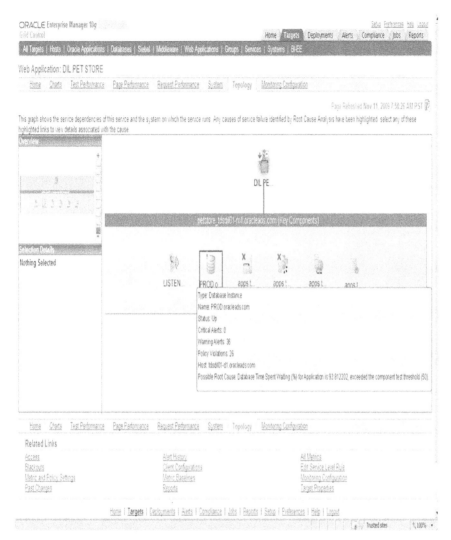

Figure 8.38: *Targets..Service Topology*

Root Cause Analysis (RCA)

Figure 8.38 exhibits that the selected service DIL PET STORE (colored in red on your screen) is down, and the cause of the service failure has been identified by the Root Cause Analysis feature to be the database instance component of the service. This component is highlighted with a red box and when you move your mouse pointer to this box, a floating message appears. The message explains that the possible root cause of the service failure is that the database time spent waiting for the application was above 93%, and this has exceeded the component test threshold of 50%.

Root Cause Analysis is obviously a powerful feature in OEM Grid Control which automatically examines service failures and looks at the metric data of all the components in the service, such as each component's availability, performance and configuration details. It then helps to eliminate any side effects or symptoms of the real root cause of the issue. For example, a database service may appear to be down, but this may be due to its listener not accepting requests rather than the database instance itself which may be up and running.

Without Root Cause Analysis, the trouble-shooting DBA would have to manually check every component of the service to determine which one was actually the cause of the service being down. This would be especially troublesome in complex cases. So using Root Cause Analysis would actually allow a much faster identification of the cause, followed by a resolution of the issue.

In the case of a service which is down, the Root Cause Analysis results are also displayed prominently on the Service Home Page, as can be seen in Figure 8.39.

Figure 8.39: *Root Cause Analysis on Service Home Page*

It is possible to drill down on the Root Cause Analysis Details link on this page to see the actual detailed analysis steps, examining the key components of the service one by one, and their component tests, in an attempt to analyze the root cause of the failure in a logical manner.

A good use of Root Cause Analysis would be to determine the issues for complex aggregate services which are combinations of services with a large number of hardware, software and network components. This may include non-Oracle targets which can also be identified as the root cause by this process. This is indeed a feature that could be very useful to the IT management: to know immediately what went wrong and to ensure that it is fixed as soon as possible.

Service Level Agreements (SLAs)

Perhaps the most nagging question in the minds of IT management is how to efficiently manage and monitor the Service Level Agreements (SLAs) in force in the company. A SLA is an important agreement of a particular level of service between the customer and the service provider. This agreement states the service standards, such as level of availability and the performance of the service, that the service provider has promised to provide to the customer.

This may happen for external customers, or it may be so for internal customers, with the IT department in the company taking on the role of the service provider to its internal consumers. But whether it be for internal or external customers, if the SLAs in force are not met, there may be financial, and in extreme cases, legal repercussions to the service provider. Hence, tracking these SLAs is a top priority for IT management.

How do you manage and monitor the SLAs? The process of managing service levels is known as Service Level Management (SLM) by setting service goals, measuring these service goals, and ensuring their maintenance. Happily, the task of managing the company-wide service levels is made a lot easier by OEM Grid Control.

This is achieved by the service level rules that can be set at the Service Home page, as seen in Figure 8.37 in an earlier section in this chapter.
In these service level rules, you can specify an expected percentage which is known as the expected service level. Then the availability or non-availability of the service over time for the agreed business hours/days and the performance achievements or non-achievements during this period are used to compute the achieved Actual Service Level seen on the Service Home page.

To drill deeper into the service level rule, click on the link on the Actual Service Level figure, in this case 100%. The page that appears shows the Service Level Details (Figure 8.40). This page shows that there are no service level issues for this service. There are also no performance issues, and there has been no blackout of the service for scheduled maintenance. The Business Hours/Days are also seen to be 24 by 7, and the expected service level is 85%.

Figure 8.40: *Service Level Details*

Click on the Edit Service Level Rule button on this page. This displays Figure 8.41 where you can edit the rule.

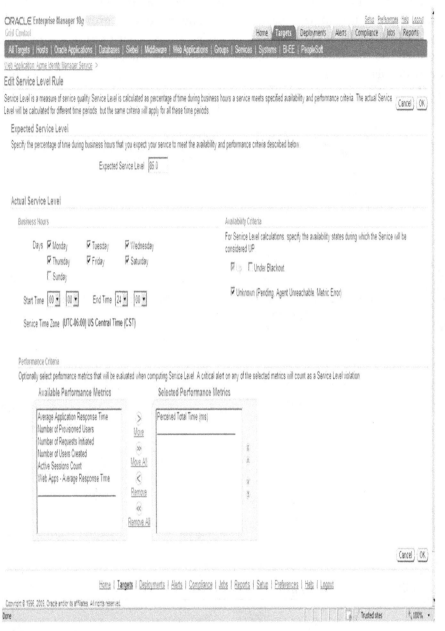

Figure 8.41: *Edit Service Level Rule*

On this page, you can set the expected service level and the business hours/days for the availability of the service to 24/7 or perhaps only 5 days a week, 9 to 5 as per the service level requirements.

You can choose to include or exclude the under blackout time (scheduled maintenance) from the calculation of the total availability. Likewise, you can also include or exclude the unknown states of the service, i.e. if the service was in a pending state (Agent information not yet uploaded), the Agent was unreachable for some reason, or if there was a metric error during the gathering of the metrics by OEM.

Performance metrics can also be selected from a list of available metrics. These metrics have warning and critical thresholds that can be set. The performance metrics are then used for the monitoring of the service. This is the method by which the SLAs are defined in OEM Grid Control. The SLA is defined by the expected service level percentage and the business hours/days to be in effect; for example, 99% service availability for 24/7. The SLA can then be enhanced with performance metric objectives. These are all used to calculate the actual service level.

For example, if a critical threshold is reached in any of the performance figures, then the calculation of the actual service level would be adversely effected. In the end the desired service level would not be achieved, thereby resulting in a violation of the Service Level Agreement (SLA).

Thus, as can be seen, OEM Grid Control offers a comprehensive solution for managing and monitoring the SLAs in force in the organization, and this is definitely a boon to IT management who now have a complete record of their SLA meets and failures, all such events being recorded in the OEM Repository.

Reports That Save Money

It is well known that, traditionally, projects have always insisted on huge SAN allocations of disk space to be on the safe side for future growth, and that DBAs managing the databases in the project have followed this up by pre-allocating their tablespaces. While this is practical thinking for the DBA world, i.e. get whatever space you can for it may not be there tomorrow, it actually leads to a lot of space wastage. SAN disk space is extremely expensive, and this has led to millions of dollars of extra SAN costs per year in large corporate sites. Consequently, IT management worries a lot about future budgets and escalating SAN costs.

The same managers would be very glad to know that Grid Control supplies out-of-the-box reports to monitor the database space usage across any database in the company, and potentially nip such issues in the bid. One example is the Database Tablespace Monthly Space Usage report (Figure 8.42) that shows the allocated space, the used space and the free space in GB with the total used percentage and as a monthly cumulative. This helps in understanding if space has been over allocated in any database; for example, this would be indicated if the used percentage was consistently seen as only 25% or below in all the tablespaces.

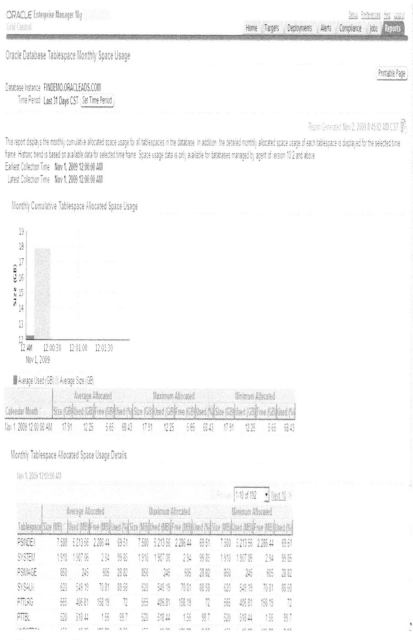

Figure 8.42: *Reports..DB Tablespace Monthly Space Usage*

Another interesting report for IT management (C-Level or below) would be the Services Monitoring Dashboard report. This is seen in Figure 8.43 where you can select any service to include in the report.

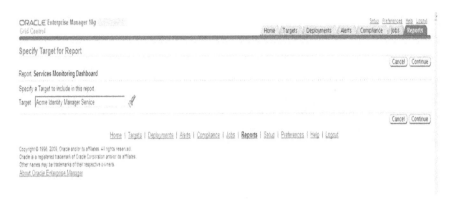

Figure 8.43: *Report..Services Monitoring Dashboard..Specify*

The Dashboard report then appears as in Figure 8.44. The report provides at a glance the service performance, the usage and business indicators, and also the service levels in the previous 24 hours, 17 days and 31 days. This tells you immediately if the service levels are being met. In this case, it is 100% and is excellent proof of having met the SLAs and can be provided to the customer.

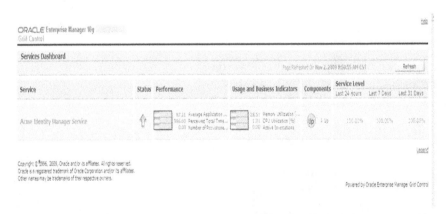

Figure 8.44: *Report..Services Monitoring Dashboard Example 1*

Another example of the Services Monitoring Dashboard report is seen in Figure 8.45 where an aggregate service is seen showing the service levels of its component services. In this case, you can notice at once that one of the services, the Acme OAM Identity service, has not met its service levels in the last 31 days, and this would be a further cause for investigation.

Figure 8.45: *Report..Services Monitoring Dashboard Example 2*

Another useful report for IT management is the Compliance Evaluation (Group) report. As the name suggests, this works with a target group and displays the non-compliance of any target in the group, the compliance score and also the summary of the Violated Rules as seen in Figure 8.46.

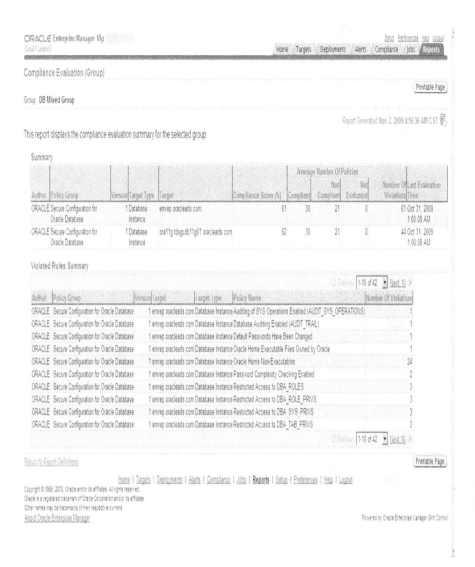

Figure 8.46: *Reports..Compliance Evaluation (Group)*

And finally, the Security Policy Compliance report (Figure 8.47) is a master report that charts the security policy compliance score of all targets against time for any time period that you can set using the button Set Time Period seen on the report page. In this case, you can see that the compliance score percentage is only 70% across all targets in the selected period.

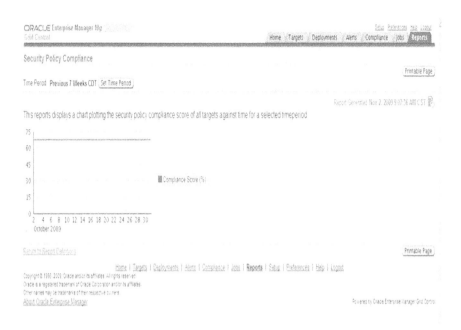

Figure 8.47: *Reports..Security Policy Compliance*

Public Access to Enterprise Manager Reports

Whatever interesting reports that may have been seen in the previous section, such as the Service Dashboard reports or the Compliance reports, can easily be made available to IT management without having them log in to OEM Grid Control.

The reports are then known as public access reports, and they are accessed directly via the Oracle Enterprise Manager Reports website, which is automatically set up on the following URL after any installation of Grid Control:

```
http://<Grid Control Server Host Name>:<Port Used>/em/public/reports
```

Allowing public access to an OEM report is easy enough. When creating or editing a report definition, simply click "Allow viewing without logging into

Enterprise Manager" on the Access page. However, note that this is only visible to OEM Administrators with a special system privilege so that confidential reports can be protected and not placed without due authorization on the publicly accessible reports website.

There are only two other factors to remember when allowing public access to the reports. First, make sure that a specific target is predefined in the report rather than allowing users to select targets at the time the report is executed. This is because public access reports do not allow selection of the targets at the time the report is executed since these reports do not log in to Enterprise Manager.

Secondly, the public access reports do not allow drill-downs, so they cannot be used to move down to the actual target pages. If you want to use the drill-down facility, the report must be executed inside OEM after logging in.

It is also possible to schedule these public access reports to be generated automatically and not on an adhoc basis by the consumer so as to place less strain on the OEM system. The generated reports are accessible on the Reports website at any point of time since they are public access reports.

Enterprise Manager Management Packs

In the course of this book, some special features of Oracle Enterprise Manager Grid Control have been examined and, at those times, the particular OEM Management Packs required were briefly mentioned so that those features could be used.

These packs deal with the database as well as Middleware. Note that the database-level packs are available only for the Enterprise Edition (EE) of the database and not the Standard Edition (SE). This is intentional because the Standard Edition does not have the licensed capabilities to support the technical aspects of the database-level packs.

A brief review of the packs are given which have proven to be more commonly used, but each pack will not be explained in detail since there are technical datasheets available for each of these packs on the Oracle Technology Network (OTN).

The first look is at the most popular duo, the Diagnostics and Tuning Packs, which have everything to do with performance.

Diagnostics and Tuning Packs

The Diagnostics Pack for databases offers automatic performance diagnostics and monitoring capabilities as an integral part of the core database engine, such as the Automatic Workload Repository (AWR), Active Session History (ASH), and the self-diagnostic engine called Automatic Database Diagnostic Monitor (ADDM). The latter can even perform clusterwide performance analysis in an Oracle 11g Real Application Cluster (RAC) database. The Diagnostics Pack also offers system monitoring of the instance and host operating system, alerts and notifications.

The pack is licensed separately as the Diagnostics Pack for Oracle Middleware, which manages and monitors any number of Oracle WebLogic server domains and Oracle Application Server farms, and assists in Java Virtual Machine (JVM) monitoring and Java application diagnostics. There is also the Diagnostics Pack for Non-Oracle Middleware to cater to other application servers.

Along with the Diagnostics Pack, the Tuning Pack for databases is the other most popular pack. It requires the former as a prerequisite. This pack offers automatic SQL Tuning with features such as the SQL Tuning Advisor, SQL Access Advisor, SQL Tuning Sets and Real-Time SQL Monitoring along with a useful Object Reorganization wizard.

Among these, the SQL Tuning Advisor is able to perform statistics analysis (find objects with stale or missing statistics), access path analysis (find possibilities for new indexes), SQL structure analysis (suggest restructuring of some SQL statements), and also SQL Profiling. The latter feature was introduced in 10g and enables tuning of SQL statements without changing the application code, and as such would be of great benefit to tune the SQL in packaged or vendor applications where the code cannot be changed easily.

An important matter to note at this point is that the 10g/11g utilities such as AWR, ASH, ADDM, and the numerous SQL Advisors also have a command line interface. Some people are under the wrong impression that if OEM is not used, these utilities are free. Not really since any use of these utilities at the

---

SQL command line on any production or test database requires you to be licensed to use the OEM Tuning and Diagnostic Packs because it means you are accessing and using the APIs of these Diagnostics and Tuning Pack features. The license is, therefore, required regardless of the access mechanism.

Finding Performance Issues Quickly

Now examine how the Diagnostics Pack can help solve a database issue fast and easy with a minimum of fuss. Say there is an important production database that is behaving badly and the users are complaining of poor response time from the database. The application manager rings up the DBA and asks them to investigate the performance degradation.

The DBA takes a quick look at the Database Performance page in Grid Control and immediately realizes there is a huge spike in application waits (the red-colored part of the Average Active Sessions graph in Figure 8.48).

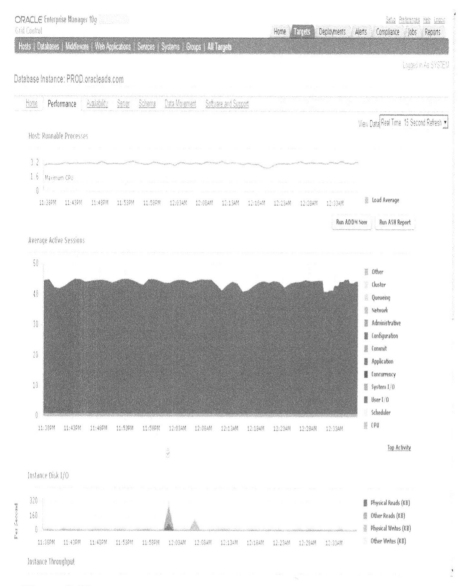

Figure 8.48: *Database..Performance: Application Waits Spike*

The DBA drills-down on this spike and Figure 8.49 appears, showing that most of the application waits are *enq: TX - row lock contention* waits. The shaded area of the graph can be dragged across the time line with the mouse. As this area is moved, the corresponding Sessions and SQL statements appear below.

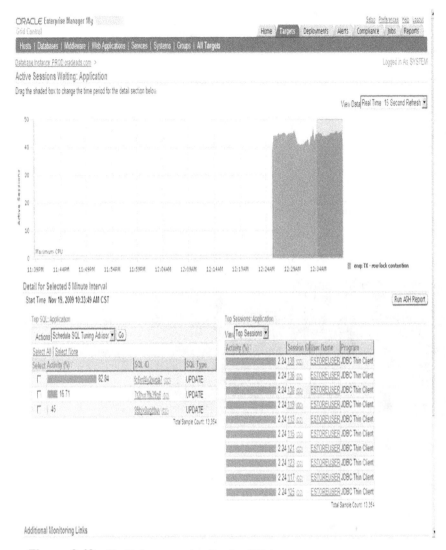

Figure 8.49: *Drill-down on Application Waits*

You can click on the SQL ID in the Top SQL: Application list in Figure 8.49. This displays the actual SQL that is causing the issue, and the sessions that are all issuing this SQL (Figure 8.50).

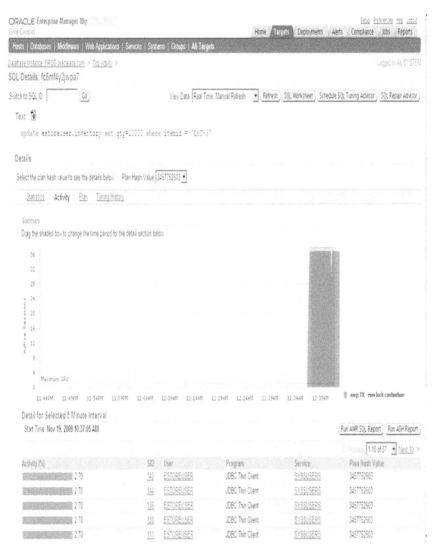

Figure 8.50: *SQL Details Pertaining to the SQL ID*

From the performance page and drill-downs, the issue has been identified to be row lock contention and also found the SQL statement responsible. Now see what ADDM says. On the Database Home page, click Advisor Central under Related Links. On this page (Figure 8.51), ADDM and the different advisors available can be seen and also the ADDM auto runs.

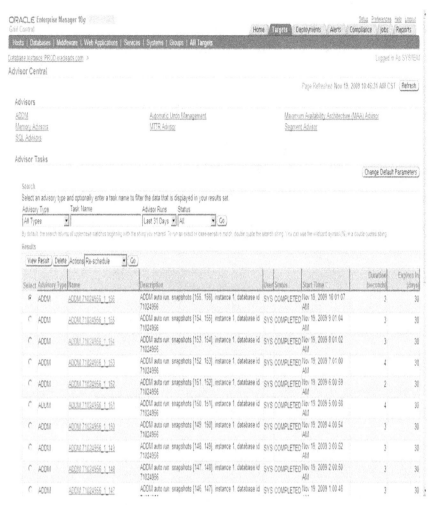

Figure 8.51: *Advisor Central Page*

Click on the most recent ADDM auto run. This brings up the ADDM Findings page (Figure 8.52). As this shows, ADDM has discovered a number of issues which are listed in the ADDM Performance Analysis section. One of the findings in the list is about *row lock* waits and another finding is about hard parses.

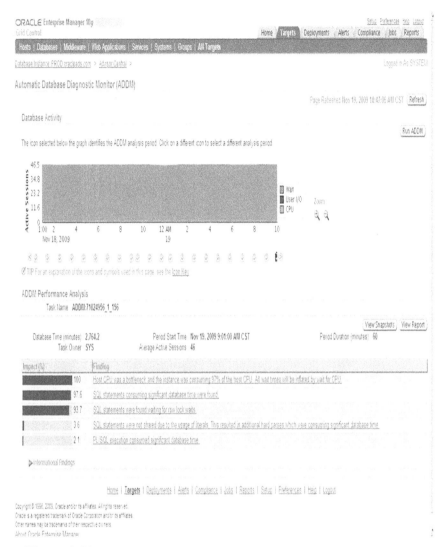

Figure 8.52: *ADDM Auto Run Findings Page*

Drill-down on the finding about the *row lock* waits. This brings up the ADDM Performance Finding Details page (Figure 8.53) that identifies the actual table object with significant row contention and the list of SQL statements that are all blocked on row locks. The recommendation is to check the application logic.

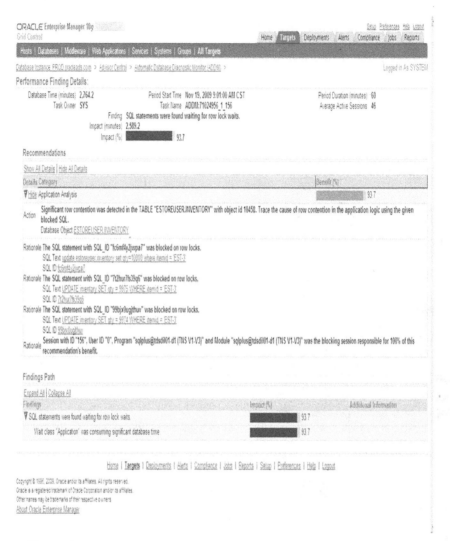

Figure 8.53: *ADDM Performance Finding Details - Row Locks*

Again from the ADDM Findings page (Figure 8.52), drill-down on the finding about the hard parsing. The Finding Details page that is displayed recommends two possible actions; either use bind variables in the application logic instead of literals, or you can set the parameter *cursor_sharing* to *force* (Figure 8.54).

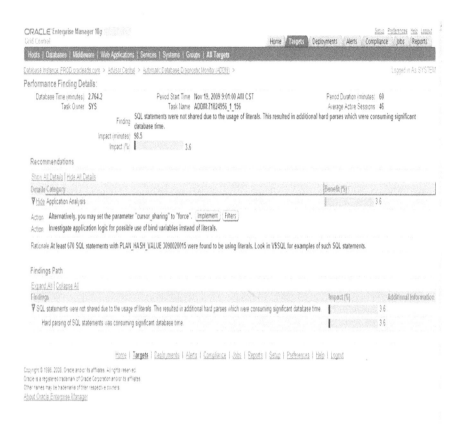

Figure 8.54: *ADDM Performance Finding Details - Hard Parses*

It is now known that the application may need to change, but the row lock issue has to be resolved immediately. So, move back to the Database Performance page. On that page under the Additional Monitoring Links section, click on Blocking Sessions. This brings up the list of blocking sessions, if any, in the current database instance (Figure 8.55). It appears that Session Id 156, username SYS, is blocking 44 sessions.

Enterprise Manager Management Packs **373**

Figure 8.55: *Additional Monitoring Links..Blocking Sessions*

Go ahead and kill Session ID 156 using the Kill Session button.

The session is marked for a kill. Refreshing the same screen again after a few seconds by using the Refresh button shows that there are no more blocking/blocked sessions in the database instance. The Database Performance page starts to show a dramatic drop-off in application waits as well as the load average (Figure 8.56).

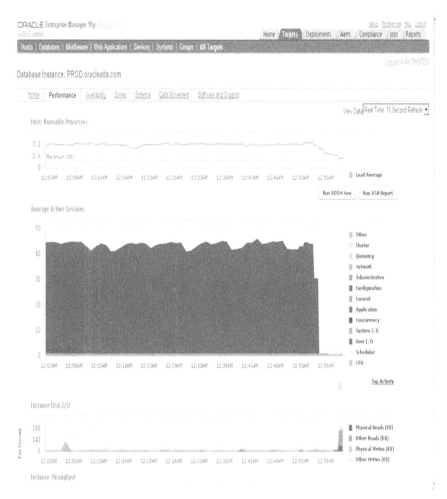

Figure 8.56: *Database Performance - End of Spike*

Drilling-down again to the Application Waits page shows that the *enq: TX - row lock contention* waits have also disappeared for the current part of the graph (Figure 8.57). The crisis is over! OEM Grid Control and its packs have greatly assisted in this scenario to find a quick diagnosis and solution.

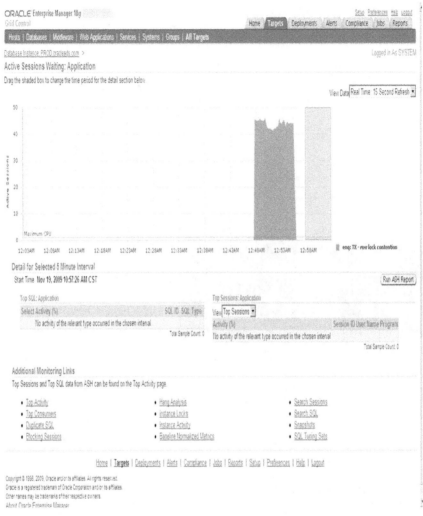

Figure 8.57: *No More Application Waits*

The New Real-Time SQL Monitoring

Real-Time SQL monitoring was introduced for 11g databases and allows you to track the details of SQL execution of long-running SQL statements, meaning five seconds or more or using parallel execution, so you know exactly what is happening. This is a very useful feature for those long-running batch jobs which appear to be frozen, but in reality may be running extremely slowly. Do not kill these jobs until you know the facts.

This new feature can be accessed via the SQL Monitoring link under the Additional Monitoring Links section on the Database Instance Performance page in Grid Control 10g Release 5. In Grid Control 10g, the link only appears for an 11g database target. The feature is, of course, also accessible in Database Control 11g, which would work only on 11g databases.

Selecting the SQL Monitoring link brings up the Monitored SQL Executions page (Figure 8.58). The SQL statements that have completed execution are marked with a tick mark, and the ones with the circular rotating icon are currently being executed. You can change the page refresh to be as low as five seconds or refresh manually.

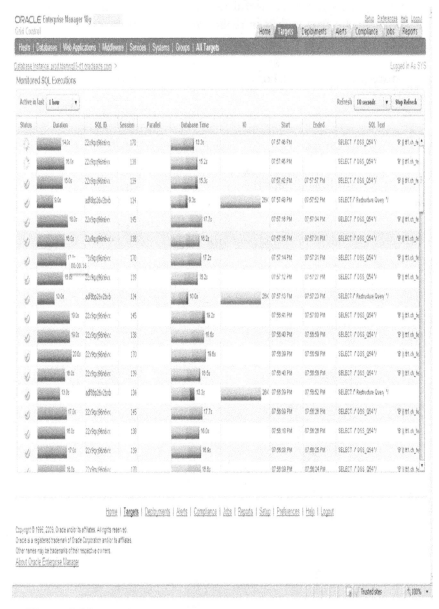

Figure 8.58: *Monitored SQL Executions*

Drill-down on any of the SQL ID links. This displays the Monitored SQL Execution Details page (Figure 8.59). This shows the actual steps of the execution plan and the time taken for each step. This particular SQL statement shown in Figure 8.59 has completed successfully as is indicated by the tick mark.

Figure 8.59: *Monitored SQL Execution Details*

If the SQL statement is currently in progress, as indicated by the circular rotating icon at the top, then the Monitored SQL Execution Details page is also refreshed automatically and shows the actual running steps in the execution plan (Figure 8.60).

Figure 8.60: *Monitored SQL Execution Details in Progress*

In the Plan Statistics section in Figure 8.60, the currently executing steps are indicated by green-colored arrows which change dynamically as per the refresh interval. As and when the columns such as Actual Rows, Memory, and Temp (temporary tablespace space used) are refreshed with the latest data, they are shaded momentarily in green.

Now it is really possible to know where we are in the execution plan. This is an excellent feature for real-life situations with long-running reports and queries where the question asked often by management is: What is our situation?

As can be seen, this is a SQL statement that is using a parallel degree of three, and the Parallel Query Coordinator can be seen in the execution plan. The current executing steps also show the parallel slave processes in action. Besides, a small worker icon, signifying the slave, indicates which of the steps are related to parallel query execution.

Notice that a new Parallel tab is visible on this page in the case of this statement since it is using parallel query. The Parallel tab was not visible in the previous Figure 8.59, where there was a statement that was not using Parallel Query. Select the Parallel tab. This shows the actual working and progress of the parallel query coordinator and each parallel server process (Figure 8.61).

Figure 8.61: *Monitored SQL Execution Details - Parallel Tab*

Provisioning and Patch Automation Pack

Now you come to the Provisioning and Patch Automation Pack. This pack is used for deployment of software, applications and patches. You can provision the entire software stack including the OS, Middleware, Oracle Home and even Oracle single-instance and clustered databases by using the concept of the Software Image Library, patched and standardized Gold images and the use of cloning. Bare Metal Provisioning of the Linux OS is possible via a standardized PXE (Preboot Execution Environment) booting process.

After provisioning, you can also use the pack to patch your single-instance and clustered databases very efficiently, and you can also patch your Automatic Storage Management (ASM) installations as well as the Oracle Clusterware. This is done using highly sophisticated and customizable deployment procedures. How to use these procedures in detail has been covered in Chapter 6 in this book. Operating systems can also be patched. This includes Linux, Solaris and Windows.

The Provisioning and Patch Automation Pack includes the Critical Patch Facility which keeps you aware of what Oracle Homes need to be patched with the latest Critical Patch Updates (CPUs) released by My Oracle Support (formerly Oracle Metalink). This can be done either via a direct connection to the Oracle internet site or in an offline upload mode.

Configuration Management Pack

The Configuration Management Pack is available in two flavors: for Oracle databases and for applications. Together, these enable you to capture and centralize configuration information about all the IT resources in the company, provided they have been added to the OEM repository.

The Configuration Management Pack for databases captures changes on the Oracle database, host and operating system. It allows historical change tracking and configuration comparisons between different systems or as compared to a Gold configuration. This helps you to find out what has changed in the configuration and what exact time the change has taken place; therefore, greatly assisting in troubleshooting when some system has stopped working.

The pack includes real-time configuration monitoring via the Configuration Change console which provides continuous detection, validation and reporting of any authorized and unauthorized configuration change. This allows the company to be fully compliant with regulatory standards like Sarbanes-Oxley, PCI and ITIL. These compliance frameworks require continuous change detection and reporting.

The Configuration Management Pack for applications was acquired by Oracle from mValent and offers the Application Configuration console that is used for application level configuration management. This is for all Oracle and non-Oracle software except the Oracle database, which is covered by the related Pack for databases. You can do everything that you could in the latter such as configuration comparisons, change history, real-time change tracking, and configuration compliance, and in this case, it is for all the software on your systems.

Since August 2010, the Configuration Management Pack for applications has been combined into the new Oracle Application Management Suites that will be explained later on in this chapter.

Change Management Pack

The Change Management Pack for databases is used to automate the deployment of planned schema-level changes from development to production. A dictionary baseline is used to capture the schema (metadata) definitions and such a baseline can be propagated easily to any target database. The pack enables you to compare the metadata definitions and track production changes in a single database including initialization parameter changes, new indexes or changes in PL/SQL code like packages, procedures and functions.

If the *enable_ddl_logging* parameter is set to TRUE in 11g, then schema changes can be tracked in real time. Wrong changes can then be corrected easily by regenerating the corresponding database objects from the dictionary baseline. You can easily reverse-engineer the database and schema definitions, capture and version baselines, and compare databases and schemas or baselines. It is also possible to copy database objects with no data, full data, or a subset of data, and modify objects on multiple databases.

One of the most useful features of the Change Management for databases is the impact analysis it can perform. If an application upgrade takes place on a test system, the pack will automatically identify all dictionary changes; therefore, you can know which part of the application upgrade is causing the most impact. Then that part of the application can be thoroughly tested.

On the other hand, the Change Management Pack for applications deals with the Oracle E-Business suite and helps to manage E-Business customizations by bundling them into patches. This pack also assists in the automation of the application of patches on E-Business and has a setup manager for creating projects of extracts to aid in deployment.

Since August 2010, the Change Management Pack for applications has been combined with the Oracle Application Management Suite for E-Business. This will be examined in a later section in this chapter.

Data Masking Pack

The Data Masking Pack enables centralized masking of confidential data in test and development databases or databases supplied to external vendors and third parties. The masking is defined using out-of-the-box masking formats via the OEM console, thereby storing all masking information centrally and not in the dispersed and manual scripts that were traditionally used.

Condition-based masking is possible. The process is irreversible, and it replaces the confidential data with scrubbed but realistic-looking data using masking rules. Database integrity rules are also followed when the masking process takes place.

When the database is cloned from production using OEM, the masking can be executed as an integrated part of the cloning process, or it can be run independently. This helps in complying with privacy and personal information laws such as Sarbanes-Oxley (SOX) and the Payment Card Industry Data Security Standard (PCIDSS).

There is also a very useful search function that allows you to query the data dictionary of any database and identify the tables and columns that need to be masked since they may be carrying confidential data.

Other Management Packs

The Oracle Linux Management Pack is available exclusively for Oracle Unbreakable Linux Basic or Premier support customers at no additional licensing cost. The Pack allows Bare Metal Provisioning and patching of the Linux operating system as well as monitoring of the servers and their administration. A standardized PXE (Preboot Execution Environment) booting process technique is used to achieve this.

The Oracle VM Management Pack allows management of virtualized environments using Oracle VM including the availability and performance monitoring of the virtual machines and configuration management of these machines. Provisioning of virtual machines from a software library of Oracle VM templates, live migration of guest machines to other servers for maintenance activities, and patching of these machines is also possible via the VM Management Pack.

Oracle Real User Experience Insight (RUEI), built using state-of-the-art Network Protocol Analysis (NPA) technology, can be used to perform a powerful analysis of your network and business application infrastructure, allowing you to monitor the real user experience using a passive monitoring approach. No modification, changes, or instrumentation of the application are required to achieve this monitoring.

Special Oracle RUEI accelerators are currently available for Oracle Peoplesoft, Oracle E-Business Suite, Oracle Siebel, and Oracle JD Edwards EnterpriseOne. With these accelerators, out-of-the-box monitoring and real user experience insight are provided specifically for these packaged applications.

In Release 1 of Oracle Enterprise Manager 11g Grid Control, Oracle has included the new 6.5 version of Oracle RUEI. This includes the capability of business transaction management: you can easily drill-down to and monitor transactions through different tiers of IT, and you can also manage your business service levels in a more sophisticated manner. This will be examined further in the next chapter.

The Service Level Management Pack (SLM) is responsible for monitoring the availability and performance of services and for making sure service level goals have been met. Tests can be made from remote locations using beacons. All services can be modeled using a topology viewer, and the Root Cause Analysis feature can be used to pinpoint the exact cause of any service failure. Reporting on service level goal achievements is through Services Dashboards, which are customizable reports. These have been seen in the previous sections.

Since August 2010, the Service Level Management Pack has been combined into Oracle RUEI. This now offers a complete end user monitoring solution that includes the synthetic testing of SLM along with the real user testing of RUEI. Synthethic transactions that are created and generated from SLM are understood by RUEI, which can then analyze these separately from any operations from real users.

Application Management Packs help manage Oracle applications such as the E-Business Suite, PeopleSoft Enterprise, Siebel, JD Edwards EnterpriseOne and Oracle Communications Billing & Revenue Management. Before August 2010, to achieve change management and configuration management for these applications, separate packs such as the Change Management and Configuration Management Pack for applications were available. Since that date, these have been combined into new Oracle Application Management Suites.

These suites are available for Oracle E-Business Suite, Siebel, PeopleSoft and JD Edwards EnterpriseOne and include the capabilities from the corresponding Application Management Pack, Configuration Management Pack for applications, Real User Experience Insight (RUEI) as well as the RUEI Application Accelerator that are all included in the suite for that application. Besides, the Oracle Application Management Suite for Oracle E-Business also includes change management features combined from the Change Management Pack for Oracle E-Business.

Other packs include the Business Intelligence Management Pack, Management Pack Plus for SOA, and other middleware management packs for Oracle WebLogic Server, Coherence and so on. There is also the Diagnostics Pack for Oracle Middleware and the Diagnostics Pack for Non-Oracle Middleware. These packs feature Java application diagnostics, Java virtual machine (JVM) monitoring and also management and monitoring of Application server.

Since August 2010, the Oracle Management Pack for Identity Management Plus is the new name for the Management Pack for Identity Management. This now supports more updated technology such as Oracle Identity Manager (OIM), Oracle Access Manager (OAM) and Oracle Adaptive Access Manager (OAAM) as part of the new 11g release of Oracle Identity Management. This is in addition to support for Oracle Internet Directory (OID), Oracle Virtual Directory (OVD) and Oracle Identity Federation (OIF).

The Oracle Application Testing Suite consists of Oracle Load Testing, Oracle Functional Testing, and Oracle Test Manager. Test scripts are used in the Oracle Load Testing Pack to automate testing of web applications, web services and packaged Oracle applications. Tens of thousands of users can be simulated on test hardware with minimal specifications, and bottlenecks can be easily identified.

On the other hand, functional and regression testing can be fully automated by the Oracle Functional Testing Pack using the OpenScript integrated scripting platform, and this can literally reduce testing time by half.

To build the entire testing process, you can use the Oracle Test Manager. This can manage test assets as well as control test execution with the ability to create testing activity reports. There are also Oracle Testing Suite accelerators (functional and load testing) for Siebel, Oracle E-Business and Web Services.

The new Oracle Application Testing Suite Release 9.1 is included in Oracle Enterprise Manager Grid Control 11g Release 1. In this version, test scripts can be generated based on real user actions. Also, middleware diagnostics can be accessed during load testing to aid in diagnosis of performance issues in the application. Other new features of Release 9.1 are as follows: applications based on Oracle Application Development Framework (ADF) have a new testing accelerator, and there is also a new test starter kit for Oracle E-Business Suite R12 applications. Thus, the testing effort is greatly simplified.

Note that all the available OEM Management Packs and their Data Sheets can be seen on the Oracle Technology Network at the following URL: http://www.oracle.com/technology/products/oem/ datasheets.html.

Management Connectors

Management connectors hook up Oracle Enterprise Manager to other HelpDesk or management systems and enable sharing of critical alert information. The connectors are available for products such as Remedy HelpDesk, Microsoft Operations Manager, PeopleSoft Enterprise HelpDesk, Siebel HelpDesk, HP ServiceCenter, HP ServiceManager, and HP OpenView Operations.

For example, suppose you have installed the management connector for Remedy HelpDesk, a popular support case management system in use in many companies. After the management connector is installed, Remedy incidents can be automatically generated based on OEM Alerts. When the alerts are cleared, the Remedy incidents can be automatically closed.

Both the OEM console and Remedy console can be launched from one another to enable quicker resolution of the actual issue.

The OEM Ops Center is included for the first time in Grid Control 11g Release 1. The Ops Center is used to manage Sun hardware, the Solaris OS, Oracle VM for SPARC (the new name for Solaris Logical Domains or LDoms), and Solaris Containers. The Ops Center will be covered more in the next chapter.

The connection between Ops Center and Grid Control is via the Oracle Management Connector for Ops Center, and this enables the Ops Center to forward event notifications, such as OS performance indicators or hardware issues, to Grid Control where they are raised as alarms. This is a first level of integration that will hopefully be followed by a deeper level of integration in the future.

System Monitoring Plug-ins

Then there are the system monitoring plug-ins. These enable monitoring, and not management, of non-Oracle products via the OEM console. Some Oracle products are also included, such as the Times Ten In-Memory Database Plug-in, to monitor the Oracle Times Ten In-Memory database and the Exadata Storage Server Plug-in to monitor the Exadata Storage server.

There are plug-ins available for other vendor database products such as Microsoft SQL Server, Sybase, and IBM DB2. Plug-ins are also available for Microsoft products such as Exchange Server, Active Directory, BizTalk Server, Commerce Server, IIS Server, ISA Server, and the .NET Framework.

Plug-ins are available to monitor storage products such as the EMC Symmetrix DMX, EMC CLARiiON, EMC Celerra, the NetApp Filer, and also load balancers such as the F5 BigIP Local Traffic Manager along with non-Oracle middleware such as IBM Websphere MQ, IBM WebSphere Application Server, Apache Tomcat and the JBoss Application Server.

The plug-ins can also monitor Linux Hosts, Unix Hosts, Windows Hosts, the VMware ESX Server, Check Point Firewall, and the Juniper Netscreen Firewall. All these plug-ins are from Oracle. There are also third-party plug-ins, such as the NimBUS SAP Plug-In, to monitor SAP R/3 and the MySQL Plug-in from the Pythian group. These plug-ins are developed by Oracle Partners.

April 2010 and the release of OEM Grid Control 11g Release 1 saw a number of partners releasing new plug-ins. These are primarily intended to monitor third-party storage such as IBM Storage, NEC Storage, Veritas Storage, Pillar Axiom as well as HP Storageworks. A complete list of all plug-ins can be seen on the OTN-based Grid Control Extensions Exchange at the following URL: http://www.oracle.com/technology/products/oem/extensions/index.html.

Present Uptake and Future of Enterprise Manager

A lot of things about Oracle Enterprise Manager have been explored in this book. What about its current usage in the IT world? The fact is that both Grid Control and Database Control uptake is steadily increasing in companies throughout the world like an unstoppable but beneficial juggernaut. Database Control is often the first step to move to a centralized Grid Control site.

Since the days of the first release in the early years of the new millennium, Grid Control gained acceptance with many DBA teams who started to use this product for their day-to-day database administration tasks and found it a lot better than their manual, scripting days. This author was very much one of the DBAs in those days who experienced first-hand the benefits of the Manage Many as One philosophy of Grid Control: the time savings, the reduction of

---

errors, and the automation which assisted in many a dull DBA task such as the patching of hundreds and thousands of databases.

Now, in the days of OEM 11g Grid Control and beyond, you can well say that Enterprise Manager is a permanent fixture of the present and future DBA who is now known as DBA 2.0 as compared to the previous DBA 1.0 who used to do everything manually.

Conclusion

In this chapter, the many ways Oracle Enterprise Manager Grid Control can be used by System Administrators, DBA troubleshooters, Regulators and IT managers has been introduced. You have seen Real User Experience Insight (RUEI), how entire systems and services can be monitored, Root Cause Analysis (RCA) to find out the cause of issues quickly, and the setting up and management of Service Level Agreements (SLAs).

Also, the different OEM management packs, in particular, the Diagnostics and Tuning Packs including the new Real-Time SQL Monitoring in 11g were covered. The other packs such as the Provisioning and Patch Automation Pack, the Configuration Management Pack, the Change Management Pack, the Data Masking Pack and other Management Packs were explained along with the Management connectors and the System Monitoring Plug-ins.

In the next and final chapter, the new version of OEM 11g Grid Control that was released in April 2010 will be examined; specifically, its new features and the new techniques of installation of this version.

The New Enterprise Manager Grid Control 11g

Released in April 2010 after a lot of anticipation, the most comprehensive corporate management and monitoring solution is out: Oracle Enterprise Manager 11g Grid Control Release 1. It just gets better and better.

This chapter will go through the highlights and all the pack enhancements in the new version, then take a look at the changed installation and administration techniques. Finally, it will closely examine the integration with My Oracle Support (MOS) in the new version before concluding this book.

Highlights of the New Version

The new version of OEM is based on Oracle WebLogic Server (WLS) 11g Release 1 Enterprise Edition (10.3.2) instead of the earlier Oracle application server used by Oracle Enterprise Manager 10g Grid Control. Hence, it can use all the performance and memory management benefits that are associated with Oracle WLS, the new engine of OEM. It should be noted at this point that a restricted use license of Oracle WLS is included with OEM, i.e. it cannot be used for domains other than the Enterprise Manager domain.

Oracle WLS 11g is considered to be the fastest application server in the market and delivers proven best performance. At the heart of any Java-based enterprise software is a Java Virtual Machine (JVM) which interfaces between the application server and the hardware. Oracle Jrockit, included with Oracle WLS 11g, is clearly the fastest JVM in the industry. Tuned and optimized to a great extent, it delivers the speed that no competing JVM can deliver.

However, Oracle JRockit is not certified at this point in time to be used with Oracle Enterprise Manager 11g. Hopefully, this will change in the future.

Oracle Coherence is also part of WebLogic Suite 11g, and this is responsible for pooling all the available memory across servers and making it available to the applications. The shared pool of memory can then contain data needed by the applications. Since this data is brought closer to the applications for processing, it will reduce queries to the database and improve performance. Clustering is also included with Oracle Coherence, meaning the cached data is replicated across servers and will not be lost if any of the servers fails. Due to this clustering, the application can have more concurrent users without performance degradation.

You could install OEM 11g Grid Control on an Oracle WebLogic Server cluster, but you cannot take advantage of the cluster configurations at this point of time. However, again hopefully, this could be a possibility in the future.

Security enhancements in the new release include TLS (Transportation Layer Security) protocol support for communication between the OEM components (OMS and Agents). There is also support for auditing a subset of operations in Grid Control. This includes monitoring-related operations such as the application of monitoring templates or the editing of monitoring settings for a target.

High Availability enhancements in the new release include the ability to update Oracle Management Service (OMS) properties without any downtime, simplified addition of a new OMS to an existing OMS, and easier Server Load Balancing (SLB) configuration. There are several other powerful features in the new release and they are listed in the following sections.

Improved Middleware Management

Application grid environments or private clouds often use Oracle WebLogic Server (WLS) as the base. The provisioning of such deployments can be greatly simplified by the new OEM 11g Release 1 as also the management of the whole stack. In this release, you get enhanced support for managing Oracle Fusion Middleware 11g. This includes full configuration management and provisioning for large Oracle WLS and Oracle Service-Oriented Architecture (SOA) Suite environments. OEM 11g now supports Oracle SOA 11g, Oracle WebCenter 11g, Oracle WLS 10.3.x, and Oracle Identity and Access Management (IAM) 11g.

SOA management in OEM 11g includes management of composite services, component services, the SOA engine, and service metrics. It also includes Enterprise Service Dashboards, configuration management and deployment automation of SOA applications along with SOA instance tracing across domains.

There is now a brand new SOA Suite 11g target type, and this provides detailed management capabilities for Oracle SOA Suite 11g including the capability of cloning and provisioning of 11g SOA composites. There is a new enterprise-wide centralized SOA view of all web services from SOA 11g, BPEL 10g, Oracle Service Bus (OSB), and Oracle WLS.

The new version of Enterprise Manager also boasts enhanced management of Oracle WLS 11g. For example, there is improved and simplified discovery of Oracle WLS including support for versions 11g, 10.X, 9.x, and 8.1.x. Each managed Oracle WLS server can be monitored independently if so required. Several Oracle WLS domains can be added in a single operation and as the membership of the domains change, there is a continuous rediscovery of the Oracle WLS domains.

As part of the new Oracle WLS management capabilities, there is no dependency on the admin server for monitoring. Also, configuration management and provisioning of Oracle WLS can be performed. Configuration management, in this case, means it is possible to track Oracle WLS installations and the applied patches across the domains in an enterprise. Additional configuration information is also collected about resource adapters, web services, node manager, and machines.

With regards to the provisioning capabilities via new supplied deployment procedures, it is now possible to clone the Oracle Fusion Middleware 11g SOA Suite including Oracle WebLogic Domain and also to scale up any Oracle WebLogic Domain. There are customizable performance summaries, and the possibility of continuous monitoring of Oracle WLS since each managed server can be monitored even when the admin server is down. Request monitoring and tracing is also possible.

Coherence Management, with a new Coherence dashboard, now includes the ability to start/stop nodes, or start/stop the entire cluster. It is possible to automatically start new nodes in the form of a corrective action when any nodes crash.

New Database Management Capabilities

Full support is provided in OEM 11g Grid Control for the new features in Oracle Database 11g Release 2, and this includes diagnostics, tuning, compression (the new Compression Advisor), real-time change detection, and flexible server partitioning using the new database feature of instance caging.

Performance diagnostics now boast the new capability of Active Reports. These are interactive reports for off-line viewing and analysis that can be emailed to different people in an XML format for analysis with full drill-down capabilities to the SQL plan level, even if OEM 11g is not installed at the receiver end.

These Active Reports build on the Real-Time SQL monitoring capabilities in the Oracle Database 11g Release 1 described in an earlier chapter. The Real-Time SQL monitoring is also enhanced in the new version to monitor entire blocks of PL/SQL application code that were not able to be monitored with the previous version.

The SQL Tuning Advisor in Enterprise Manager 11g is now able to take advantage of new capabilities in Oracle Database 11.2 that support an automatic degree of parallelism. For the identified Top SQL, available CPUs on the server are taken into account to suggest an appropriate degree of parallelism. The SQL Tuning Advisor is also able to suggest alternative execution plans using historical performance data as well as real-time data.

Global AWR and ASH reports are available for easier RAC system diagnostics. The enhanced ADDM can analyze locking sessions across RAC instances. ADDM is also backward compatible and can now analyze snapshots from earlier database versions. ADDM reports have been enhanced with impact breakdown among multiple dimensions such as SQL, Service, and SID. Besides, ASH can now be used for tuning Oracle Data Guard standby databases.

For Oracle Exadata Version 2, Enterprise Manager 11g features Exadata-aware Real-Time SQL monitoring and I/O resource management for this new and powerful database machine. Using the storage monitoring plug-in, the performance monitoring you perform can drill down to the Oracle Exadata storage cell level to diagnose performance issues. Configuration changes can also be captured and, incredibly, you can now provision the entire database machine through OEM 11g.

Oracle Clusterware, used in Oracle Real Application Clusters (RAC), can be monitored and managed by OEM in this new version. Besides, the ASM Cluster File System introduced in Oracle Database 11.2 can now be fully administered and monitored using OEM 11g. Security enhancements in this case allow separation of duties between the storage administrator and the DBA.

The High Availability (HA) console introduced in OEM 10g Release 5 is enhanced with the ability to convert a single instance database on a file system to a RAC database on ASM failing over to a standby database on ASM. This process is fully automated by the deployment procedures in OEM 11g. These procedures are called directly from the HA console or the Maximum Availability Architecture (MAA) Advisor page, and this is described in a later section in this chapter.

The OEM Support Workbench is enhanced to cover ASM instances and also boasts of better diagnostics for memory related errors, i.e. *ORA-4031* or *ORA-4030*. The compression schemes introduced in Oracle Database 11.2 are now accessible in OEM 11g via the new Compression Advisor, which can be used to analyze objects and recommend appropriate compression schemes.

The Oracle Database Resource Manager is now enhanced to support the new feature of instance caging introduced in Oracle Database 11.2. This limits each database to certain numbers of CPUs and is much more flexible than server partitioning and less resource-intensive than the Hypervisor-based Virtual Machine technology.

New Features in the Data Masking Pack

The Data Masking capabilities now have OEM command line (EMCLI) support for data masking actions so that these can be executed in nightly batch jobs. One of the most important enhancements to the Data Masking Pack in OEM 11g Grid Control is the ability to perform heterogeneous data masking on different databases such as IBM DB2 and Microsoft SQLServer via Oracle Database Gateways.

This needs the respective OEM plug-ins for these databases. You need to install Oracle Gateway 11.2 for SQL Server for connecting to MS SQL Server and the Oracle Gateway 11.2 for DRDA for connecting to IBM DB2. This also will need a staging Oracle database where the actual masking will take place.

It should be noted here that DRDA (Distributed Relational Database Architecture) is OpenGroup's published architecture for connectivity to databases including DB2 for z/OS and OS/390, DB2/400, and DB2 Universal Database. Using the gateway, the DRDA database servers can be accessed from any platform on which Oracle is supported.

Other new features in the Data Masking Pack include a data preserving shuffle, SQL expression based Mask Formats, pre-masking scripts and random decimal number generation.

New Features in Change Management

In the realm of the OEM 11g Change Management Pack, the brand-new and exciting feature is Real-Time Schema change detection. For example, new or dropped indexes, changes to tables, procedures, triggers or functions are all detected.

The Change Management Pack in the new release also has the feature of Schema Change propagation, allowing you to propagate your planned schema changes from your baseline database to multiple database destinations. This avoids the risks of flat files used for schema changes that can be easily tampered with.

Schema baselines can also be imported and exported from files if so required. There is a new Meta-Data API for XML Based Schema Object Comparisons.

Widespread Management of Hardware, Virtualization and Operating System

The entire lifecycle of physical and virtual Oracle Sun environments is managed by OEM Ops Center (formerly Sun Ops Center). This manages Oracle Sun hardware, Oracle Solaris, Oracle VM for SPARC (previously called Logical Domains or LDoms) and Solaris Containers. As a result, customers can utilize their Sun systems to the fullest extent. The OEM Ops Center appears in Figure 9.1.

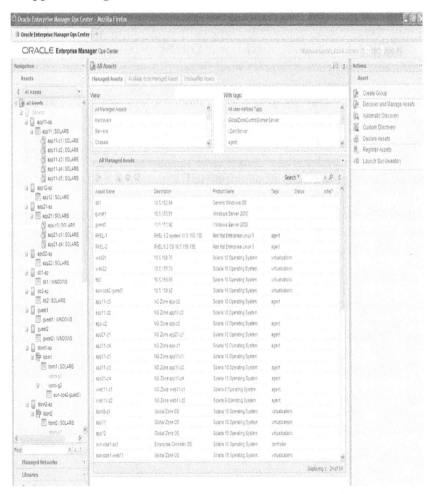

Figure 9.1: *Oracle Enterprise Manager Ops Center*

Hardware level events can now be centrally monitored via Grid Control since the first level of integration between OEM Grid Control and OEM Ops Center has been achieved. This is via the Enterprise Manager Management Connector for Ops Center; notifications from the Ops Center can now be exposed as Grid Control Alerts, alerting the DBA to issues at the deeper hardware/firmware level. Logically, you can guess that further integration is on the way.

The new OEM Packs for Ops Center are:

1. OEM Ops Center Provisioning and Patch Automation Pack: This allows managing the packages/RPM and patches, and includes Firmware management, Fault management, OS monitoring and provisioning. Also, compliance, governance and audit besides other capabilities such as Service Processor (SP) Active Management for the Sun ILOM (Integrated Lights Out Management) facility are managed.

2. OEM Ops Center Virtualization Management Pack (requires the above Ops Center Provisioning and Patch Automation Pack): This allows full lifecycle management of the Oracle VM Server for SPARC and the Oracle Solaris container with capabilities for snapshots, backup and restore, creation and use of templates, and virtual appliances. Storage management for VMs and Virtual Network management is included as well as warm and cold migration, guest provisioning, and the use of virtual resource pools.

Ops Center can, therefore, manage both physical and virtual Oracle systems, such as SPARC & X86 servers, Solaris OS, Oracle Enterprise Linux, Solaris Containers and Oracle VM Server for SPARC. Besides, heterogeneous management features include the ability to also manage Red Hat Linux, SUSE Linux, and Windows via the System Center Configuration Manager (SCCM)). Figure 9.2 shows a glimpse of the virtualization management capabilities of OEM Ops Center.

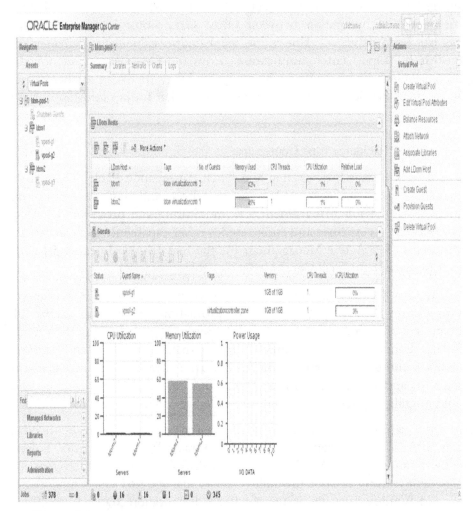

Figure 9.2: *Ops Center Virtualization Management*

Simplified Discovery is another key feature of the Ops Center. Network-based discovery of servers, operating systems, and virtual machines is supported using different protocols such as Sun Service Tags, SSH, IPMI, and so on so that assets can be easily discovered. These powerful Asset Discovery capabilities of OEM Ops Center are displayed in Figure 9.3.

Figure 9.3: *Ops Center Custom Asset Discovery*

The discovered assets are then displayed in a hierarchical manner, showing servers and their corresponding operating systems and virtual machines. Key system data such as CPU, memory, and software is also captured in the discovery process. Assets are intelligently grouped together; for example, by hardware platform or groups can be manually defined based on geography or other criteria.

With regards to provisioning capabilities, automated provisioning (simple) of operating systems for both bare metal and virtual servers is provided by the Ops Center as well as management of Gold image libraries. Typical manual tasks around jumpstart setup, dhcp configuration, and more can be automated by the Ops Center. The target system or systems to provision can be selected, the appropriate image can then selected, and the Ops Center will do what is needed with a press of the Start button.

Another important aspect is that full Firmware provisioning and updating is also possible with the Ops Center. Figure 9.4 displays the OS provisioning capabilities of OEM Ops Center.

Figure 9.4: *Ops Center OS Provisioning Capabilities*

Intelligent patch and configuration management is another of Ops Center's most powerful features. This is achieved by using a unique intelligent knowledge base to manage patches and configurations, connected to patch repositories from major operating system vendors. Using an analysis engine which is highly advanced, the patch information along with the system information is analyzed to find dependencies and patch requirements. The end result is that it accurately finds the specific patch updates required for any of the systems. Administrators can then schedule the patch updates across the systems. Patch application simulation and rollback are also possible.

Comprehensive out-of-the-box audit reports are provided by Ops Center to ensure that systems are able to meet compliance requirements. Also in this regard, new systems can be easily configured as per configuration profiles that follow security and compliance requirements.

Hardware and OS monitoring of managed systems is another powerful capability of the Ops Center. An agentless approach is used, capturing various efficiency and health metrics; for example, power consumption, temperature, voltage, fan speed, and so on.

Operating systems are monitored and their memory, and CPU load are captured. Real-time event thresholds can be set for parameters and historical analysis is also possible, both online or the data can be downloaded for offline analysis.

Enhancements to Application Testing Suite (ATS)

Included in the OEM 11g Release 1 Grid Control is the new Oracle Application Testing Suite (ATS) Release 9.1. This features Functional and Load Testing for packaged and custom web applications and is an important part of the Oracle Application Quality Management (AQM) suite along with Oracle Real Application Testing and the Data Masking Pack.

In this new version of Oracle ATS, real user actions can automate test script generation since load test scripts for ATS can be automatically generated by Oracle Real User Experience Insight (RUEI) sessions.

Oracle ATS 9.1 can now assist in finding performance bottlenecks during a load test by directly accessing OEM J2EE Middleware performance diagnostics. There is also a new ServerStats profile, and this is used for monitoring the Oracle database during a load test. The new version boasts the use of OpenScript which is a standard Java-based scripting platform as opposed to proprietary scripting languages used by other testing products as such languages would have a steeper learning curve.

Scripting enhancements include a new OpenScript Tree View debugger, a new script assets manager, enhanced support for creating shared script functions, and result code verification for advanced scripting. New testing accelerators are available to simplify testing of applications based on Oracle ADF, supporting both functional and load testing.

Also, in order to help reduce the testing effort, a new test starter kit for Oracle E-Business Suite R12 (12.1.1) applications is also provided for functional testing. This provides sample test scripts for Oracle EBS 12.1.1 applications based on the EBS Vision database.

Enhancements to Oracle RUEI 6.5

OEM 11g also carries a new release 6.5 of Oracle RUEI for user experience management. The new version of Oracle RUEI boasts drill-down integration to Oracle Enterprise Manager 11g Release 1 Grid Control for Java (JVM) diagnostics, Application modeling and Request Monitoring.

This integration is seen in Figure 9.5.

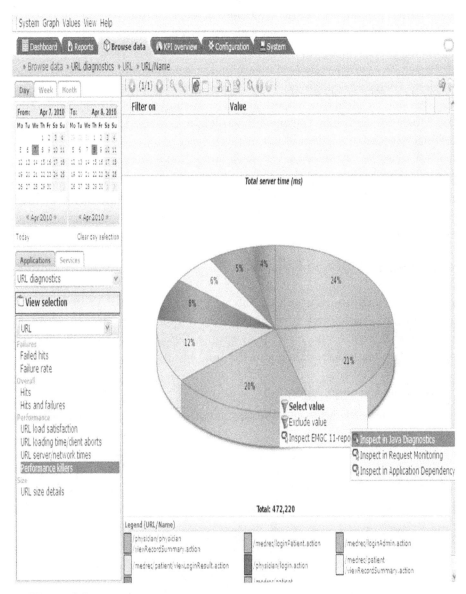

Figure 9.5: *RUEI 6.5 Integration with Grid Control Java Diagnostics*

Oracle RUEI 6.5 now has externally viewable dashboards, creation of custom dashboards, the ability to moving between previous actions in the data browser, an improved session diagnostic display and search, and a fully translatable GUI into simplified Chinese. The ability to create a new dashboard and publish it externally at an URL with anonymous access allowed is seen in Figure 9.6.

Figure 9.6: *RUEI 6.5 - Creating a New Dashboard*

Integration is also offered with EBS, Siebel Management Packs, the Grid Control Beacon Service Test and with the My Oracle Support (MOS) portal as well as integration with the Oracle Application Testing Suite (ATS) script setup. There are considerable improvements for EBS, Siebel and PeopleSoft Accelerators. The WebDav protocol is supported along with Oracle Single Sign-On (SSO) and Oracle Access Manager (OAM) logins to RUEI.

Oracle RUEI now also allows diagnostics of the network configuration and user specific data access per application. TCP traffic snapshots can be created either based on all traffic or with only the collector's currently defined filters applied.

Business Transaction Management (BTM)

Oracle Business Transaction Management (BTM) is offered in the new version with the ability to drill-down to and monitor transactions through different tiers as well as more powerful business service management. The new catchword is Business Driven Application Management. This capability is enhanced through the acquisition of AmberPoint, a provider of leading software for Service-Oriented Architecture (SOA) management. This is now a part of OEM Grid Control in the form of BTM.

The abilities of Oracle BTM are real-time tracking of each transaction, and the ability to follow transactions across all infrastructure and applications: Application Servers, Applications, Enterprise Service Bus' (ESBs), Business Process Managers (BPMs), and so on. You can see how powerful this is going to be.

The solution leverages message content; that is, the business value flowing through the application. This is done without modifying or tagging the messages using a non-invasive technology that does not break applications. The Oracle BTM screen seen in Figure 9.7 gives a tantalizing glimpse of what is available.

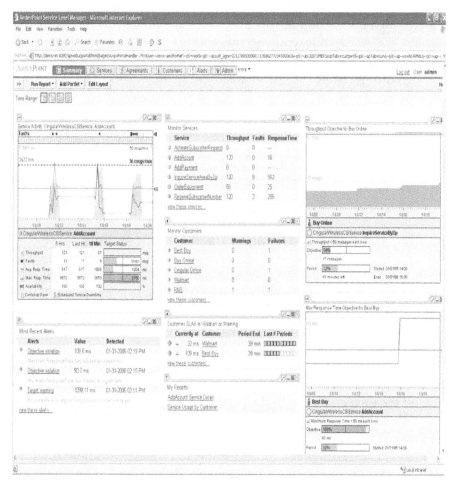

Figure 9.7: *Oracle Busines Transaction Management (BTM)*

As can be seen in Figure 9.7, the product offers performance metrics, monitors against baselines and thresholds, and Service Level Agreements (SLAs).

Preventative and corrective actions can also be enabled so that violations are not just reported after it is too late. For example, throttling and alerts can be triggered before SLA failure in the case of Platinum-level SLA customers. It is, therefore, possible to enforce service level agreements in real time.

Historical reporting is also possible. There is a central view of failed transactions with a transaction history and a message flow per transaction. You can drill into the transaction content and context. This allows you to avoid manually searching through log files on separate machines. Ad-hoc transaction searches are also possible; for example, transactions with faults or slow response times.

The product provides business impact insight, such as who uses what, when it is being used and how much is being used, with a detailed end-user impact including exceptions, SLA violations and the like. It also clearly shows the business value flowing through the system: total orders, claims, failures and more.

Provisioning and Patch Automation Pack Enhancements

One of the most important enhancements of the OEM Provisioning and Patch Automation Pack is the integration with My Oracle Support (MOS) and Community Forums. This integration of the 11.1 version with MOS is vastly improved with new components such as complete patching lifecycle automation, SR integration, patch conflict checking and merge request filing. There is also a community-based console integrated with Oracle Forums so that members of the IT community can share their knowledge and best practices and their experience with the patches.

In an automated workflow, patches can be selected, validated and deployed across the complete IT infrastructure with the automated workflow using the sophisticated and customizable deployment procedures. This helps to minimize the risk as well as the effort required to implement recommendations and fixes. In a later section in this chapter, this new integration of Enterprise Manager with My Oracle Support will be examined more closely.

Smart Configuration Management is now possible and includes comprehensive configuration lifecycle management. Components are discovered and changes detected in real-time for compliance. Millions of customer configurations can be concurrently analyzed and this provides the IT team with real-time notification of impending problems.

There is a brand new feature in RAC provisioning deployment procedures called a Profile which lets you record all inputs in the deployment procedure interview and use it for later repeated deployments, thereby automating the task even further. This is known as Profile-driven RAC provisioning and there are four out-of-box profiles available.

Other Provisioning and Patch Automation Pack enhancements are support for 11.2 databases such as out-of-place patchsets, Rac Grid Plug and Play (GpNp) support during provisioning and scale-out, and the ability to configure either admin-managed or policy-managed databases. ASM provisioning is now supported as well as Clusterware provisioning with Grid Naming Service (GNS) support.

Weblogic provisioning makes it also possible now for you to clone from a reference Gold installation of WebLogic, and you can easily scale out and scale back your WebLogic installation using OEM 11g Release 1 Grid Control. Even the Sun Oracle Database Machine in Exadata V2 can be provisioned in the new version using a special deployment procedure.

It should be mentioned here that the Oracle Home Clone wizard has not been certified with 11.2 databases. This wizard has been deprecated since OEM Grid Control 10.2.0.4 and will not be certified for any new versions of databases, Middleware or any other Oracle software. Instead, use deployment procedures; the existing Oracle Database Provisioning procedure can now be used to provision 11.2 databases that are single-instance (non-RAC). You can refer to My Oracle Support Note 737939.1 for the certification details for the clone wizard and deployment procedures.

There is now a new deployment procedure called Oracle Grid Infrastructure Provisioning for standalone servers that can be used to provision Grid Infrastructure for Single Instance Databases, and a new deployment procedure Oracle Grid Infrastructure/RAC Provisioning to provision 11.2 RAC databases and Grid Infrastructure.

The other existing deployment procedures, One Click Extend Cluster Database and Delete/Scale down Oracle Real Application Clusters, have been certified with Oracle 11.2 RAC clusters in the new version. Another new feature is the capability of dynamic prerequisites. This means OEM can download the latest versions of prerequisites and tools for the RAC provisioning feature and then use those versions.

So far as server provisioning is concerned, the Provisioning Pack now supports Bare Metal Provisioning for Oracle VM 2.2 and Oracle Enterprise Linux 5. Besides, it can perform provisioning of Linux, Solaris and Windows as guest Virtual Machines (VMs) on Oracle VM servers. The patching plans now support Oracle Database 11.2. The existing patching procedures will also patch the Oracle RAC stack including Oracle Grid infrastructure for both RAC and non-RAC databases.

Service request submission and reporting is greatly simplified with auto population of service requests and reporting of service requests by configuration.

Integrated Application-to-Disk Management

One of the other catchwords in the new OEM 11g is Integrated Application-to-Disk management. The Oracle stack is now managed from top to bottom (application to disk) and this includes the Oracle Database, Oracle Fusion Middleware, Oracle Applications, Oracle Solaris and Oracle Enterprise Linux as well as Oracle VM and, of course, the Oracle Sun Servers.

This integrated management of the complete stack assists the IT administrators in quickly arriving at the root cause of any issue. Also, many issues can now be automatically resolved using OEM 11g. The JVM Diagnostic and Composite Application Monitoring and Modeler tools, used for Java application and composite management, need no longer be installed and maintained separately since they have been integrated into OEM 11g.

Enhancements to Identity Management Pack

In the new version, the Identity Management plug-in is no longer required. The discovery of all components of the Oracle Identity Management Suite can be performed from within the OEM 11g Release 1 Grid Control console. A new enterprise-wide view of Oracle Identity Management is available via an Identity and Access page that provides a centralized glimpse of all Oracle Identity Management 10g and 11g components. From this Identity and Access page, users can discover Identity Management components and create systems and services based on the underlying dependencies. The overall health of the Identity Management environment can also be monitored from this page with performance management and monitoring for all the Identity Management 11g components. This includes performance metrics and drill-down into statistics.

Configuration management of Identity Management components can also be performed such as keeping track of configuration changes, snapshots of configurations, and comparison of component configurations. There is also an Enhanced ADF-based Interface for managing Fusion Middleware with features such as the ability to customize home page views via drag and drop of regions and context sensitive menus.

Enhancements to Real Application Testing

In the new OEM 11g version, Database Replay now supports the shared-server database architecture and also the Streams apply workload. At the API level, replay filters are supported. The replay compare period report has been enhanced, and there are now OEM pages for replay divergence analysis.

The SQL Performance Analyzer (SPA) has also been enhanced to allow multiple test executions; this is for the purpose of improved trial accuracy. Active Reports are also supported for SPA. Two workloads can now be analyzed using SQL Tuning Set (STS) comparisons. Custom workflows can now be created for different scenarios for database upgrade. Finally, SPA now allows Exadata Simulation for the purpose of DSS or Data Warehouse workloads.

New Plug-Ins

OEM 11g now has a number of new plug-ins developed by partners to monitor third-party storage such as IBM, NEC, HP and such as can be seen on the OEM Grid Control Extensions Exchange webpage on OTN: http://www.oracle.com/technology/products/oem/ extensions/index.html.

More New Features   -

A complete list of new features in OEM 11g can be seen in the newly released documentation at this link: http://download.oracle.com/ docs/cd/E11857_01/em.111/e11982/ whats_new.htm#CHDCIDIG.

This is indeed the new age of OEM 11g.

Installation Techniques for the New Version

The installation for the new version is somewhat different from the previous versions of OEM. In fact, a lot different.

First and foremost, OEM 11g Grid Control does not use Oracle Application Server as in the 10g version, so it cannot use the OEM OC4J (Oracle Containers for J2EE) since OC4J is the J2EE runtime component of Oracle Application Server. Instead, the new version of OEM is based on Oracle WebLogic Server (WLS) 11g Release 1 Enterprise Edition (10.3.2).

Another difference is obvious: the OC4J Application Server software was always included in the earlier OEM 10g distribution. However, in the case of the new version, the Oracle WLS software is not included on the OEM 11g software distribution. Instead, it must be downloaded separately and pre-installed before OEM 11g can be installed.

The good news is that from OEM Grid Control 11.1 onwards, full future patchsets will be made available for download. There will no longer be a requirement to install the base release as was the case in the previous 10g version. For example, to install OEM Grid Control 10.2.0.5, you first had to install the earlier 10.2.0.3 or 10.2.0.2 release depending on your platform, and then you could patch it to 10.2.0.5. This will no longer be the case in OEM 11g and future versions of OEM.

Another welcome piece of news is that Oracle VM (Virtual Machine) templates are now available for rapid deployment of Oracle Enterprise Manager 11g. Now take a look at the installation of the new version.

Installing Oracle WebLogic Server

The first step is to ensure that Oracle WebLogic Server (WLS) 10.3.2 (*Oracle Fusion Middleware 11g Release 1 Patch Set 1*) is pre-installed on the server where OEM Grid Control will be installed. You must download the software separately from the OTN site as follows:

```
Oracle WebLogic Server 11gR1 (10.3.2) + OEPE - Package Installer.
```

This download includes the Oracle WebLogic Server 11gR1 (10.3.2) package installer, as well as Oracle Enterprise Pack for Eclipse 11g (11.1.1.1). The latter is Oracle's free Eclipse-based Integrated Development Environment (IDE) for Java Enterprise Edition (EE), Web Application, and Web Service development deploying to Oracle Weblogic Server.

The recommendation from Oracle is to install OEM 11g Grid Control on a dedicated Oracle WebLogic Server instance. If Oracle SOA Suite 11.1.1.2.0 is already installed on an Oracle WebLogic Server instance, then do not install Grid Control on this. This is because, at this point in time, OEM Grid Control and Oracle SOA Suite cannot exist together, the reason being that the *oracle_common* property is used by both the SOA Suite Administration Server and the OEM Administration Server.

The workaround, if it becomes necessary to use the same Oracle WebLogic Server instance, is to first deinstall the Oracle SOA Suite. Then you can remove the *oracle_common* value from the Oracle WebLogic Server so it can be used again by the OEM Administration Server.

Make sure that you are installing Weblogic Server 10.3.2 and not the later version 10.3.3. If you install the 10.3.3 version, then this will have the after-effect that the OEM 11g install will fail at the stage of configuration assistant OMS Configuration, and the installation log will show the following error:

```
severe: omsca-err:securing of oms failed.
```

In this case, you must deinstall everything and try again with the correct version of WebLogic 10.3.2.

Install WebLogic Server 11g Release 1 Enterprise Edition (10.3.2) using the following steps. As the Oracle user, execute the file that you have downloaded:

```
./oepe111130_wls1032_linux32.bin
```

This starts the Oracle Installer for WebLogic (Figure 9.8). Note that the Oracle Inventory location is not required even if this is the first installation of Oracle software on the server. This signifies that Oracle WebLogic does not use the Oracle Inventory location at this point in time, unlike most other Oracle software.

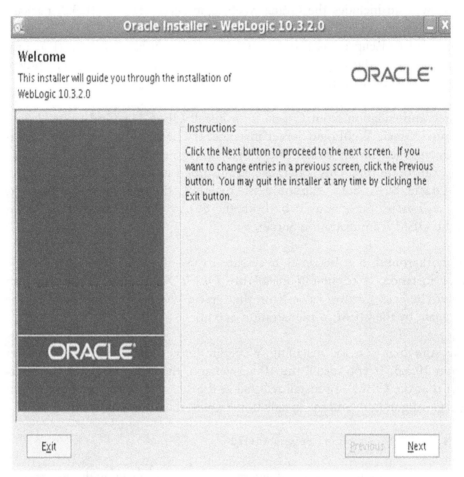

Figure 9.8: *Oracle WebLogic Installer*

Click Next. In Figure 9.9, you are asked to choose a Middleware Home Directory where WebLogic 10.3.2.0 will be installed.

Figure 9.9: *Create a New Middleware Home*

You decide to use */u01/app/oracle/product/middleware* as the Middleware Home Directory. Click Next. The Security Updates screen appears (Figure 9.10).

Oracle Installer - WebLogic 10.3.2.0 _ X

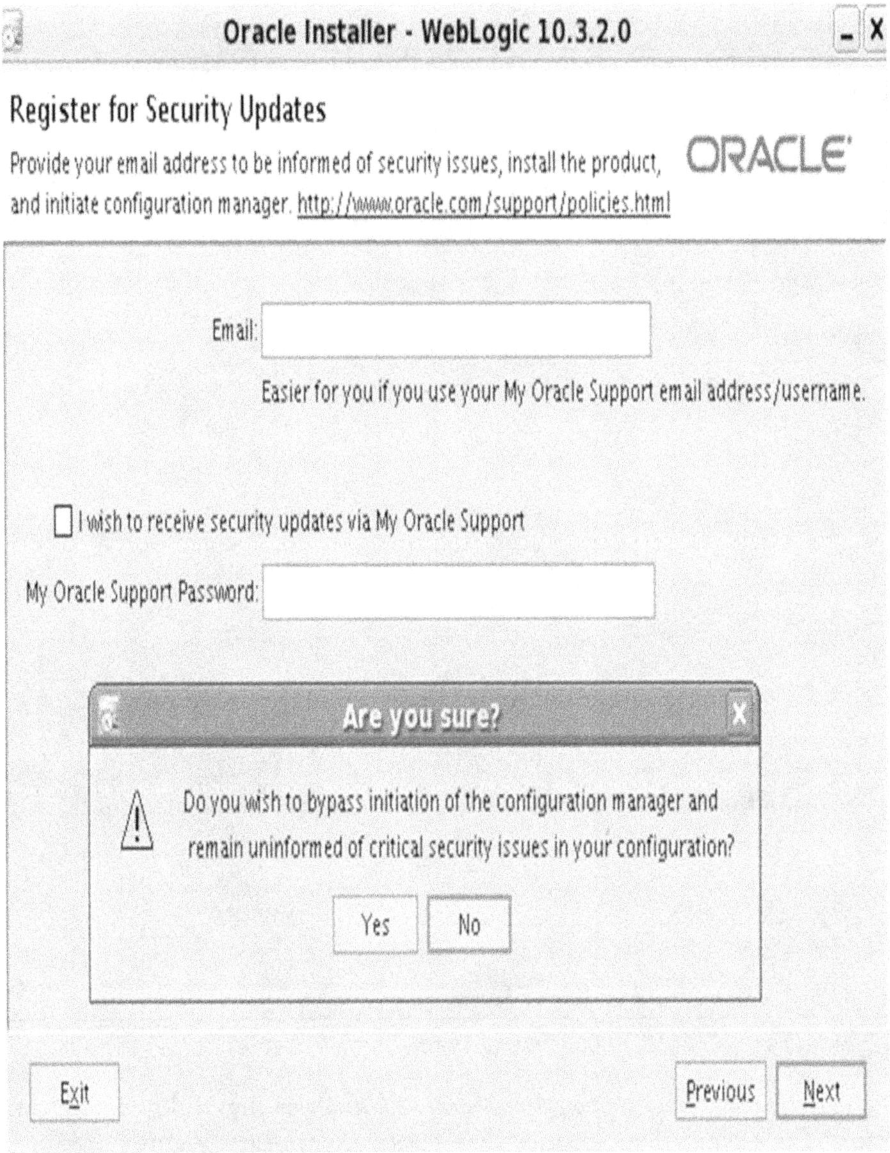

Register for Security Updates

Provide your email address to be informed of security issues, install the product, ORACLE
and initiate configuration manager. http://www.oracle.com/support/policies.html

Email: [   ]

Easier for you if you use your My Oracle Support email address/username.

☐ I wish to receive security updates via My Oracle Support

My Oracle Support Password: [   ]

Are you sure? X

⚠ Do you wish to bypass initiation of the configuration manager and
remain uninformed of critical security issues in your configuration?

Yes   No

Exit   Previous   Next

Figure 9.10: *Security Updates Screen*

This enables you to connect to Oracle Support and receive security updates
and start the Oracle Configuration Manager. In this case, you decide to go
ahead without this facility.

In production, it would greatly help with Oracle Support Service Request (SR) resolution if you were to use the Oracle Configuration Manager in conjunction with Oracle Enterprise Manager to send production configurations to Oracle Support and assist in resolving support cases via the Enterprise Manager Support Workbench.

The Install Type screen now appears (Figure 9.11). You must choose the *typical* installation. But if you use a *custom* installation, make sure that that you choose the same components that get installed in the typical installation.

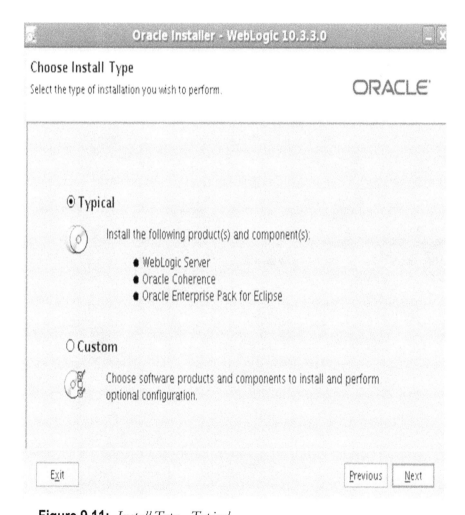

Figure 9.11: *Install Type - Typical*

In the next screen (Figure 9.12), ensure that the installation is under the Middleware Home Directory that is displayed on this screen. For example, if you specify the following directory, then the installation of Grid Control will create a new domain and the existing domains will not be used, which is what is wanted.

```
/u01/app/oracle/product/middleware/wlserver_10.3
```

You can also specify the directory for Oracle Enterprise Pack for Eclipse on this screen.

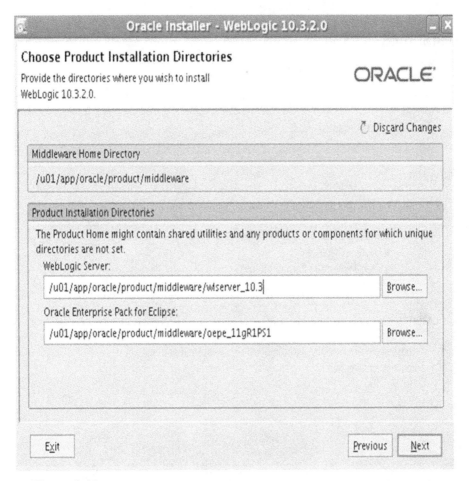

Figure 9.12: *Product Installation Directories*

Click Next. This takes you to the Installation Summary screen (Figure 9.13).

Figure 9.13: *Installation Summary*

The installation of Oracle WebLogic Server now starts and quickly progresses (Figure 9.14).

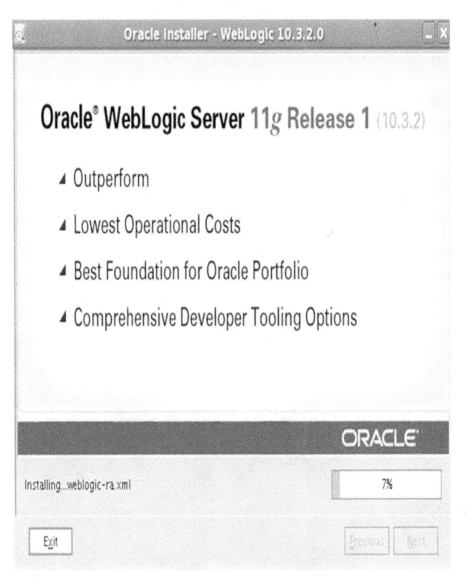

Figure 9.14: *Installation Progress*

Finally, the installation completes (Figure 9.15).

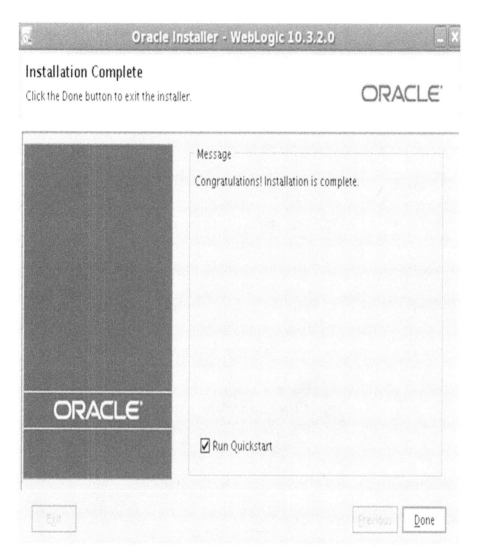

Figure 9.15: *Installation Completion*

The Oracle WebLogic Quick Start screen now appears where you can create domains and access the documentation (Figure 9.16). At this point, you do not need to do anything on this screen.

Figure 9.16: *WebLogic Quick Start*

Applying Oracle WebLogic Patches

The next step is to apply necessary patches to the Oracle WebLogic Server installation you have just completed.

The Oracle WebLogic Server Patch requirements are that you must apply Patch ID WDJ7 on the Oracle WebLogic Server home using the Oracle Smart

Update utility. This should be done before the installation/upgrade of Oracle Enterprise Manager 11g Grid Control. This patch is necessary to fix the following bugs: 8990616, 9100465, and 9221722 and is explained in the My Oracle Support note 1072763.1. The Oracle Smart Update Installing Patches and Maintenance Packs Guide for Release 3.2.1 explains the steps of using Oracle Smart Update: http://download.oracle.com/docs/cd/E15523_01/doc.1111/e14143/ toc.htm.

To run Oracle Smart Update, move to the *bea_home* (the Oracle WebLogic Server home) and then to the *utils/bsu* subdirectory under that home. From there, you can start Oracle Smart Update with the *bsu.sh* command as follows:

```
cd /u01/app/oracle/product/middleware/utils/bsu
./bsu.sh
```

The first thing that Oracle Smart Update asks you are your credentials for My Oracle Support. As soon as you log in to My Oracle Support, the Oracle Smart Update utility begins refreshing patch information as can be seen in Figure 9.17.

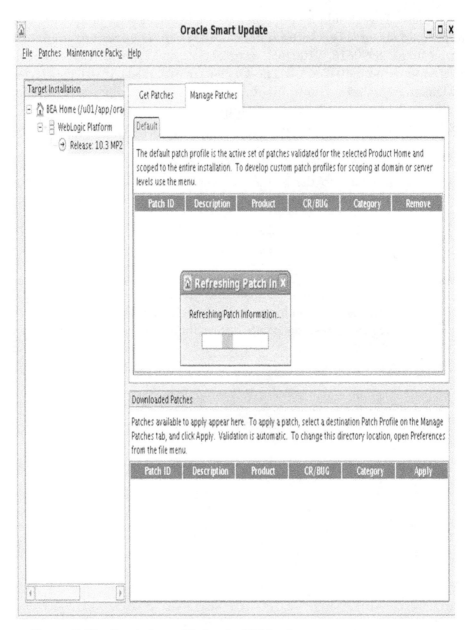

Figure 9.17: *Oracle Smart Update for WebLogic*

When the refreshing is over, move to the Get Patches tab. This shows the patches currently available from Support (Figure 9.18).

Figure 9.18: *Get Patches Tab*

Click on the Download Selected button. After the download is complete, the downloaded patches immediately appear in the Get Patches tab (Figure 9.19). These can now be applied to the installed components.

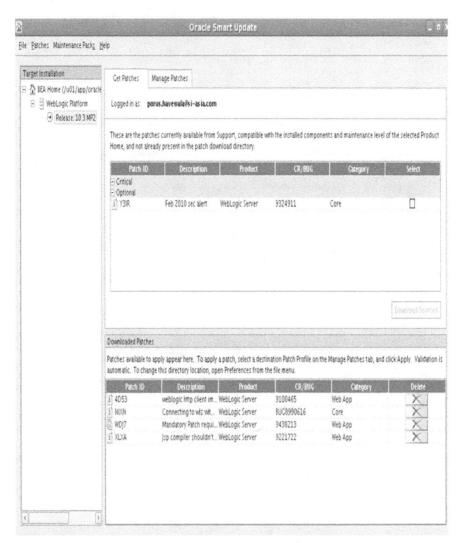

Figure 9.19: *Downloaded Patches in Get Patches Tab*

Move to the Manage Patches tab again. Here, you can see the list of downloaded patches with an Apply button against each patch as displayed in Figure 9.20:

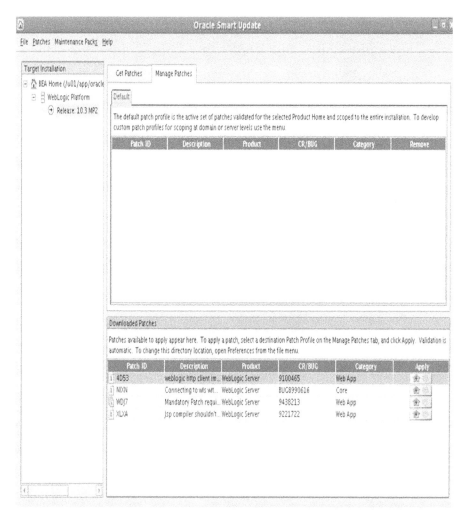

Figure 9.20: *Manage Patches Tab with Patches to Apply*

Click on the Apply button against the WDJ7 patch. Validation is performed to see if there are any conflicts, and the patches are then applied one by one. The patches now appear under the Default section on the Manage Patches tab (Figure 9.21).

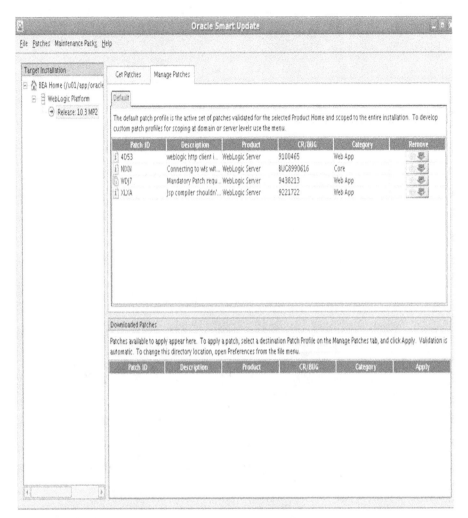

Figure 9.21: *Patches After Application*

At this point, you have succeeded in patching the Oracle WebLogic Server to the required level.

One more check is required on the server where Oracle WebLogic Server is installed. You must make sure that the entropy pool value is greater than 400. Run the following command to verify this value.

```
cat /proc/sys/kernel/random/entropy_avail
```

The value is definitely greater than 400 in this case.

Installing Database and Patches

You now need an Oracle database in which the OEM repository will be installed. Document ID 412431.1 in My Oracle Support lists the databases that can be used for the repository. This is the OEM Grid Control Certification matrix. As per this note, the supported database versions for the repository are 10.2.0.4, 11.1.0.7 and 11.2.0.1. The Enterprise Edition must be used and the database can be a Real Application Cluster (RAC) database or can be a single instance.

As expected, the Application Server stack version supported is Oracle WebLogic Server (WLS) 11g R1 PS1 (10.3.2). The supported browsers are Internet Explorer 7.0/8.0, Firefox 3.0/3.6 and Safari 4.0. Note that My Oracle Support requires Adobe Flash Player version 9.0.115 or above. You can use a database on the same server where you are installing OEM 11g, or you can use a separate server. This makes it possible to follow the techniques for scalable architecture for large sites as explained in Chapter 2 of this book.

The database is effectively separated from the Oracle Management Service, and you can have one or more management services on different servers pointing to the same management repository. *If you are thinking of using* Oracle Database 11g Release 1 (11.1.0.7.0), then you must make sure that the patch for bug 9066130 is applied to the database software. Or if you are using Oracle Database 11g Release 2 (11.2.0.1.0), then the patch for bugs 9002336 and 9067282 must be applied. For more information about these patches, you can see Document ID 1073166.1 in My Oracle Support.

As the first step, install Oracle Server 11.2 Enterprise Edition and create an Oracle 11.2 database with SID emrep. This will be used as the OEM repository. Then you can download and apply the patches for bugs 9002336 and 9067282 as noted above. The database emrep is now patched and ready to be used as the repository for OEM.

Oracle Enterprise Manager 11g Install

You can now start the main OEM 11g Grid Control install. After downloading the software and unzipping it to a directory on your server, simply run the *runinstaller* command. This starts the installation (Figure 9.22).

```
./runInstaller
```

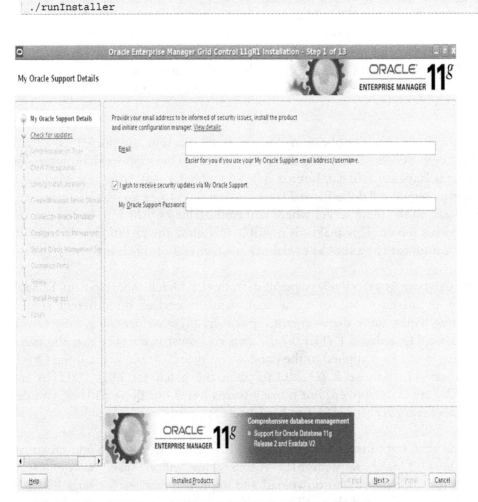

Figure 9.22: *Enterprise Manager 11g Installation Screen*

Click Next. The Check for updates screen appears (Figure 9.23).

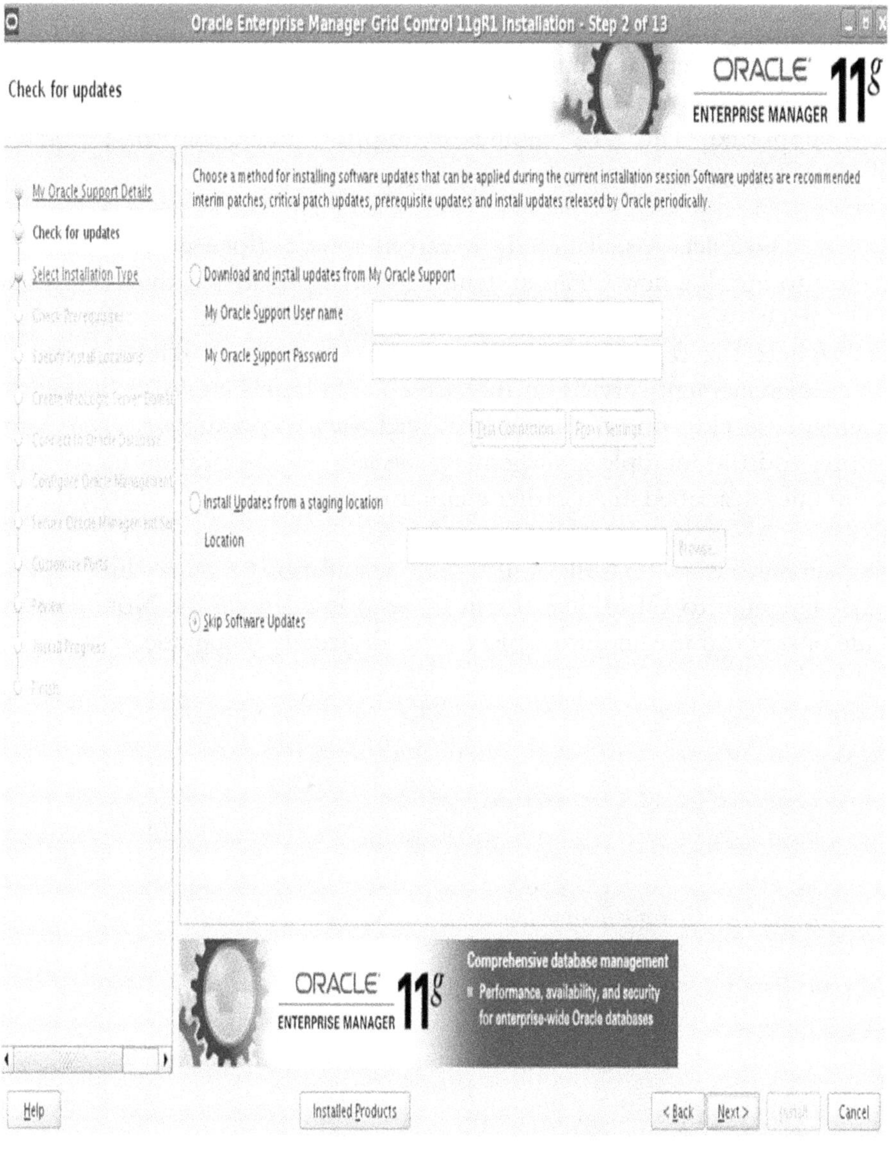

Check for updates

ORACLE 11^g
ENTERPRISE MANAGER

- My Oracle Support Details
- Check for updates
- Select Installation Type
- Check Prerequisites
- Specify Install Locations
- Create WebLogic Server Domain
- Connect to Oracle Database
- Configure Oracle Management
- Secure Oracle Management Service
- Customize Ports
- Review
- Install Progress
- Finish

Choose a method for installing software updates that can be applied during the current installation session Software updates are recommended interim patches, critical patch updates, prerequisite updates and install updates released by Oracle periodically.

○ Download and install updates from My Oracle Support

My Oracle Support User name [_____]

My Oracle Support Password [_____]

[Test Connection] [Proxy Settings]

○ Install Updates from a staging location

Location [_____] [Browse]

◉ Skip Software Updates

ORACLE 11^g
ENTERPRISE MANAGER

Comprehensive database management
■ Performance, availability, and security
for enterprise-wide Oracle databases

[Help]   [Installed Products]   [< Back] [Next >] [Install] [Cancel]

Figure 9.23: *Software Updates*

On this screen, you can decide that software updates will be automatically installed while the installation of OEM 11g Grid Control is in progress. You need to select the source from either My Oracle Support (username and password required) or you can use the updates from a staging location.

This auto-update feature is a new feature in OEM 11g Release 1 and will allow you to download the latest version and bug fixes via recommended product one-off patches. Metadata-only changes, such as updates to prerequisite checks, can also be downloaded in this way. Oracle Universal Installer changes are also supported. This all combines to improve the quality of the actual install of OEM.

Click Next. The Select Installation Type screen appears (Figure 9.24). You can now select to install a new OEM system. As noted previously, this requires an existing Oracle WebLogic Server installation as well as an existing Oracle database where the repository will be created. Or you can select to add an additional management service on this screen. This can be used to install the management service on a second or third server pointing to the same repository, and the multiple management services can be load balanced using the techniques described in an earlier chapter of this book.

If your server has an existing OEM 10g installation, then a third option appears: Upgrade to OEM 11g as can be seen in Figure 9.24. Note that the Upgrade option can use an out-of-place (non-destructive) upgrade.

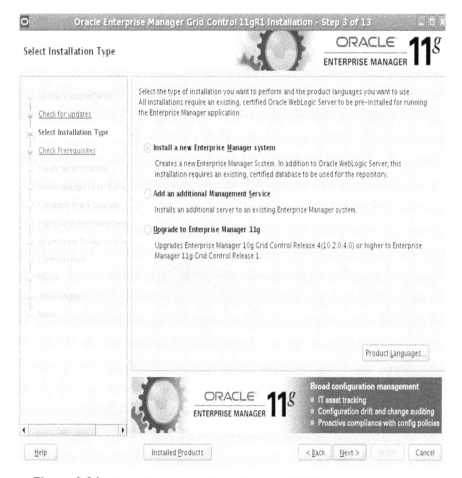

Figure 9.24: *Select Installation Type (Existing EM10g Server)*

There is no longer any option on the Select Installation Type screen to only install the OEM Agent, as was the case in previous versions. For installing OEM Agents, the Agent Push (Deploy) Application is recommended; this can be called from the Deployments tab of Grid Control and requires SSH equivalence.

Note that if there is no previous version of OEM 10g Grid Control on the server, then the installation type options dynamically change and do not include the Upgrade option. This is seen in Figure 9.25.

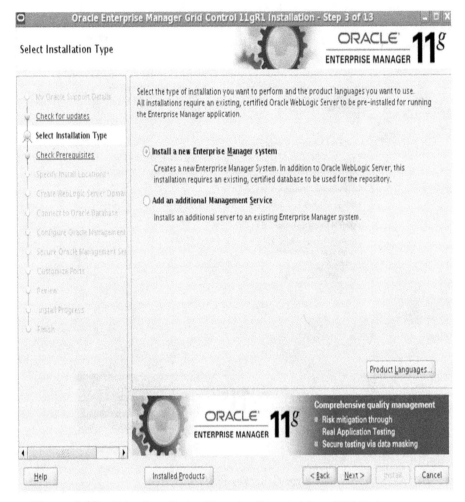

Figure 9.25: *Select Installation Type (on Server with no EM10g)*

In the next screen, the Prerequisite Check appears (Figure 9.26). All checks have succeeded.

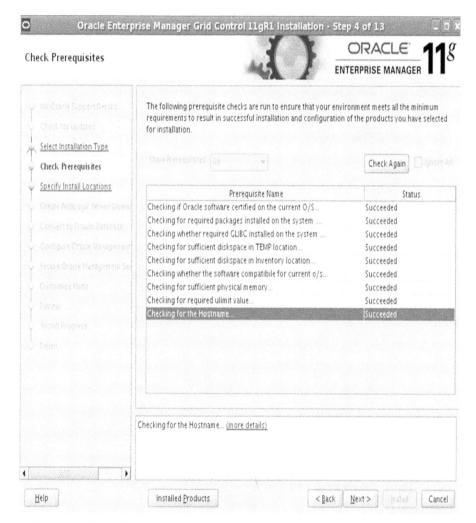

Figure 9.26: *Check Prerequisites*

Next, the locations for the Middleware Home and the OMS instance base location can be specified (Figure 9.27).

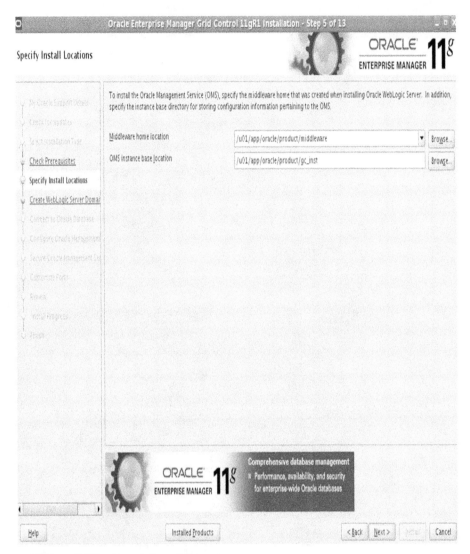

Specify Install Locations

ORACLE 11*g*
ENTERPRISE MANAGER

To install the Oracle Management Service (OMS), specify the middleware home that was created when installing Oracle WebLogic Server. In addition, specify the instance base directory for storing configuration information pertaining to the OMS.

My Oracle Support Details

Check for updates

Select Installation Type

Check Prerequisites

Specify Install Locations

Create WebLogic Server Domai

Connect to Oracle Database

Configure Oracle Management

Secure Oracle Management Ser

Customize Ports

Review

Install Progress

Finish

Middleware home location   /u01/app/oracle/product/middleware   ▼   Browse...

OMS instance base location   /u01/app/oracle/product/gc_inst   Browse...

ORACLE 11*g*
ENTERPRISE MANAGER

Comprehensive database management
▪ Performance, availability, and security
for enterprise-wide Oracle databases

Help   Installed Products   < Back   Next >   Install   Cancel

Figure 9.27: *Specify Install Locations*

On this screen, you must specify the Oracle Middleware Home location from the previous installation of Oracle WebLogic Server, and this will be where the Oracle Management Service (OMS) home and the Oracle Management Agent home will be created as oms11g and agent11g, respectively.

The Oracle Middleware home location is the home used when you had installed Oracle Weblogic Server 10.3.2 (Oracle Fusion Middleware 11g Release 1 Patch Set 1). The Installation wizard automatically detects this home and presents it to you on this screen so that you can verify that it is fine.

If you have selected the option to install an additional management service or upgrade it (the third option), then you must make sure the Middleware home location used is the same as the Middleware home location specified for the first Management Service installation. This ultimately means that Oracle WebLogic Server 10.3.2 must be installed in the same path on the second or third servers.

What is the Oracle Management Service instance base location also specified in Figure 9.27? This specifies the location where the configuration information of the Management Service is stored. The default location is under the parent directory of the Oracle Middleware home. You can accept the default location, or you can choose another location but ensure that the new location has write permission.

The next screen (Figure 9.28) is where you specify the WebLogic Server Domain that is to be created. The domain name is set to be GCDomain (Grid Control Domain).

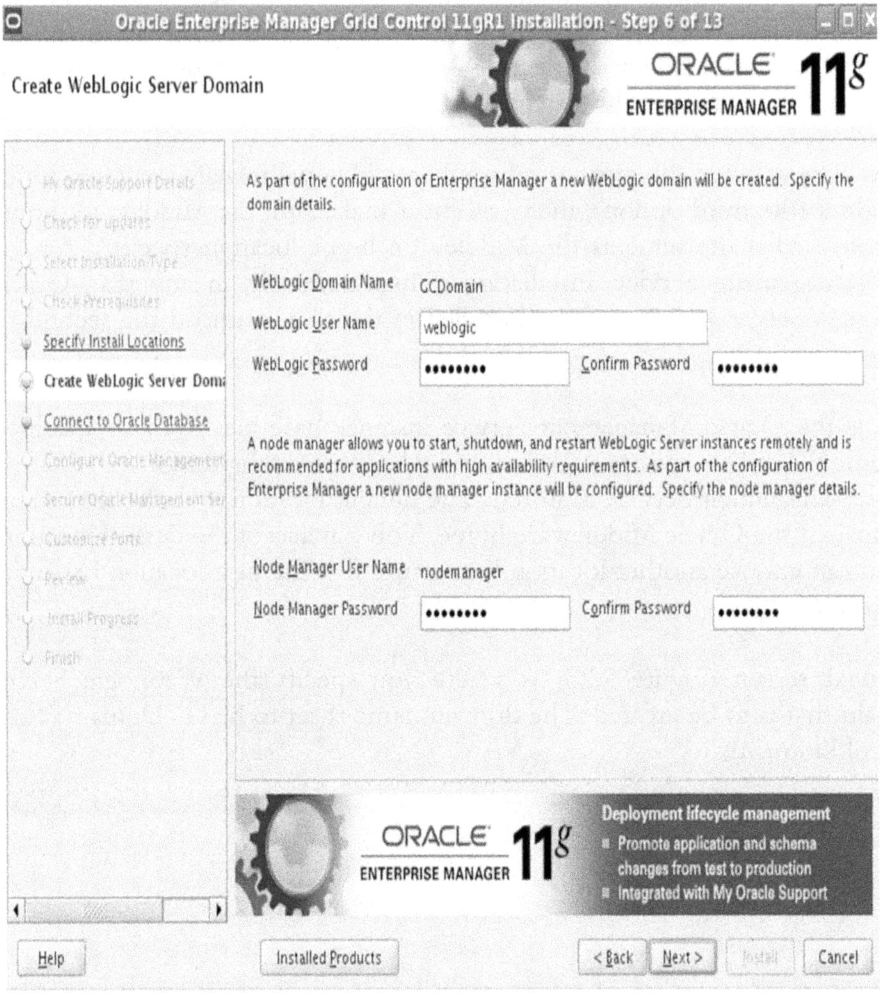

Create WebLogic Server Domain

ORACLE *11⁸*
ENTERPRISE MANAGER

My Oracle Support Details

Check for updates

Select Installation Type

Check Prerequisites

Specify Install Locations

Create WebLogic Server Doma

Connect to Oracle Database

Configure Oracle Management

Secure Oracle Management Ser

Customize Ports

Review

Install Progress

Finish

As part of the configuration of Enterprise Manager a new WebLogic domain will be created. Specify the domain details.

WebLogic Domain Name   GCDomain

WebLogic User Name   weblogic

WebLogic Password   ••••••••   Confirm Password   ••••••••

A node manager allows you to start, shutdown, and restart WebLogic Server instances remotely and is recommended for applications with high availability requirements. As part of the configuration of Enterprise Manager a new node manager instance will be configured. Specify the node manager details.

Node Manager User Name   nodemanager

Node Manager Password   ••••••••   Confirm Password   ••••••••

ORACLE *11⁸*
ENTERPRISE MANAGER

Deployment lifecycle management
* Promote application and schema changes from test to production
* Integrated with My Oracle Support

Help   Installed Products   < Back   Next >   Install   Cancel

Figure 9.28: *Create WebLogic Server Domain*

On this screen, you can also specify the Node Manager details. This is required for restarting WebLogic Server instances remotely and aids in High Availability environments. A new Node Manager instance will be configured by this installation. Move to the Next screen (Figure 9.29) where you now specify the repository database details including the name of the database: emrep.

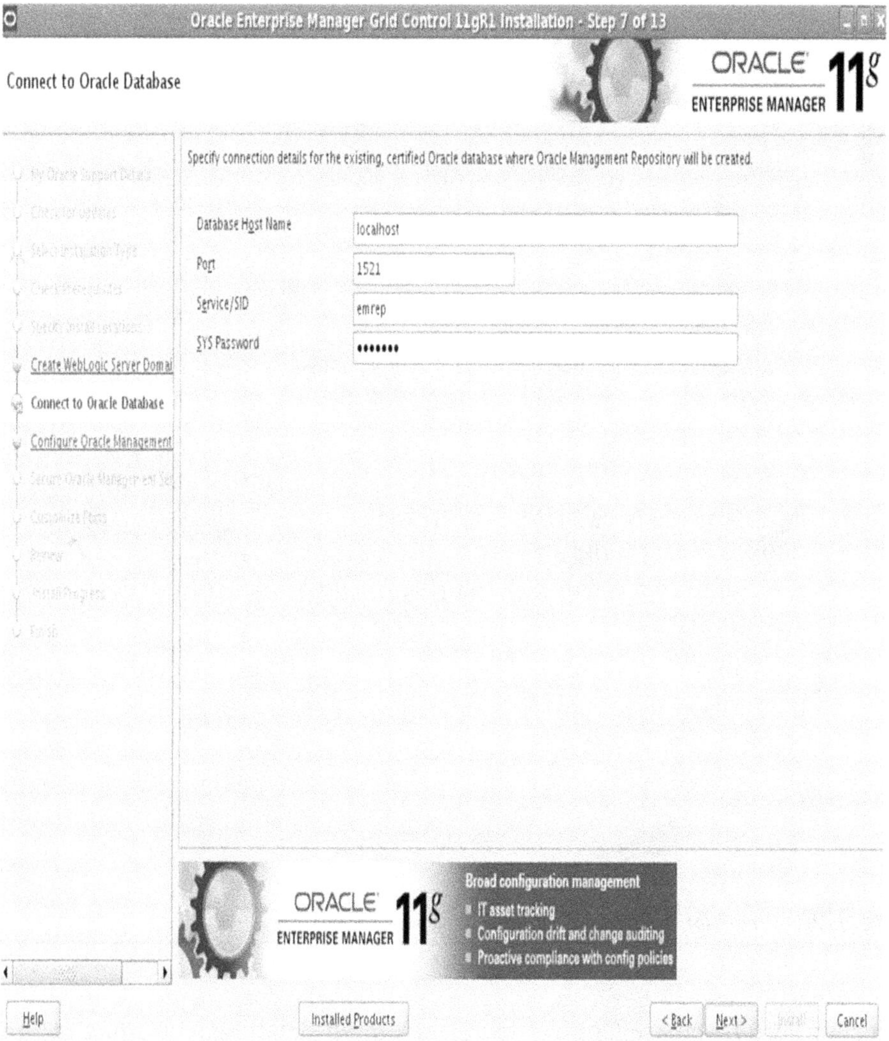
Oracle Enterprise Manager Grid Control 11gR1 Installation - Step 7 of 13
Connect to Oracle Database
ORACLE ENTERPRISE MANAGER 11g
Specify connection details for the existing, certified Oracle database where Oracle Management Repository will be created.
Database Host Name
localhost
Port
1521
Service/SID
emrep
SYS Password
Create WebLogic Server Domai
Connect to Oracle Database
Configure Oracle Management
Broad configuration management
IT asset tracking
Configuration drift and change auditing
Proactive compliance with config policies
Help
Installed Products
< Back
Next >
Cancel

Figure 9.29: *Specify Repository Database*

When you click on the Next button, you hit an error (Figure 9.30). This is because Database Control is already configured on the emrep database. In fact, the 11.2 database installation that you completed just before this does not allow you to create a database without either Database Control or Grid Control configured.

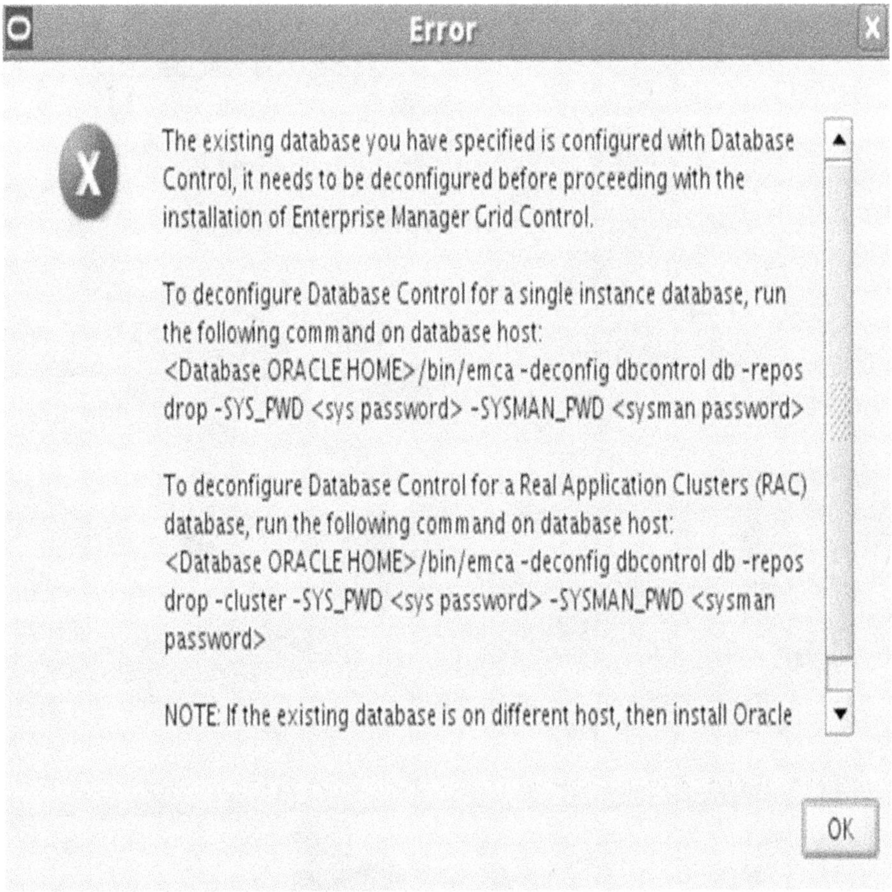

Error

The existing database you have specified is configured with Database Control, it needs to be deconfigured before proceeding with the installation of Enterprise Manager Grid Control.

To deconfigure Database Control for a single instance database, run the following command on database host:
<Database ORACLE HOME>/bin/emca -deconfig dbcontrol db -repos drop -SYS_PWD <sys password> -SYSMAN_PWD <sysman password>

To deconfigure Database Control for a Real Application Clusters (RAC) database, run the following command on database host:
<Database ORACLE HOME>/bin/emca -deconfig dbcontrol db -repos drop -cluster -SYS_PWD <sys password> -SYSMAN_PWD <sysman password>

NOTE: If the existing database is on different host, then install Oracle

OK

Figure 9.30: *Error for Existing Database Control*

To deconfigure Database Control from the emrep database, you must run the commands as follows in a different terminal window as the Oracle UNIX user:

```
[oracle@localhost ~]$ emca -deconfig dbcontrol db -repos drop -sys_pwd
oracle1 -sysman_pwd oracle1

started emca at may 18, 2010 10:59:48 pm
em configuration assistant, version 11.2.0.0.2 production
copyright (c) 2003, 2005, oracle.  all rights reserved.

enter the following information:
database sid: emrep
listener port number: 1521
```

```
do you wish to continue? [yes(y)/no(n)]: y
may 18, 2010 10:59:58 pm oracle.sysman.emcp.emconfig perform

info: this operation is being logged at
/u01/app/oracle/cfgtoollogs/emca/emrep/emca_2010_05_18_22_59_45.log.
may 18, 2010 10:59:58 pm oracle.sysman.emcp.util.dbcontrolutil stopoms
info: stopping database control (this may take a while) ...
may 18, 2010 11:00:07 pm oracle.sysman.emcp.emreposconfig invoke
info: dropping the em repository (this may take a while) ...
may 18, 2010 11:03:39 pm oracle.sysman.emcp.emreposconfig invoke
info: repository successfully dropped
enterprise manager configuration completed successfully
finished emca at may 18, 2010 11:03:45 pm
```

Database Control has now been deconfigured from the emrep database and you can continue with the Grid Control installation and put the repository on this database. However, when you click on the Next button again, you find that more errors appear (Figure 9.31). These have to do with certain parameter settings that exist in the emrep database.

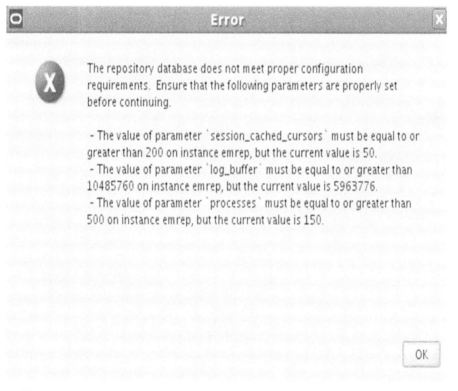

Figure 9.31: *Error for Database Configuration*

To fix these parameter settings, run the following commands:

```
SQL>
alter
 system set session_cached_cursors  = 200 scope=spfile;

System altered.

SQL>
alter
 system set log_buffer=10485760 scope=spfile;

System altered.

SQL>
alter
 system set processes=500 scope=spfile;

System altered.
```

Now the Next button throws up another error, this time having to do with the size of the undo tablespace (Figure 9.32).

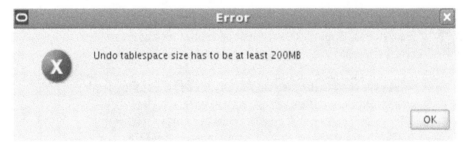

Figure 9.32: *Error for Undo Tablespace*

This is fixed by the following command:

```
alter database datafile '/u01/oradata/emrep/undotbs01.dbf' resize 200M
```

You now arrive at the Configure Oracle Management Repository screen (Figure 9.33). Here, you enter the SYSMAN password and also the OEM tablespaces. Note that there are now three tablespaces as compared to the two in the earlier OEM 10g Grid Control version.

Password warnings appear throughout the installation screens; at least eight characters, beginning with a letter and at least one numeric value must be used to specify a password.

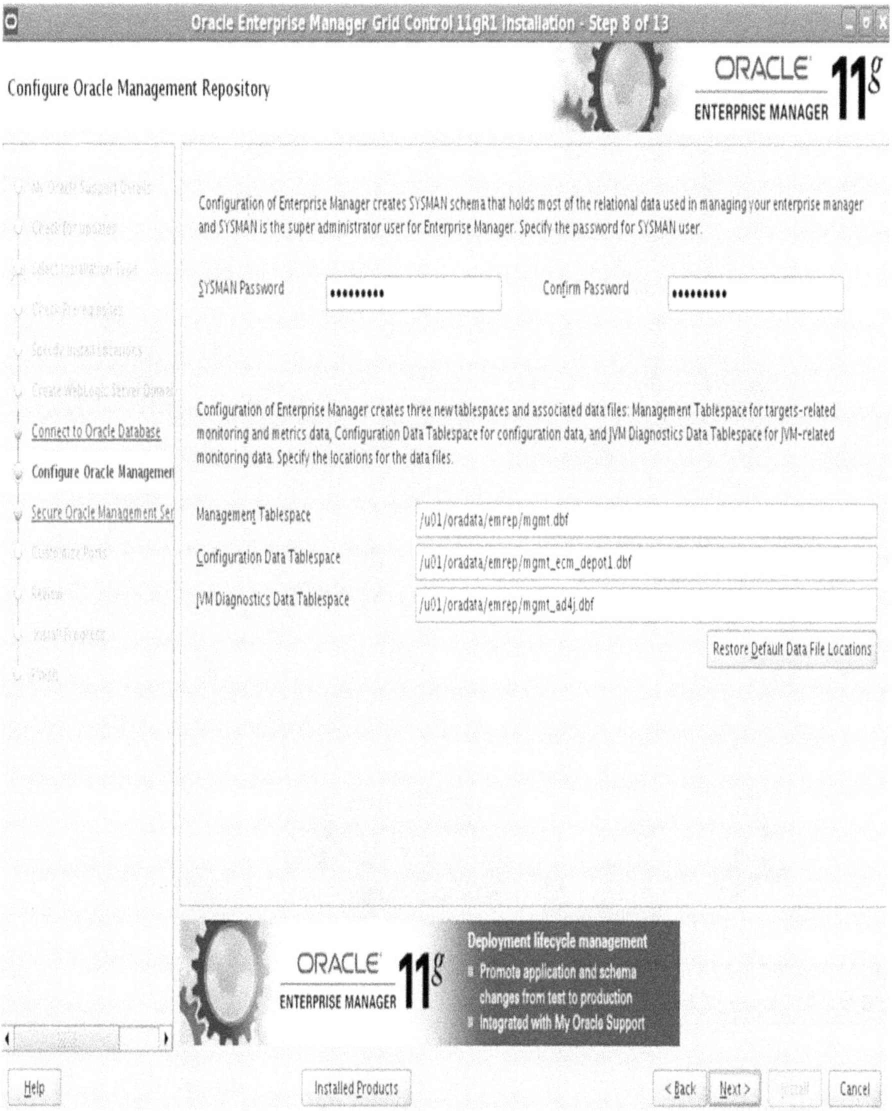

Figure 9.33: *Configure Oracle Management Repository*

Click Next. The Secure Oracle Management Service screen appears (Figure 9.34).

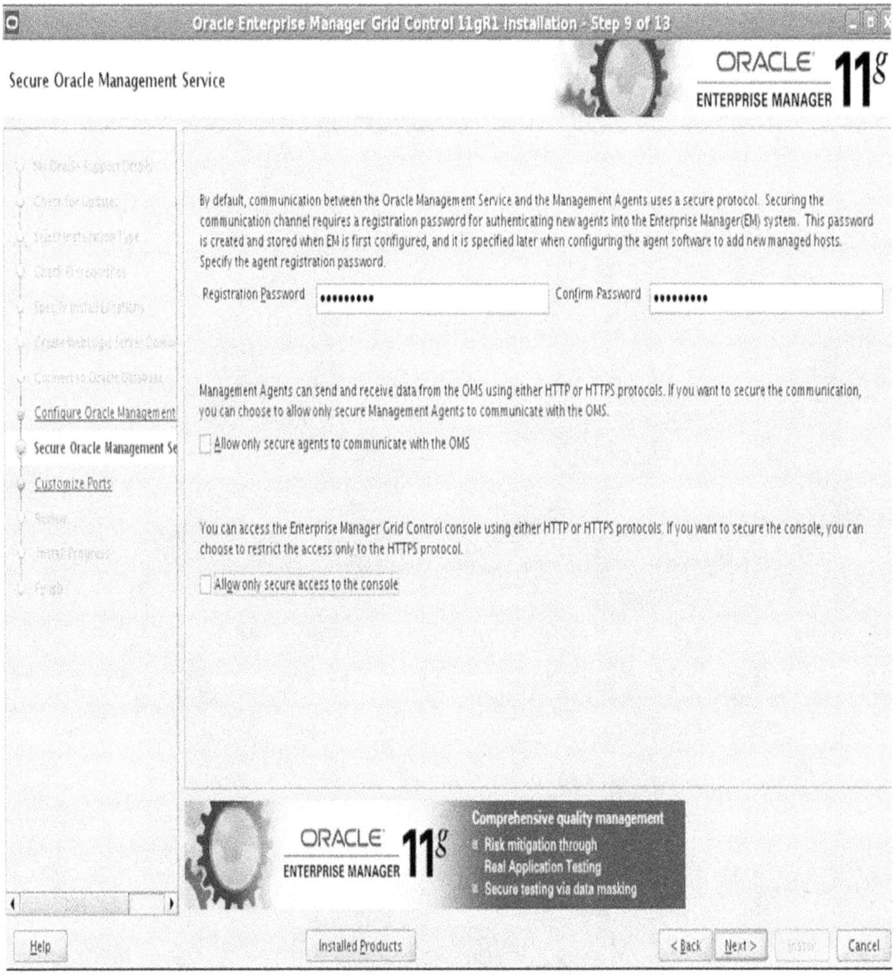

Figure 9.34: *Secure Oracle Management Service*

On this screen, specify the Registration Password for the Agent. You can also specify to allow only secure Agents to communicate to the OMS, and whether to allow only secure access via HTTPS to the Enterprise Manager console.

The next screen that appears is the Customize Ports screen (Figure 9.35). This shows the various ports to be used along with the recommended port range. This makes it a lot easier in OEM 11g Release 1 to customize the ports.

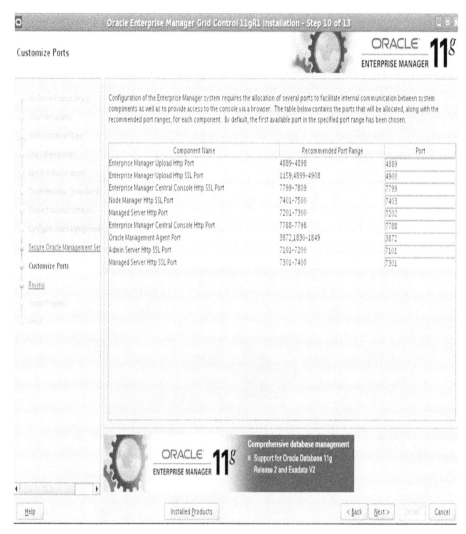

Figure 9.35: *Customize Ports*

You can now review the installation (Figure 9.36). It is observed that at least six GB will be needed for the installation of the OMS Home and the Agent Home.

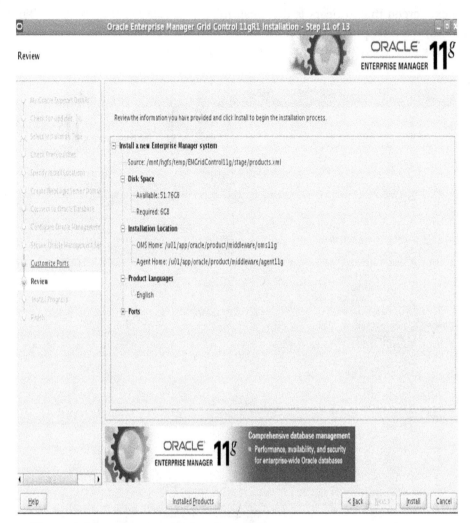

Figure 9.36: *Review Installation*

The installation now begins to progress (Figure 9.37). The Oracle Management Service is installed first, followed by the Oracle Management Agent. You may notice the new Webtier Home.

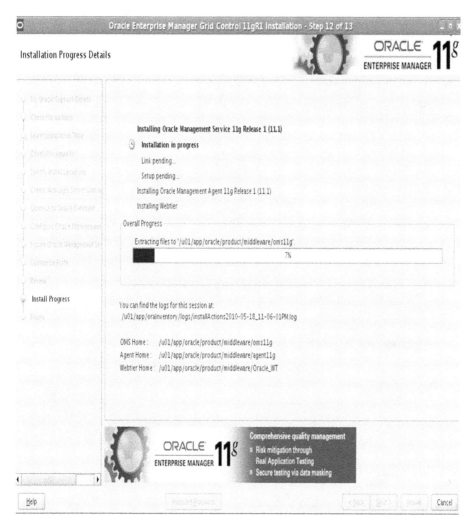

Figure 9.37: *Installation Progress Details*

You now need to execute certain configuration scripts as the root UNIX user (Figure 9.38).

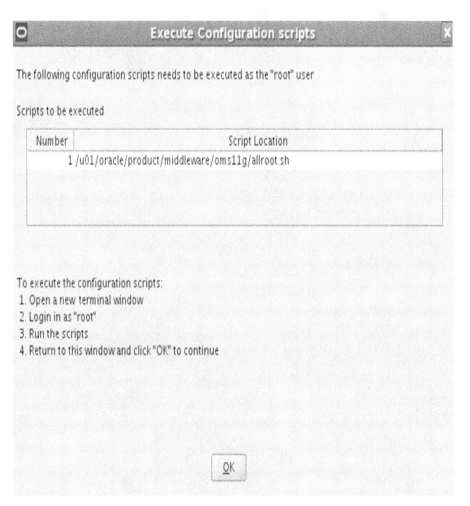

Figure 9.38: *Execute Configuration Scripts*

After executing these scripts, the installation resumes. The configuration assistants now start (Figure 9.39).

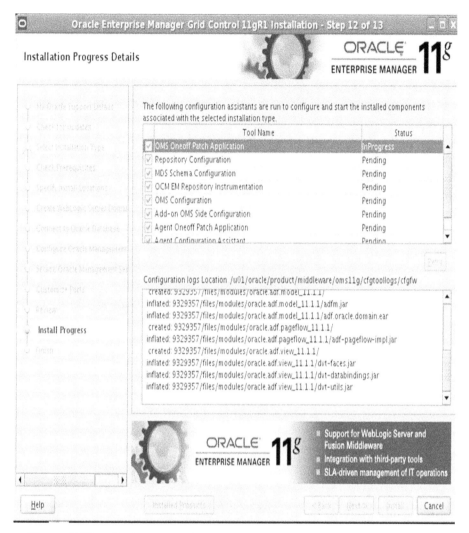

Installation Progress Details

ORACLE 11g
ENTERPRISE MANAGER

The following configuration assistants are run to configure and start the installed components associated with the selected installation type.

Tool Name	Status
OMS Oneoff Patch Application	InProgress
Repository Configuration	Pending
MDS Schema Configuration	Pending
OCM EM Repository Instrumentation	Pending
OMS Configuration	Pending
Add-on OMS Side Configuration	Pending
Agent Oneoff Patch Application	Pending
Agent Configuration Assistant	Pending

Configuration logs Location /u01/oracle/product/middleware/oms11g/cfgtoollogs/cfgfw

```
created: 9329357/files/modules/oracle.adf.model_11.1.1/
inflated: 9329357/files/modules/oracle.adf.model_11.1.1/adfm.jar
inflated: 9329357/files/modules/oracle.adf.model_11.1.1/adf.oracle.domain.ear
 created: 9329357/files/modules/oracle.adf.pageflow_11.1.1/
inflated: 9329357/files/modules/oracle.adf.pageflow_11.1.1/adf-pageflow-impl.jar
 created: 9329357/files/modules/oracle.adf.view_11.1.1/
inflated: 9329357/files/modules/oracle.adf.view_11.1.1/dvt-faces.jar
inflated: 9329357/files/modules/oracle.adf.view_11.1.1/dvt-databindings.jar
inflated: 9329357/files/modules/oracle.adf.view_11.1.1/dvt-utils.jar
```

ORACLE 11g
ENTERPRISE MANAGER

- Support for WebLogic Server and Fusion Middleware
- Integration with third-party tools
- SLA-driven management of IT operations

Help   Installed Products   < Back   Next >   Install   Cancel

Figure 9.39: *Configuration Assistants in Action*

These configuration assistants are responsible for the OEM repository creation, OMS configuration and so on.

When complete, the installation of Enterprise Manager 11g Grid Control is finally over. You now have a working OEM system and can use all the features described in the previous chapters. Log in to the Grid Control console.

Oracle Enterprise Manager 11g Install

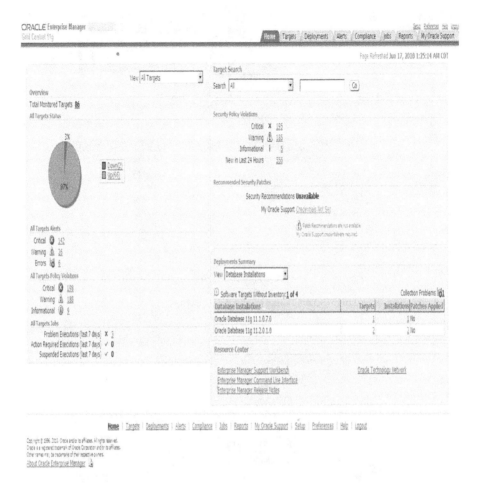

Figure 9.40: *The New Grid Control 11g Console Home Page*

Deinstallation of Oracle Enterprise Manager 11g

In this version, you can easily deinstall OEM 11g Grid Control if you want to. Simply run the command:

```
./runInstaller -deinstall
```

You then click on the Installed Products button, select the products you want to deinstall and then click on the Remove button. This will perform the deinstallation of the products.

Upgrade to OEM 11g

Concerning upgrading to OEM 11g Grid Control from an existing 10g installation, the following points need to be made:

- You need to be on OEM 10.2.0.4 or 10.2.0.5 to upgrade to OEM 11g, and your repository database version must be Oracle Enterprise Edition 10.2.0.4 or above.

- The upgrade is an out-of-place upgrade; that is, it creates a new OEM 11g Oracle Home.

- The configuration data from the previous installation is moved to the new installation, and the OEM 10g repository is upgraded to the 11g repository version at the end of the process.

Close Integration with My Oracle Support

The Grid Control console home page in this new 11g version is seen in Figure 9.40. Notice the new tab on the screen labeled My Oracle Support. This gives an indication of the close integration of Grid Control with My Oracle Support (MOS) from this release onwards. No other IT vendor today completely integrates management and support in the way OEM 11g Grid Control does.

When you move to the My Oracle Support tab on the home page, you are asked to log in directly to MOS as can be seen in Figure 9.41.

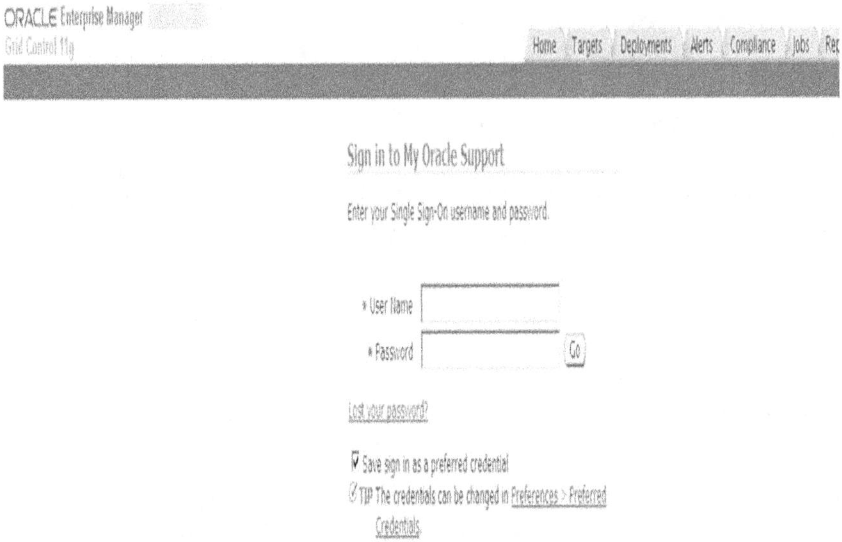

Sign in to My Oracle Support

Enter your Single Sign-On username and password.

* User Name

* Password   [Go]

Lost your password?

☑ Save sign in as a preferred credential

✎ TIP The credentials can be changed in Preferences > Preferred
Credentials.

Figure 9.41: *The New My Oracle Support (MOS) Tab*

After logging in to MOS with your Oracle Single Sign-On (SSO) username and password, move to the Patches and Updates sub-tab under the main My Oracle Support tab. This now appears with a lot of patch information (Figure 9.42).

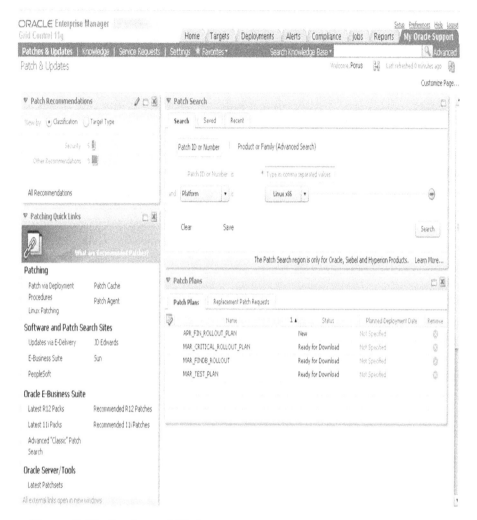

Figure 9.42: *Patches and Updates*

Click on the All Recommendations link in the Patch Recommendations section. This takes you to the screen in Figure 9.43, which shows a list of all patch recommendations for all the managed targets in your OEM system. The list includes Oracle Critical Patch Updates (CPUs), Patch Set Updates (PSUs), and other recommended patches and bundles.

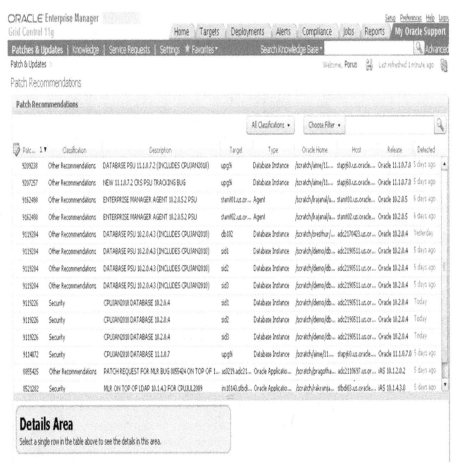

Figure 9.43: *Recommended Patches List*

Selecting any patch from the list of recommended patches shows a few options such as Full Screen, Add to Plan, or Download. This is seen in Figure 9.44. You can now select Full Screen to see all the patch details.

Figure 9.44: *Selecting a Patch From the List*

This bring up detailed information about the patch from My Oracle Support, such as the list of bugs resolved by the patch, download trends of the patch and even community reviews from Oracle Forums so you can build on community experience and contribute your own feedback. This is seen in Figure 9.45.

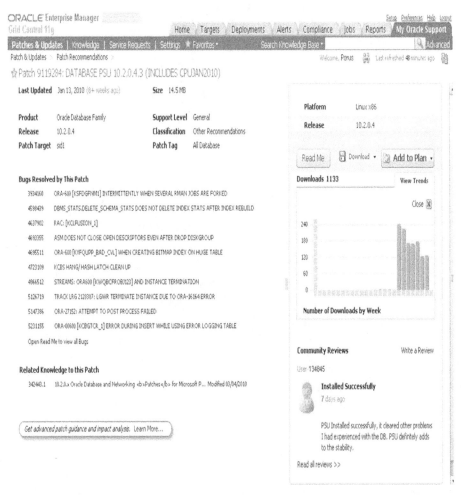

Figure 9.45: *Detailed Patch Information*

You also have the ability to add the patch to a plan on this page. This is a new concept in My Oracle Support: using a patch plan, you can build a collection of patches that can then be applied to the appropriate targets using OEM in a specific period of downtime. You can create a new plan, add the patch, and then validate the patches in the plan for any conflicts either amongst the new patches or with the patches already applied. This is seen in Figure 9.46.

Figure 9.46: *Patch Validation*

After validation, if there is a conflict, you can file a Merge Request directly from OEM and you do not have to raise a separate Service Request (SR) in My Oracle Support for this. Alternatively, if there is a merge patch already available for the conflict, the merge patch will be shown and you can replace the conflicting patches with the merge patch.

Once the patches are validated to be conflict-free and are ready for deployment, you can select the patches and then click on the Run Procedure option (seen in Figure 9.47) which goes ahead and starts the powerful and customizable deployment procedures that have been seen in an earlier chapter of this book.

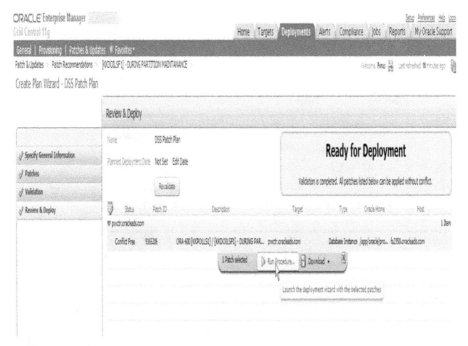

Figure 9.47: *Run Deployment Procedure*

The next screen (Figure 9.48) shows the appropriate deployment procedure being selected; in this case, the Patch Oracle database procedure for a standalone database. The deployment procedure is then responsible for applying the set of patches in the plan to the appropriate targets.

Figure 9.48: *Patch Oracle Database Deployment Procedure*

As is obvious, there is now an excellent integration of OEM 11g Grid Control with My Oracle Support (MOS), making the patching experience even more seamless and efficient. This can be truly called Patch Automation: reducing manual labor and making the life of the DBA easier and better.

Grid Control Administration Changes

OEM 11g Grid Control has introduced certain changes in the way the background administration is handled. Thanks to Werner De Gruyter of Oracle Corporation for suggesting and supplying the material for this section.

Controlling the Oracle Management Service (OMS)

In OEM 10g Grid Control, controlling the Oracle Management Service (OMS) also involved controlling the OPMN (Oracle Process Management

Notification) stack which was installed and configured with Oracle Application Server. In the new 11g version of Grid Control, this has been replaced with the Oracle WebLogic server. Therefore, stopping and starting the stacks between the two versions has changed.

In OEM 10g Grid Control, the commands were as follows:

Stopping the entire stack	*<OMS Home>/opmn/bin/opmnctl stopall*
Starting the entire stack	*<OMS Home>/opmn/bin/opmnctl startall*
Stopping and starting OMS only	*<OMS Home>/bin/emctl stop oms* *<OMS Home>/bin/emctl start oms*
List status of EM Infrastructure	*<OMS Home>/opmn/bin/opmnctl status –l*

In OEM 11g Grid Control, the commands used are:

Stopping the entire stack	*<OMS Home>/bin/emctl stop oms –all*
Starting the entire stack	*<OMS Home>/bin/emctl start oms*
Stopping and starting OMS only	*<OMS Home>/bin/emctl stop oms* *<OMS Home>/bin/emctl start oms*
List status of EM Infrastructure	*<OMS Home>/bin/emctl status oms -details*

As can be seen, the new version's *emctl start* command takes care of the entire stack and starts the necessary components behind the scenes. No other command, such as *opmnctl* in the previous version, is needed.

Setting Parameters for the OMS

In OEM 10g Grid Control, a file had to be manually edited in order to change parameters for the management service such as the loader threads or job threads or other things. The parameters were manually changed in the *emoms.properties* file in this version.

However, in the new 11g version of Grid Control, the file has disappeared and all the parameters for the management service are now stored in the Grid Control repository. Issue an *emctl* command to change the parameters directly in the repository using the SYSMAN password. This means centralization of parameter values and also greater security. This also applies to setting logging and tracing parameters for the management service.

In OEM 10g Grid Control:

To set or modify a property value for the management service (OMS)	Manually edit the *emoms.properties* file
To list all the properties and their values for the management service	Manually go through *emoms.properties* or write your own shell script to parse the file
To set or modify logging or tracing parameters for the management service	Manually edit the *emomslogging.properties*

In OEM 11g Grid Control:

To set or modify a property value for the management service (OMS)	*<OMS Home>/bin/emctl set property -name <name> -value <value> -module emoms*
To list all the properties and their values for the management service	*<OMS Home>/bin/emctl list properties*
To set or modify logging or tracing parameters for the management service	*<OMS Home>/bin/emctl set property -name <name> -value <value> -module logging*

Changed Locations of Log and Trace Files

In OEM 11g Grid Control, the location of the log and trace files has been changed drastically due to the use of the new WebLogic Server stack. There is now a separation of static and dynamic information, i.e. the code and runtime, respectively. The steps to find the locations are as follows.

First examine the *emInstanceMapping.properties* file. This is found in the *<OMS Home>/sysman/config* directory. The internal ID, i.e. OMS name of the OMS, can be found in this file as well as the name and location of the file with the port numbers and directory locations used by this particular OMS. As an example, the entry for the first OMS *emgc_oms1* can appear as follows:

```
emgc_oms1=/oracle/gc_inst/em/emgc_oms1/emgc.properties
```

The listed file can now be opened to reveal the directory and port information for the OMS. There are three important properties in this file, *em_instance_home*, *em_domain_home* and *em_webtier_insthome* that will assist in finding the log files. The locations are as follows:

In OEM 10g Grid Control:

OMS Application Log files Location	*<oms home>/sysman/log*
OMS JAVA Application Log files Location	*<oms home>/j2ee/j2ee/oc4j_em/log/ oc4j_em_default_island_1*
Application Stack Log files Location	*<oms home>/opmn/logs*
Apache (HTTP Server) Log files Location	*<oms home>/apache/apache/logs*

In OEM 11g Grid Control:

OMS Application Log files Location	*<em_instance_home>/sysman/log* as an example: */oracle/gc_inst/em/emgc_oms1/sysman/log*
OMS JAVA Application Log files Location	*<em_domain_home>/servers/<oms id>/logs* as an example: */oracle/gc_inst/user_projects/domains/gcdomain/ servers/emgc_oms1/logs* Note: The Node Manager will write the log and trace files in the same location as above.. The Node Manager will also write to *<em_domain_home>/servers/<oms id>/sysman/log* as an example: */oracle/gc_inst/user_projects/domains/gcdomain/ servers/emgc_oms1/sysman/log*
Application Stack Log files Location	*<gc_inst>/domains/gcdomain/servers/emgc_adminserver/logs* This is the directory for the 1st OMS which is the one with the Admin server. As an example: */oracle/gc_inst/user_projects/domains/gcdomain/ servers/emgc_adminserver/logs*
Apache (HTTP Server) Log files Location	*<em_webtier_insthome>/diagnostics/logs/ohs/ohs1* as an example: */oracle/gc_inst/webtierih1/diagnostics/logs/OHS/ohs1*

SQL*Plus Absence from OMS Home

In OEM 11g Grid Control, the SQL*Plus command line utility is no longer available in the *bin* directory of the OMS Home. There are two major effects of this change that are explained below.

In the case of patching, you will not be able to run the post-install SQL file using SQL*Plus. Instead, you will have to use the Repository Creation Utility (RCU) to execute the SQL post-install files. The patch *readme* will explain how to run this utility.

The second effect of the absence of SQL*Plus is on Enterprise Manager Diagnostics (EMDIAG). This is a troubleshooting kit provided by My Oracle Support to diagnose and fix issues with agents and targets.

Normally, EMDIAG was manually installed by the Grid Control administrator in the OMS Home where it used SQL*Plus to run scripts to get formatted output about agent and target information from the repository. However, because SQL*Plus is no longer present in the OMS Home and RCU does not provide formatted SQL output like SQL*Plus, it is no longer possible to install EMDIAG in the OMS Home.

Rather, EMDIAG must now be manually installed in a different location; use the Oracle home of the repository database. EMDIAG will then be able to use SQL*Plus from that home to access the repository and produce the reports.

Increasing the JAVA Heap Size of the OMS

In the case of OEM installations that are responsible for managing and monitoring a large number of targets or using many of the advanced techniques described in this book, it is possible to change the application server's standard out-of-box heap size of 512 MB to a higher value. This is done by changing the configuration of the application server. This was done in OEM 10g Grid Control by editing the *<OMS home>/opmn/conf/opmn.xml* file and changing the *-Xmx* parameter to *-Xmx1024M* for the *OC4J_EM* application.

In the case of the new OEM 11g Grid Control, the correct procedure to increase the heap size is to edit the *startEMServer.sh* file in the

<em_domain_home>/bin directory, and add the following lines immediately before the last line in the file:

```
if [ "${server_name}" != "emgc_adminserver" ] ; then
   user_mem_args="-xms256m -xmx1024m -xx:maxpermsize=512m -
xx:compilethreshold=8000 -xx:permsize=128m"
   export user_mem_args
fi
```

High Availability Console

The High Availability (HA) console and the Maximum Availability Architecture (MAA) Advisor were introduced in OEM 10g Release 5 and their capabilities are enhanced in the current 11g release. The importance of these concepts, and their ease of implementation in OEM, necessitates a brief description before concluding this book.

Select a database target and move to the Availability tab. The links for the High Availability console and the Maximum Availability Architecture Advisor are both seen on this page. Click on the High Availability Console link, and the console appears as in Figure 9.49.

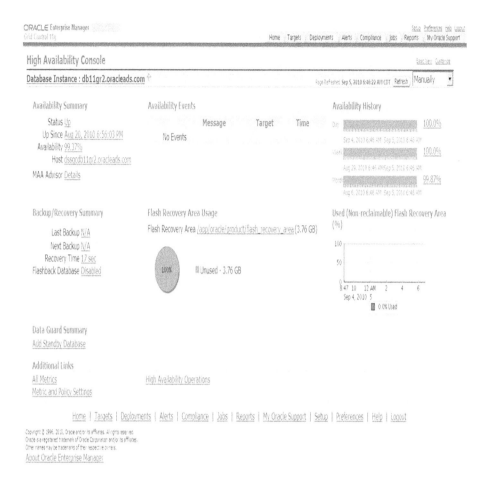

Figure 9.49: *High Availability Console*

The HA console is obviously a dashboard where you can monitor all your HA components for this database target. The console is fully customizable; notice the Customize link at the top corner. Using this link, it has been decided to show historical charts which appear under the Availability History section on the console page.

The HA console displays a summary view of all the Data Guard and RAC (if any) setups for your database target with corresponding charts, the Backup/Recovery summary of the database, and the Flash Recovery Area usage. Availability related events are also seen on the HA console.

Assistance for implementing a HA system is provided via recommendations from the new Maximum Availability Architecture (MAA) Advisor in Grid Control. HA configuration best practices and standards can be easily understood and implemented using the MAA Advisor. Click on the MAA Advisor details from the HA console or from the Database..Availability tab. This brings up the recommendations or solutions list as seen in Figure 9.50.

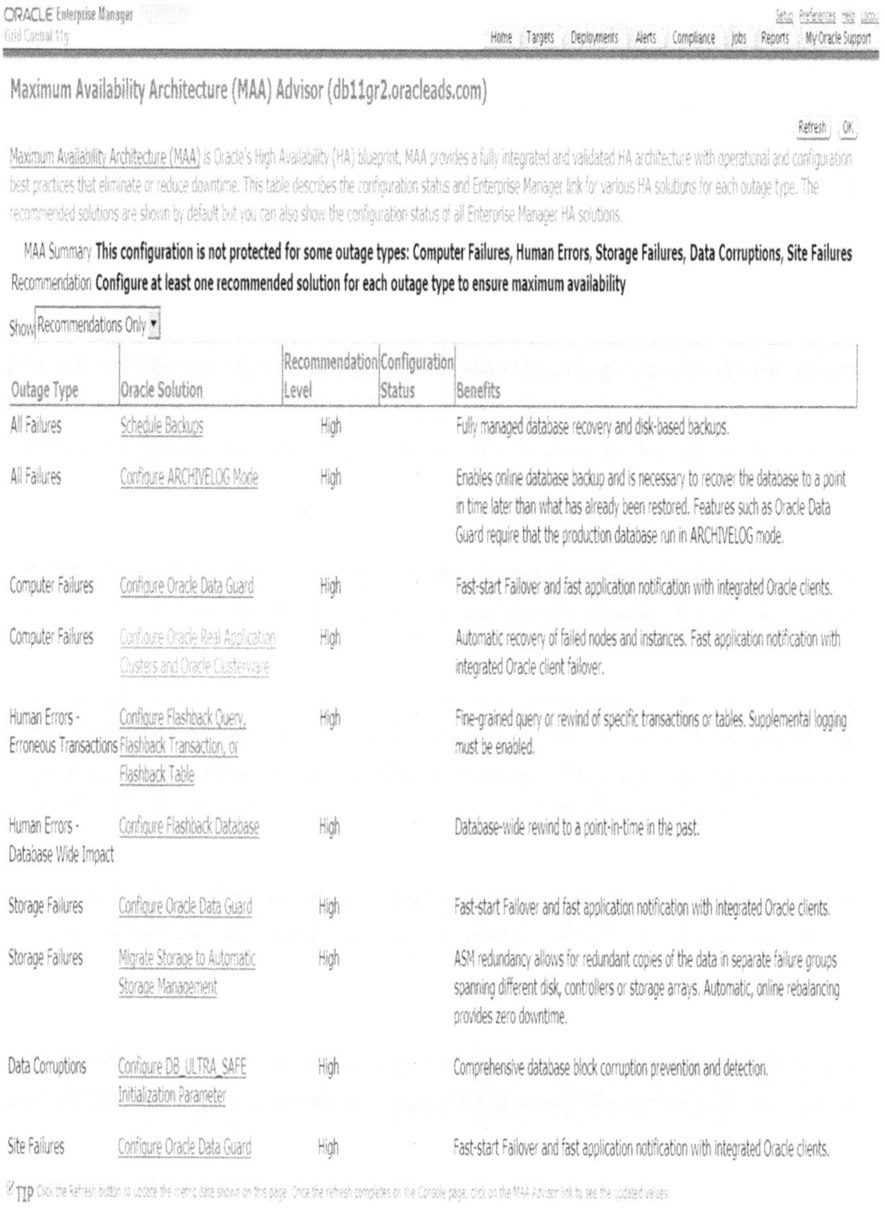

Maximum Availability Architecture (MAA) Advisor (db11gr2.oracleads.com)

Refresh OK

Maximum Availability Architecture (MAA) is Oracle's High Availability (HA) blueprint. MAA provides a fully integrated and validated HA architecture with operational and configuration best practices that eliminate or reduce downtime. This table describes the configuration status and Enterprise Manager link for various HA solutions for each outage type. The recommended solutions are shown by default but you can also show the configuration status of all Enterprise Manager HA solutions.

MAA Summary **This configuration is not protected for some outage types: Computer Failures, Human Errors, Storage Failures, Data Corruptions, Site Failures**
Recommendation **Configure at least one recommended solution for each outage type to ensure maximum availability**

Show Recommendations Only ▼

Outage Type	Oracle Solution	Recommendation Level	Configuration Status	Benefits
All Failures	Schedule Backups	High		Fully managed database recovery and disk-based backups.
All Failures	Configure ARCHIVELOG Mode	High		Enables online database backup and is necessary to recover the database to a point in time later than what has already been restored. Features such as Oracle Data Guard require that the production database run in ARCHIVELOG mode.
Computer Failures	Configure Oracle Data Guard	High		Fast-start Failover and fast application notification with integrated Oracle clients.
Computer Failures	Configure Oracle Real Application Clusters and Oracle Clusterware	High		Automatic recovery of failed nodes and instances. Fast application notification with integrated Oracle client failover.
Human Errors - Erroneous Transactions	Configure Flashback Query, Flashback Transaction, or Flashback Table	High		Fine-grained query or rewind of specific transactions or tables. Supplemental logging must be enabled.
Human Errors - Database Wide Impact	Configure Flashback Database	High		Database-wide rewind to a point-in-time in the past.
Storage Failures	Configure Oracle Data Guard	High		Fast-start Failover and fast application notification with integrated Oracle clients.
Storage Failures	Migrate Storage to Automatic Storage Management	High		ASM redundancy allows for redundant copies of the data in separate failure groups spanning different disk, controllers or storage arrays. Automatic, online rebalancing provides zero downtime.
Data Corruptions	Configure DB_ULTRA_SAFE Initialization Parameter	High		Comprehensive database block corruption prevention and detection.
Site Failures	Configure Oracle Data Guard	High		Fast-start Failover and fast application notification with integrated Oracle clients.

TIP Click the Refresh button to update the metric data shown on this page. Once the refresh completes or the Console page, click on the MAA Advisor link to see the updated values.

Figure 9.50: *MAA Advisor Details*

From the MAA Advisor page, it is possible to click on any of the recommendations or solutions listed in order to implement that solution. This includes database actions such as configuring Oracle Data Guard, setting archivelog mode, enabling Flashback capabilities, setup and scheduling of RMAN backups, migration of database storage to ASM, or even conversion to Oracle Real Application Clusters (RAC).

Hence, it can be seen that single instances can be easily converted to MAA-compliant systems with minimal downtime using the powerful workflows and provisioning features in OEM 11g Grid Control, which are callable from this page.

Book Conclusion

In this concluding chapter, several new features and versions of Oracle Enterprise Manager products such as the OEM Ops Center, Oracle ATS, Oracle RUEI, Oracle BTM and so on have been featured. Also demonstrated have been the changed installation and administration techniques for the new version of OEM 11g Grid Control, the close integration of this version with My Oracle Support (MOS), and also the enhanced capabilities of the High Availability (HA) console to convert to MAA-compliant systems.

In the entire book, you have seen how the DBA can benefit from OEM Grid Control by using this product for the practical tasks in the day-to-day life of database administration. You saw how database backups, patching of databases, and creation of standby databases can be streamlined, and how entire software homes and databases can be automatically provisioned.

These are nitty-gritty tasks but they combine to take up a lot of DBA time until Grid Control automation and its Manage Many as One approach came along to considerably alleviate the issue. Also shown were the benefits of Grid Control to the Unix System Administrator, the company regulators (for compliance), and finally the IT management for the purpose of their SLA management. You have seen the number of OEM Management Packs, management connectors and system monitoring plug-ins steadily increase for a lot of non-Oracle products, so much so that there are few products today that cannot be monitored by OEM Grid Control and new plug-ins are being developed every year.

For OEM Grid Control and its ambition to be the Enterprise Management System of choice, it can be truly said that it has progressed well on that path and the sky is truly the limit for future versions of the Oracle Enterprise Manager product.

I hope you have enjoyed this book. Please feel free to recommend it to your friends. You can also regularly visit the Oracle Enterprise Manager Blog of the author at the following URL to comment on the book or on Enterprise Manager in general:

```
http://enterprise-manager.blogspot.com/
```

As the blog itself describes, it is the first and only fully dedicated to discussions on the fantabulous Oracle Enterprise Manager Grid Control, Oracle's Enterprise-wide Management System.

Index

About the Author

Porus Homi Havewala

Porus Homi Havewala works as a Senior Manager (Database Management) in the Enterprise Technology team of Oracle Corporation based in Singapore, and specializes in Oracle Enterprise Manager. He is an Oracle Employee ACE and was previously awarded the prestigious "Oracle ACE Director" title by Oracle USA. He has extensive experience in Oracle technology since 1994, including as a Senior Production DBA, Senior Database Consultant, Database Architect, E-Business Technical DBA, Development DBA, and Database Designer Modeler. He has also worked in Oracle India in the ACS (Advanced Customer Services) department and is an enthusiast for Oracle technology, especially Oracle Enterprise Manager Grid Control and RMAN, on which he has conducted seminars for large MNCs and implemented powerful enterprise tools.

Mr. Havewala has worked with the first production Grid Control site in the world, Telstra, the largest telecommunications company in Australia. He has published numerous articles on Grid Control and RMAN on OTN, and created the world's first blog dedicated to Grid Control, showcasing podcasts exclusively based on this technology. There are only about 100 Oracle ACE Directors in the entire world and Mr. Havewala was the very first Oracle ACE and ACE Director in Singapore; a recognition of his outstanding achievements in the Oracle world. Prior to Oracle Corporation, he was employed at S&I Systems, an Oracle Platinum partner in Singapore.

www.ingramcontent.com/pod-product-compliance
Lightning Source LLC
Chambersburg PA
CBHW081455050326
40690CB00015B/2802